From Fetish to Subject

From Fetish to Subject

Race, Modernism, and Primitivism, 1919–1935

CAROLE SWEENEY

PRAEGER

Westport, Connecticut
London

Library of Congress Cataloging-in-Publication Data

Sweeney, Carole.
From fetish to subject : race, modernism, and primitivism, 1919–1935 / Carole Sweeney.
p. cm.
Includes bibliographical references and index.
ISBN 0–275–97747–1
1. Blacks. 2. Primitivism. 3. Civilization, Modern. 4. Imperialism—Social aspects. I. Title.
HT1581.S94 2004
305.896—dc22 2004012290

British Library Cataloguing in Publication Data is available.

Library of Congress Catalog Card Number: 2004012290
ISBN: 0–275–97747–1

First published in 2004

Praeger Publishers, 88 Post Road West, Westport, CT 06881
An imprint of Greenwood Publishing Group, Inc.
www.praeger.com

Printed in the United States of America

The paper used in this book complies with the Permanent Paper Standard issued by the National Information Standards Organization (Z39.48–1984).

10 9 8 7 6 5 4 3 2 1

This book is dedicated to my family, Doug and Pascale,
to my father, and to the memory of my mother Agnes Sweeney.

Contents

Abbreviations

RMN *La Revue du Monde Noir*

DA *La Dépêche Africaine*

LD *Légitime Défense*

n. pag. indicates no page available in original archival material
n.d. indicates no date available in original archival material

Acknowledgments

I owe many people thanks for their encouragement and support during the process of this book. Firstly, thanks to my editor at Greenwood, Marcia Goldstein, and my project coordinator at Impressions, Brenda Scott, both of whom were always transatlantically efficient and approachable. Thanks to friends and colleagues at the University of Southampton who have ensured a lively intellectual and social context for this work, in particular Nicky Marsh, Carrie Hamilton, Vivienne Orchard, Florence Myles and Jackie Clarke. Thanks also go to Maria Lauret who has seen and aided the transformation of this project over the years. Lastly very special thanks to Pascale and Doug whose love, humour and conversation have sustained me.

I am grateful to the Modern Languages at the University of Southampton for granting me study leave to complete work on the book. And to Cornelia for making it possible to go to the Schomburg Centre in Harlem to complete archival research during that leave.

I would also like to thank the British Academy for a grant to complete research for this book in the Schomburg Center for Black Culture in Harlem.

Some material in this book has appeared elsewhere in substantially revised form. They are:

Nottingham French Studies. "Resisting the Primitive: The Nardal Sisters, *La Revue du Monde Noire* and *La Dépêche Africaine*" Vol. 43, No. 2, Summer, 2004.

Journal of Romance Studies. "'I'll say it's getting darker and darker in Paris all the time' *négrophilie* and Inter-war France" Vol. 1 No. 2, Autumn 2001.

Introduction

> Other regions give us back what our culture has excluded from its discourse.
> —Michel de Certeau

In *L'Afrique fantôme* (1934), a surrealist account of the 1931–33 ethnographic mission to Dakar-Djibouti, Michel Leiris recounts his formative experiences in Parisian bars and cabarets in the postwar years of the early 1920s. Describing his "abandonment to the animal joy of experiencing the influence of a modern rhythm" in Montmartre *bars nègres,* Leiris characterises the pleasures of *la culture nègre* as a locale of uninhibited spontaneity, an uncensored and libidinous space functioning as the antithesis to the moribund intellectualism of the subject of modernity (54). Depicting Western culture as spiritually destitute and dominated by an arid consumer capitalism, Leiris's portrayal of modern urban life as decrepit, inauthentic, and devoid of vitality was a common theme in French cultural life in the years immediately following the First World War. This sense of exhaustion and depletion was expressed by writers on the left and the right alike, and in the case of the latter it was often accompanied by a sense of reactionary anxiety over the survival of the European "race" itself. Leiris's reminiscences are suggestive of a set of reactions to the postwar moment when a kind of "all pervasive, collective, and incurable shell shock" from Ypres and the Somme stalked European capitals (T. Miller 24). Postwar France was a ravaged society, broken by long years of fighting and facing a lost generation of men. The very reality of the immediate postwar moment seemed irrevocably altered; this was a world in which, as Walter Benjamin has memorably said, "nothing remained but the clouds" (*Illuminations* 84). The promises of Enlightenment universal reason and the idea of history as progress lay buried with the young soldiers who had perished in the trenches. The interwar years were a "between-the-acts" epoch of immense changes in cultural, political, and socioeconomic spheres; an era in which narrative and aesthetics seemed to have exhausted their own forward momentum and needed a more "elementary art" that would "save mankind from the folly of these furious times" (Arp 39). This simpler, more essential art was not to be found within clotted realms of bourgeois ideology, in "the sclerotic liberal-moral-humanistic ideal of freedom," but from without (Benjamin, *One Way Street* 236). The years between 1907 and 1935 saw a movement outside of the West and its epistemological geographies to the figure and the text of the racial other against and through which the subject of modernity could be reread and reinterpreted. These years saw a re-conceptualisation of the category of race that underwent significant changes in both definition and inscription as a wave of cultural primitivism reverberated through high, popular, and mass culture in Paris. Broadly referred to in histories of the period as *négrophilie,* this term, first used by Jean Laude to describe a prewar interest in *l'art nègre* in the visual arts, loosely translates as a cultural fascination with blackness as a free-floating signifier for a more pervasive sense of otherness.[1] Leiris's peregrinations around the bars and *bals* of Montmartre, commonly dubbed Harlem-sur-Seine, took place at a time when *négrophilie* was at its height. Josephine Baker was poised to make her début in the *Revue Nègre,* jazz was the *musique branché* for the cognoscenti, and René Maran's "véritable roman" *nègre Batouala* won the prestigious Prix Goncourt. The space and the sign of the racial "other," now made more materially available through the systematic colonial plundering of the spoils of empire, seemed to offer the potential of rejuvenation for a dilapidated Western modernity lying in ruins after la Grande Guerre. But during this time a real black presence was growing in France. Colonial ex-soldiers and black American conscripts and enlistees who remained in France after the end of the First World War began to rub shoulders in Paris with a small group of *évolués,* beneficiaries of the colonial policy of *assimilation,* from Africa and the Caribbean. These groups would form the basis for political and aesthetic black diasporic activism that wrote back against *négrophilie* from within its own discourses.

The negrophile aesthetic valorisation of a particular version of blackness did not of course translate into enlightened political policies around race and cultural difference either domestically or in the colonised territories. Although images of so-called primitive races shifted from negative to positive connotations, first in the cultural domain and then only very slowly on a political level, the incidence of popular cultural primitivism in itself did not alter the material or political conditions of French colonial subjects overseas. *Négrophilie* did, however, constitute a significant shift in representations and conceptualisations of race, which would continue to reverberate long after the faddish fascination for *les nègres* had diminished. Public attitudes towards the postwar *dette du sang*, the presence of Senegalese *tirailleurs*, and black American ex-soldiers in France after the war shifted from the overt racism of the nineteenth century to a more paternalistic benevolence that constructed *les nègres* as infantile and picturesque, in the fashion of the Banania *tirailleur* declaring in pidgin French, "Y'a bon!" (Dewitte 12).[2] The widespread popularity of *l'art nègre* and *le jazz hot* in the clubs and salons of bourgeois Paris did not make fashionable Parisians aware of the 1919 Pan-African Congress in Versailles led by W. E. B. DuBois or the formation of the Union Inter-Coloniale in 1921. While black American jazz musicians and entertainers were lauded in Paris in the 1920s, in North Africa, for example, an anti-imperial rebellion, la Guerre du Rif, led by the outlawed Abdel El Krim, was brutally suppressed in 1925 by the French military supporting Spanish forces. As Josephine Baker, the living embodiment of modern primitivism, was taking Paris by storm with her music-hall hit chanson "J'ai deux amours" and her slave-chic attire, the Institut Pasteur hosted a conference on so-called racial hygiene that explained the public health problems of the immigrant population in France.[3] Most striking of all perhaps is the fact that a popular cultural negrophilia existed alongside a gradual resurgence of aggressively xenophobic nationalism in France, promulgated by the Catholic republicanism of Charles Maurras's L'Action Française and other ultra-right extraparliamentary leagues such as La Cagoule. While African Americans were being fêted in cosmopolitan Paris, Senegalese soldiers who had fought for France in the war were denied citizenship or war pensions. North African workers brought into France during the war from the colonies were now being ousted in favour of a more controllable European migrant workforce of Poles and Czechs, whose cultural differences could be more easily assimilated (Dewitte 19).

Critics have described *négrophilie* as a patronising lionisation of certain aspects of black culture and identity, both real and imagined, that simply inverted the essentialist taxonomies of earlier derogatory racial typologies around "blackness." This is a position summed up rather caustically by Lemuel A. Johnson, who notes that "the concerns of the age had inverted the very means of denigration, transforming them into the attributes of a Messiah" (95). Johnson is deeply suspicious of a passing cultural trend that suddenly declares "black is good," and describes primitivism of the 1920s as "a one dimensional taste for the exotic and the picturesque" in which the mercurial tastes of a white urban public momentarily celebrates the particular essence of blackness previously denigrated and scorned (95–99). However, I argue here that the cultural primitivism of the early twentieth century was not simply a naïve "love of black culture" by a small group of avant-gardists, nor does it refer to a more popular black influence on *les années folles* or the jazz age. *Négrophilie* was a modernist primitivism, brimming with the dynamic and vigorous energies and contradictions of all the various strands of modernisms, and as such represented a more multivalent aesthetic and cultural phenomenon than earlier primitivist discourses. In previous primitivisms, black culture, in the form of a mythical Africanity, was represented as base, backwards, and lacking in any cultural presence, as opposed to the exotic categories of the Eastern, Arabic, or Polynesian, which were fascinating for their enigmatic differences and alternative knowledge systems. However, within modernist primitivism the discursive tropes around blackness began to acquire an exotic legitimacy. While this white negrophilia can be now regarded as politically problematic for obvious reasons, it was not simply coterminous with a liberal racism or colonialism. In what follows, I argue that interwar cultural primitivism developed from an initial modish interest in black cultural difference that simply inverted essentialist racial typologies into a more heterogeneous text of cultural difference that gradually opened up debates on race, colonialism, and representation of blackness. In other words, I look at *négrophilie* as both a popular interest in black cultural expression and a more heterogeneous modernist engagement with cultural and epistemological difference that represented a new transculturated aesthetic of the non-West. As the interwar period wore on, various kinds of cultural negotiation of difference emerged and opened up spaces for a counterprimitivism that constructed an anti-allegorical mode for the racial other and affirmed *real* spaces of difference.

The cultural roots of *négrophilie* have routinely been traced by art critics and historians back to the original discovery of African art, or *l'art nègre*, in Paris museums and *bistrots* around 1904 by André Derain and Maurice de Vlaminck and, of course, Picasso. The latter's first encounter with the primitive artefact has assumed a semimythological status in art history, as told in the perhaps apocryphal narrative of his serendipitous discovery of African masks in the *cabinets des curiosités* in the malodorous, cramped back annexes of the Musée du Trocadéro.[4] The implications for aesthetics would be dramatic and one could even say that without this discovery the trajectory of the modernist avant-garde would have been somewhat different. Paul Guillaume, a renowned art collector known as *le négrier* (the slaver), commented that all "the modern movement in art" was "impregnated with Africanism . . . because since Impressionism no manifestation in art could be shown that is not African in essence." "All new painters," Guillaume insisted, worked with "African emotion in a new setting" (140–41). By the early 1920s in France, primitivism was the defining mode in the visual arts and much of the early work of artists such as Braque, Léger, Brancusi, and Picasso clearly resonated with the lines and dimensions of non-Western art. What had originated in the visual and plastic arts developed in the rapidly proliferating areas of popular and mass culture into a full-blown popular phenomenon: the *vogue nègre* of *négrophilie*. From Josephine Baker's "Danse Sauvage" at the Théâtre Champs-Elysees to her *Zou Zou* film stickers on bananas and advertisements for hair pomade; images of colonial life in magazines such as *Annales* to posters advertising *Le Ballet Blanc et Noir;* the popularity of jazz and *le blackbottom* in the night-spots of Montmartre (the Harlem of Paris) to exotic African images on china tableware, the primitive, or at least its echoing archive, was suddenly everywhere. The particular type of transculturated contact of *négrophilie* that I am looking at here occurred both in popular and mass culture in magazines, films, advertising, and the music hall as well as in the galleries, salons, studios, and theatres of the avant-garde. The idea of the noble savage, sporadically fascinating to French writers since Montaigne's *Des Cannibales* in the sixteenth century and continuing in the Enlightenment tradition with Diderot, Montesquieu, Rousseau, and Voltaire, now reappeared, reconfigured to the particular dynamics of the contemporary moment. *La culte nègre* constructed the primitive figure in specific aesthetic and cultural ways, investing blackness as a trope of alterity with a doubled metaphoricity: the black body represented not only an archive of premodern history but also a blueprint for a specifically modern future. Martin Steins describes this as "[l]e mythe de l'homme primitif, découvert en Afrique, cristallisait des nostalgies européenes et faisait miroiter à une civilisation qui se découvrait en état de crise, la possibilité de retrouver une innocence, de recommencer la construction de la societé, de s'affranchir des servitudes sociales, notamment d'un monde technique" (76).

James Clifford has identified a crucial shift from an "early white negrophilia" in the 1920s to the more "complex engagement with black cultures" in the 1930s, a distinction that has not always been made in critical work in this area ("Negrophilia" 904–5). Attention to the ethnographic concept of otherness in the second interwar decade took place against the ascendant imperial rhetoric of France's *apogée coloniale* and the civilising mission of *la mère patrie*. Central to the shift from a crude, unreconstructed negrophilia that essentialised and reified the racial other to a more nuanced conceptualisation of racial subjectivity (which took place only very slowly over two distinct decades), was what Jean Laude describes as the "l'encerclement de la planète" by European colonial powers (10). Imperialism, defined here as the total set of practices, theories, and attitudes of a nation ruling over a conquered territory through the expansion of global capitalism, constituted the dominant ideological conditions in which *négrophilie* occurred.[5] More specifically, within imperialism's project, relations between coloniser and colonised and metropole and colony inflected many aspects of metropolitan cultural production in the interwar era; thus primitivism repeated certain paradigms of imperial and colonial relations in specific cultural and institutional ways. Far from stabilising and remaining static throughout France's colonial *apogée* of the 1920s and 1930s, relations between metropole and colony underwent what Edward Said calls a "Copernican change," as the inevitable consequences of *assimilation* and the *mission civilisatrice,* the ideological linchpins of French colonial policy, began to reverberate through metropolitan culture and politics (*Culture* 234). The invention, reinvention, and strategic deployment of race as a metaphor for political ideology was predicated on a set of relations between coloniser and colonised that privileged Western modernity, and in particular French republicanism, as the epistemological ideal. The triumphalist, but nonetheless anxious, narratives underpinning France's imperial *mission civilisatrice* unequivocally celebrated a rationalising, normative modernity that attempted to include, describe, and control the colonised in ways that sought to obliterate the notion of the outside and the unknown.

It has become commonplace to read that modernist primitivism was bound into and even a continuation of the colonial subjugation of peoples and cultures that was simply another, albeit sophisticated, version of the "imprisonment of the black subject" as the West's radical other (Gikandi 159). The story of the relationship between European modernism and primitivism is by now very well rehearsed, but this book suggests that many readings of this relationship have often oversimplified both terms to come up with the rather pedestrian conclusion that European modernism was in fact a cultural extension of imperialism, serving only to annex, appropriate, and silence Europe's others. Mary Louise Pratt has pointed out in *Imperial Eyes* that cultural contact is a highly complicated and complex interaction not always reducible to totalising theories of colonial discourse. These theories, embedded in a sometimes reductive postcolonial ethics, have very frequently understood modern primitivism as denigration at worst and appropriation at best. This is a situation that Fredric Jameson clearly recognises when he says, "The traces of imperialism can . . . be detected in western modernism, and are indeed constitutive of it: but we must not look for them in the obvious places, in content or in representation" (*Modernism and Imperialism* 44). Of course, empire and colonialism are the underpinning historical coordinates of modernist primitivism and are thus imbued with its ideological charges, but they cannot be reduced to simple models of complicity with the interests and activities of a rapacious colonialism. While the discourses of primitivism manage what Hal Foster calls the "ideological nightmare of a great art inspired by spoils" (199), modernism's engagement with the idea of otherness cannot be conflated into a crude model of "a Eurocentric and phallocentric category which involves a systematic preference for certain forms and voices over others" (Hebdige 177). Nor is it complicit with a stifling but unspoken orthodoxy that "consistently places the metropolitan centre over the 'underdeveloped' periphery, Western arts forms over Third World ones, men's art over women's art . . . " (Hebdige 177). This definition of modernism relies upon a caricatured version of high modernism, the aloof and glacial texts of Eliot and Pound perhaps, rather than acknowledging cross-fertilising diversity of modernisms: Dadaism (both Zurich and Paris, early and late), Vorticism, Imagism, Cubism, Expressionism, Futurism, and the later Paris-based configurations of the Surrealist Group. These different avant-garde modernisms often did not seek to perpetuate the simple binarisms of self/other or primitive/civilised but were variably engaged in registering the fracturing of hierarchical binaries and opposed the dominant fictions that kept in place a dynamics of centre and periphery. The openness of modernisms to the so-called outside left the category of difference open to all kinds of splitting and dissent that allowed for a "dialogic relation with immediate historical contexts" (T. Miller 31). This dialogism by its very nature was a space in which not one but many voices could be heard; it was a multivocal space that was by turns oppositional, internationalist, and nonhierarchical. The inherently complex nature of modernist primitivism then was often (but by no means always) a countercultural force that abhorred the silencing of colonial subjects even while their objectification was frequently central to their aesthetic.

My arguments throughout this book hope to provoke a more comparative framework in which we can read the phenomenon of early twentieth-century primitivism. Using Fredric Jameson's concept of "thinking together," I attempt to reconcile previously disparate critical and conceptual positions on these issues: race, modernism, and counter-primitivism of the black Atlantic diaspora. I want to avoid a wholesale incrimination of modernism for its appropriation of cultural difference and apparent complicity with colonial ideologies by suggesting that from within versions of modernist primitivism, there opened up radically new spaces of articulation in which counterprimitivism and anticolonialism could emerge. Far from being solipsistically obsessed with the question of autonomous apolitical form, certain forms of avant-garde modernism nurtured an emergent anticolonialism that was committed to a new poetics of race and difference and would challenge the authority of white mythologies. Too often the question of how race has functioned within modernism has focussed only on the formal aestheticisation of race, in particular blackness, as a marker of ontological crisis, leaving out, or at best subduing, the effects of a real black presence in France, which was in Fanon's words "battered down" by the weight of the stereotype. This book remaps the relationship between modern primitivism and the development within and against this modern primitivism of counternarratives by diasporic groups that worked to recover the agency and voice of the primitive and to construct an "account of the modern/primitive encounter from the 'other' side" (Foster 200). Toni Morrison describes this as a diversion of the critical focus from the "racial object to the racial subject;

from the described and the imagined to the describers and the imaginers" (90). *Négrophilie* engendered, albeit in sporadic and uneven ways, the emergence of a diasporic matrix of a black Atlanticism in which students, trade unionists, and writers began to write back against the silencing of real otherness and to mark out a space in which a counterdiscourse could be articulated. This book sets out to answer the following questions: what distinguished *négrophilie* from earlier primitivisms? What was especially modern or modernist about this form of primitivism? How can we assess this primitivism as a complex aesthetic and poetical occurrence that cannot be simply conflated with a brutishly uncaring aesthetic modernism or as a simple act of ruthless appropriation? What were the particular historical conditions that produced both primitivism and anticolonialism?

Chapter 1 sets out to dissect the term *primitive* by looking at its antecedent discourses and examining its correlative and sometimes equivalent term *exotic*. A useful schema for interrogating the representation of otherness by Western cultural texts is one in which these two foundational typologies of otherness—the primitive and the exotic—are interrogated within a broad historical matrix. The term *primitive* is associated with the "unformed and untamed realm of the pre-rational" (Williams, *Politics* 58) and a violently repressed Freudian id that is unleashed from societal interdiction. The discourses of the exotic, in contradistinction, are more concerned with difference as emblematic of a paradisal "elsewhere," a geographical otherness characterised by plenitude and harmony. Using these two discursive paradigms of racial and cultural otherness as coordinates, I examine the incidence of modern primitivism in early Zurich Dada and the emergence of a new visual aesthetic of difference. In interwar France the trope of the primitive is mediated through the aesthetics of Fauvism and Cubism and then develops into a popular and mass cultural interest in black cultural forms that has retrospectively been called *négrophilie*. This cultural phenomenon needs to be specifically understood as a response to the end of the First World War in Europe when the post-Enlightenment promises of liberal progress and endless amelioration failed in the trenches of the Somme and at Ypres. The trajectory of the *la vogue nègre* is examined within the epistemological contexts of a radical disenchantment of the Western world as argued by Adorno and Horkheimer in *Dialectic of Enlightenment*.

Chapters 2 and 3 look at a specific figure of modern primitivism: the figure of Josephine Baker, a young black American entertainer from St. Louis who became an overnight sensation with her performances in *La Revue Nègre* in 1925. Tracing her performances in the *Revue* back to her "pickaninny" and black-face routines on the American music-hall stage, I present a series of close readings of Baker's racial persona as *la petite sauvageonne* between 1925 and 1927. These readings, drawn from the popular presses and from high cultural commentary on Baker's act, interrogate how she was held up as a figure of an ancient and nostalgic past while simultaneously seen as a new model of a future aesthetic. I also assess claims that Baker's performances were subversive and parodic of racial stereotypes while situating them in the historically specific cultural contexts of interwar Paris. In 1931 Baker was elected Queen of the Colonies for the Exposition Coloniale Internationale. The misguided association of Baker, an American, with the colonies was part of her public persona in the second interwar decade; this association is examined in detail in chapter 3. Examining the overdetermined racialised discourses around Baker's body that described her performing body as a racial spectacle signified all cultural difference. I read these discourses through the colonial contexts of France in the early 1930s. This was a time when the French Empire was at its *apogée* in terms of economic profit and public approval but was starting to experience the very first rumblings of anticolonial dissent.

Chapters 4 and 5 explore the relationship between avant-garde constructions of race in political, aesthetic, and ethnographic discourses. The 1934 *Negro* anthology, an ambitious tome covering the historical, sociological, and aesthetic aspects of race and empire edited by the poet, activist, and patron Nancy Cunard, brings together a set of concerns around race, cultural difference, and imperial power in the second interwar decade. The anthology, an explicitly Communist polemic, gives space to both black and white voices from the Americas, Europe, and Africa within an agenda of radical cultural politics and political activism as exemplified by the work of the Surrealist Group. Although only partially successful in its political intervention, the *Negro* anthology was a significant attempt to challenge dominant ideologies of race and to resist the dominant ideological narratives of cultural primitivism.

Chapter 5 looks in detail at the Surrealist Group's anticolonial activities in the 1930s. Through their later affiliation with both the Communist Party and the Parti Communiste Français (PCF), the Surrealist Group attempted to unite cultural text and political context. In *Negro,* the Group offer a contemplation of the material conditions of production behind the primitive. Their contributions to the anthology were part of a wider collaboration between anticolonialist activism, in which writers such as Daniel Thaly, Léon Damas, Aimé Césaire, and Léopold Senghor were already active, and the increasingly politicised aesthetic practices of the avant-garde.

Chapter 6 considers the "voyages in" of France's assimilated *évolués.* Heirs to the spurious civilising mission of French colonial ideology, writers, artists, and activists travelled from the colonial territories of the French Empire to participate in the cultural life of the metropolitan centre. I look here at the formation and political mobilisation of a black Atlantic diasporic community in Paris and the gradual recuperation of its own agency, history, and aesthetic in the pre-négritude years. The challenge to prevailing conceptualisations of racial difference initially came from workers and student groups who found Paris Noir a fruitful transnational site of encounter for these discussions. Students from Guadeloupe, Martinique, Réunion, West Africa, Guyana, Indo-China, and Haiti were influenced in various ways by black Americans whom they encountered in Paris and by the transatlantic cross-pollination of intellectual ideas and political activism. I point out how these debates taking shape in the 1930s were not in themselves new but belonged to an older tradition of diasporic political activism begun just after the end of the First World War. Through close readings of *La Dépêche Africaine*, *La Revue du Monde Noir*, and *Légitime Défense*, I argue that these three journals are representative of an emergent Francophone black Atlanticism and thus mark an important point in the construction of a counterprimitivist discourse of race and ethnicity.

NOTES

1. The term *negrophilia* is used first in Jean Laude's *La Peinture française (1905–1914) et l'art nègre* and more recently in James Clifford's entry on negrophilia in *A New History of French Literature* (1989) and Petrine Archer Shaw's *Negrophilia: Avant-garde Paris and Black Culture in the 1920s* (2000).
2. See also Bancel and Blanchard 16.
3. See Taguieff, *Discours* 53–81, 134–60.
4. The exact origins of the primitive influence on modern art have been well documented by art historians. See Frascina and Harris; Goldwater; Kahnweiler; Krauss; Laude; and the ethnographic cultural critique of Clifford, who dates this discovery by Picasso et al. to around 1910 (*Predicament* 190). Opinions differ, however, among art historians as to the exact date, but it is certainly somewhere between 1906 and 1910. See Rubin 328–30. See also Laude for a usefully detailed history of the use of the primitive in the visual arts.
5. On theories of French imperialism and colonialism, see Betts; Brunschwig; Girardet; Persell; Andrew and Kanya-Forster; and Kiernan.

CHAPTER 1

Constructing the Modern Primitive

> And we came to the land of the Cyclopes, a fierce, uncivilized people who never lifted a hand to plant or plough but put their trust in Providence. [. . .] The Cyclopes have no assemblies for the making of laws, nor nay settled customs but live in hollow caverns in the mountain heights, where each man is lawgiver to his children and his wives, and nobody cares a jot for his neighbours.
>
> —Homer, *The Odyssey,* book ix

INTRODUCTION

For centuries, certainly since the early European conquests of the Americas, the West, a fraught and loosely generic category, has been narrating and representing its "outside"; its others. Memoirs, journals, novels, poems, travel writing, journalism, ethnographic accounts, administrative documents, and essays have all contributed to the classification, codification, and textual representation of culture and customs outside of the sphere of Europe. Contact across cultures did not, of course, take the form of unalloyed wonderment and curiosity; in fact, as we know only too well, the converse took place, as indigenous cultures, local knowledges, languages, and sometimes whole peoples were eradicated in the name of commerce, civilisation, and progress. However, alongside conquest and exploitation, the West's engagement with its others has been an elliptical movement of the self reaching out, extending out to the unknown and perhaps unknowable other. This engagement has produced a range of discursive structures and practices that have shaped Western understanding and representation of its others.[1]

The ideological and epistemological forces shaping the production of certain discourses of otherness are not fixed into an immutable iconographic vocabulary of difference but rather change over histories, geographies, and political regimes. Edward Said's seminally influential work in *Orientalism* effectively kick-started the postcolonial industry of interrogating the ideological and political production of discourses of otherness (in Said's case of the Arabic Orient), a critical practice now known as colonial discourse analysis variably employed by many critics of colonialism and postcolonialism. However, recently a number of critics, such as the anthropologist Nicholas Thomas, have alerted us to the tendency of colonial discourse analysis to fix on the negativity of European discursive practices and the "effacement of native agency" (37). To see the relationship between the imaginer and the imagined thus is to continue to privilege the totalising power of colonialism and to uncomplicate the intrinsic complexities of discourses around racial and cultural otherness. My focus here is not simply on the negativity of primitivist discourses but on the complex activities of a particular type of primitivism in the first decades of the twentieth century. I am not primarily concerned with assessing or examining the long history of changing discourses and tropes of Western primitivism—this has been carried out very comprehensively elsewhere—but on interrogating a specific point in which the relations between a "native" voice and its "describers" underwent significant changes that troubled the internal logic of the primitivism itself.[2] My emphasis is on a very specific historical period from around 1907 to 1935, with a particular focus on the interwar years in France. During this time there were significant shifts in the ways that the racial other as primitive was constructed and represented in a set of artistic and intellectual practices that can be loosely termed modernist primitivism. The category of the primitive was read in particular aesthetic and epistemological relationships to modernity and to the expressive limits of the modern subject. Modernist primitivism was not a singular activity carried out by a handful of artists and writers whose aesthetic engagement with Europe's others was predicted on a ruthless appropriation of difference for its own formally innovative agenda. Nor were modernism's interests simply in employing the trope of the primitive other as a cipher for the expression of an irrationality left over from the "internal violence of a saturated whole" (Baudrillard 10). Rather, modernist primitivism was a variety of engagements with cultural difference that jostled up against each other in a dynamic field of diverse avant-gardisms, theory and praxis, production and consumption across high and popular cultures. Stuart Hall has suggested that within culture "different currents struggle within the same ideological field, what must be studied is the way in which they contest, often around the same idea or concept." Continuing through Gramsci, he says,

"The question is [. . .] 'how these currents are born, how they are diffused and why in the process of diffusion they fracture along certain lines and in certain directions' " (*Hard Road* 327). Modernism, then, opened up a series of fractures in primitivist discourses in which the object of representation—the primitivised other—disrupted the authority of primitivism by rupturing the textual prison of an objectifying otherness.

In *The Politics* of *Modernism*, Raymond Williams recognises that an aesthetic fascination with the art of "marginal peoples" has been a consistent feature of intellectual and artistic inquiry for several historical eras in the West. The recourse to folkloric traditions and customs, he says, is a temporal one and is a desire to "reach back beyond" to a "simpler art" (58). This past, however represented, is always presented in a reflexive, sometimes dialectical, relationship to a European present that is seen to develop and change while the time of the other stands still. Whether it is the Celts, Slavs, Native Americans, Polynesians, Indians, or Africans, representations and discourses of otherness have *always* approximately divided into two generic categories of otherness: the primitive and the exotic.[3] While these two terms are in no way exclusive—in reality the borders between the two are highly pliable—they remain nevertheless useful distinctions. Broadly speaking, non-European otherness rendered as primitive has been represented as regressive and atavistic: the untutored subject of non-history whose customs and traditions have not been caught up in the idea of Enlightenment and progress, and later, modernity. The primitive is represented as the antithesis of modernity. The exotic, on the other hand, is interesting to the West for its "emblematic" qualities that suggest a more complex cultural difference. The customs and tradition of the exotic have often been represented as highly picturesque and often enigmatic mystical rituals that exist in a more elaborate social and cultural context compared to the primitive's undeveloped simplicity (Thomas 173).

The vast body of writing over the centuries on the West's encounter with its other, whether colonial or otherwise, can more or less be divided along geographical lines. Middle and Far Eastern, Polynesia, and Islamic North Africa have fallen under the category of the exotic, whereas sub-Saharan Africa and its diasporas in the Caribbean and the Americas is rendered as the primitive. In short, as Hal Foster remarks, it is typically a case of "malefic Africa versus paradisal Oceania" (188).[4] It is important to understand that the borders between these two terms are not rigid but permeable and shifting according to the ideological and historical contexts of their production. However, before embarking on a discussion of modernist primitivism, it is important to delineate two predominant tropes of otherness within primitivism: that of a regressive, untamed atavism versus the state of plenitude and harmonious simplicity of the exotic primitive.

THE PRIMITIVE AS EXORCISM

The story of Picasso's "discovery" of African and Oceanic masks in the cramped and malodorous back rooms of the Musée de Trocadéro in Paris has attained almost mythical status in the histories of modernism. Although Picasso himself was to later remark rather nonchalantly, "L'art nègre? Connais pas!" his reworkings of Grebo and Fang masks in his pathbreaking work *Les Demoiselles d'Avignon* (1907) broke with a foundational relationship between object and meaning, sign and referent, and profoundly altered the aesthetics of a whole generation of painters, writers, and intellectuals. Considered as the most seminally influential single piece of modern art in the twentieth century, art historians routinely place Picasso's completion of the painting as a determining moment in modern primitivism. The painter's own comments on the African artefacts in the Trocadéro point up a new engagement with the aesthetics of the object as other: "Men had made those masks and other objects for a scared purpose, a magic purpose, as a kind of mediation between themselves and the unknown hostile forces that surround them" (Gilot and Lake 266). *Les Demoiselles*, then, is regarded as central to the shift in signification of *l'art primitif* from a debased and unevolved fetish object to a more complex one officially ordained in the modernist canons of epistemological and aesthetic influence.

Picasso's Cubist break with mimesis in the *Les Demoiselles* was the genesis of a "strong anti-representational bias" that would, in one form or another, mark most modernist avant-gardisms (Nicholls, *Modernisms* 112). "The new modes or perception it [Cubism] offers transfigure the world and in doing so conjoin primitive and modern in an explosive union which links the 'cruelty' of seeing to a 'barbarism' which exceeds Western conventions of representation" (Nicholls, *Modernisms* 114). Here Peter Nicholls alights upon one of the two predominant understandings of primitivism within aesthetic modernism. The first is an allegorical evocation of repressed deathly and libidinal drives, the "unformed and untamed realm of the pre-rational" (Williams, *Politics* 58), that operate as a negative opposite to rationality and consciousness. Thus, Picasso's claim to André Malraux that he (Picasso) was against everything and that everything was an enemy and unknown points to the void of the negativity represented by the African masks used to denote death and disease in *Les Demoiselles*. William Rubin comments on this in the controversial volume *"Primitivism" in Twentieth Century Art:*

> We sense the thanatophobia in the primordial horror evoked by the monstrously distorted heads of the two whores on the right of the picture. . . . One can hardly imagine the fear, shock and awe that these heads must have imparted in 1907. . . . They finally conjure something that transcends our sense of civilized experience,

something ominous and monstrous such as Conrad's Kurtz discovered on the heart of darkness. (254)

If we are to focus primarily on the racialised elements in Picasso's use of the African masks, we see a particular trope of primitivism in which African, a generic term used for all black cultural signs, signifies a regressivism focussed on the notion of the primordial and the atavistic. Within this the corporeal is expressed as an almost bestial promiscuity, a wild and untamed physicaiity on the borders between the animal and the human. This is a use of the primitivised Africanity that has its roots in the nineteenth century and has most notably been the subject of intense and ongoing critical and ethical scrutiny in the case of Joseph Conrad's turn-of-the-century novella.

Heart of Darkness (1899) is perhaps one of the most cited texts of the engagement of early twentieth century with racial difference. While it may seem redundant to revisit this text after so much critical attention has been directed towards it, any serious study of the role of primitivism in the early twentieth century continues to demand an engagement with this seminal moment of representation of Africa in European culture. The novel frames the contact with the primitive as a means of exploring a fascination with the irrational, the unrestrained, but above all with death.[5] For Marlow and Kurtz, Africa represents an allegory of exorcism, an unknowable and unconfinable context in which all is possible. Conrad presents us with Kurtz's moral and psychic disintegration into native life; his mask of the European civilised self falls quickly away when confronted with the limitless possibilities of a primordial blood lust in which all "methods" are possible and nothing is prohibited. This then is the space of the untamed, violently repressed Freudian id, for which we can read the "natural" state of humanity, untouched by civilising forces. The atavistic human subject is reminiscent of some later work on dissident primitivism, for instance, in George Bataille's *Visions of Excess* (1985) in which the "abrupt violence" of cannibalism and ritualised killings become the self released from cultural and religious interdiction. Conrad's savage wild-eyed natives who inhabit the "incomprehensible frenzy" of the Congo are replayed later in Picasso's *Les Demoiselles d'Avignon* as a Cubist rendition of Grebo masks with their fetishistic suggestions of morbidity and sexual disease. We see here the figure of the primitive, an unspecified African-ness, representing the "underside of the rock of Western objectivity and aesthetics" (Torgovnick 156). The primitive as debased, abject, and thoroughly irredeemable was a recurrent trope in much of nineteenth-century Africanist writing, both in English and in French. In *The Rhetoric of Empire*, David Spurr scrutinises the rhetorical devices shaping and ordering a variety of colonial discourses in the nineteenth and twentieth centuries. He designates four main categories for the apprehension of otherness in fiction and journalism: debasement, negation, idealisation, and aestheticisation. Roughly speaking, the first two are almost purely negative and derogatory categories, while the latter are predicated on a more nostalgic desire for a return to origins and to find an originary plenitude and wholeness. Just as a primitivised blackness is depicted as the very core of ontological darkness, without light or rationality, the exotic primitive is a redemptive place flooded with light and colour.

"PARFUM EXOTIQUE": THE PRIMITIVE AS REDEMPTION

The second category of the primitive may be described as a romantic primitivism, or what Raymond Williams calls an attraction to the "vitality of the naïve" (58). In distinction to the trope of the malefic or malevolent primitive located in the heart of darkness, geographical areas denoted as exotic have tended to be in Oceania, particularly Polynesia, the Oriental Far East and Arabic Middle Eastern regions. In 1771 Bougainville (whose name itself would be associated with an eternally exotic flower) described the fragrant island of Tahiti as Garden of Eden. His encounters with the indigenous peoples was one characterised by "hospitality, ease innocent joy and every appearance of happiness . . . " (B. Smith 25). This is an erotic paradise of abundance and plenitude; a crucible of sensuality and above all harmony. Diderot's later *Supplément au voyage de Bougainville,* written in 1772 and published 1796, took Bougainville's ideas of the simple sensuality and harmonious life of the South Seas island and used it as a semi-allegorical treatise on the confrontation between mind and body, Catholicism and sexuality. The paradisal tropes of plenitude can be discerned most fully in Paul Gauguin's Tahitian painting as well as in the work of Victor Segalen (1878–1919).[6] Gauguin's' depictions of the "happy inhabitants of the unknown paradises of Oceania" may be loosely placed within a Rousseau-esque tradition of the enduring trope of the noble savage in *Discours sur l'origine et les fondements de l'inégalité parmi les hommes* (1755) (Gauguin 168–69). This exoticist tradition in painting continued in the works of Henri Matisse and Henri (Douanier) Rousseau and can also be clearly seen in a seam of exoticist poetry in early modernists such as Baudelaire and Mallarmé. Consider the following extract from Baudelaire's "Parfum Exotique":

> Quand, les yeux deux fermeé, en un soir chaud d'automne,
> Je respire l'odeur de ton sein chaleureux
> Je vois dérouler des rivages heureux
> Qu' éblouissent les feux d'un soleil monotone;

Une île paresseuse où la nature donne
Des arbres singuliers et des fruits savoureux;
Des hommes dont le corps est mince et vigoureux,
Et des femmes don't l'oeil par sa franchise étonne.[7]

The poem continues to praise the abundant charms of "charmants climats" with the perfume of "verts tamariniers" to create a poetics of absolute plenitude, the body perfectly in tune with its natural surroundings. The senses are bewitched by the landscape and the beautiful men and women whose half-naked and uninhibited indigenous bodies fill the island-scape with a surfeit of sensuality and indolence. This, then, is the essence of the exotic primitivism: the bounteous South Sea island that persists in the popular imagination even today, in which figure and the texts of the other function as a source of "originary unity, symbolic plenitude, natural vitality" (Foster 206). Romantic primitivism was an intellectual tradition less predicated on the West's relationship to a repressed or excised excess than with a search for lost origins, a desire for cohesion and wholeness in simpler social and cultural structures than those of the West. It is suggestive of the recuperability of a primal Edenic idyll and the possibility of regeneration and revivification through unthreatening sensual experience. In a sense this category does not speak *through* the figure of the other but escapes *to* it.[8] This is closer to the varieties of exoticism that have typically been found in the representation of Middle Eastern and Asian cultures, such as the trends of Japonisme, Chinoiserie, and of course Orientalism that occurred in France in both the eighteenth and nineteenth centuries.

Modernist primitivism variably employed both of these tropes of difference through the generic term *primitif* or *nègre.* Crucially, we must remember that these categories are never fixed into inviolable demarcations, as the contexts of describing otherness are always contingent upon the locale of enunciation and are moreover, as Nicholas Thomas has observed, "necessarily evaluations of prior discourse" (171). In other words, what we may categorise under the heading primitive today might be termed exotic tomorrow or in the next century. Modern primitivism in France coincided historically with the three very important things that are inseparable from both its production and dissemination, its central paradoxes as well as to its disintegration. The interwar era was the *apogée,* or apotheosis, of France's colonial empire; this was also the height of late modernism, if we take the publication of *Ulysses* in 1922 as the beginning of the later modernist period. This was also a time when technological developments in print, transport, and communications permitted a much more rapid degree of interaction on a global scale. The Atlantic and Pacific oceans, once, redoubtable barriers to easy passage and trade, became thoroughfares for ideas, influences, and movements, replacing what had once been the transporation of goods and people around the pernicious triangle of human trade between Africa, the Americas, and Europe.[9] To these developments we can add the catastrophic experiences of the First World War and the immediate postwar moments in which writers and artists sought to comprehend and represent a society devoid of all reason.

POSTWAR TRAUMA AND DISENCHANTMENT

The reverberations of the Great War continued long after the 1918 Treaty of Versailles, and this period immediately following the cessation of military hostilities was, as Tyrus Miller has noted, characterised by "a kind of all pervasive, collective, and incurable shell-shock" affecting soldier and artist alike (24). The unprecedented degradation of human life in the trenches of Ypres and the Somme was incommensurate with post-Enlightenment narratives of instrumental reason and progress. How could reason produce such murderous unreason? The idea of a history as a positivist, progressive liberalisation of the subject, as promised by the grand narratives of the nineteenth century, seemed increasingly untenable, as a generation of men met violent and untimely deaths amidst the carnage of the battlefield. Very broadly speaking, then, the immediate postwar years saw a crisis of confidence in Western modernity and the ways in which a "civilised" European subject could be imagined. Four years of military slaughter on an industrial scale had severely tried the notion of a post-Enlightenment modernity that had promised to deliver an ever-ameliorating future. How could the modern subject begin to imagine itself again amidst the fractured, dislocated historical space of the present? Walter Benjamin has famously recognised this perceptual cataclysm, remarking: "A generation that had gone to school on a horse-drawn streetcar now stood under the open sky in a countryside in which nothing remained unchanged but the clouds, and beneath the clouds, in a field of force of destructive torrents and explosions, was the tiny, fragile human body" (*Illuminations* 84). Tyrus Miller suggests that this postwar world was less determined by the organic rhythms of everyday life than by an increasing automation of the body—man as machine—in which "the distinction between the vital and the mechanic had become less sharp" (24). After the war art became a project of reimagination of this fragile humanity in which the shell-shocked subject of modernity sought reanimation and demechanisation against the "disenchantment of the world" (Adorno and Horkheimer 5).

The epistemological project of modernity posited the idea of social progress that would extend into a future of ever-ameliorating self-knowledge gained through social, political, and institutional interactions carefully administered and policed by the vigilant apparatuses of the modern nation-state. Jürgen Habermas has described modernity's project as a strong secular faith in "the extravagant expectation that the arts and sciences would promote not only the control of natural forces but also understanding of the world and of the self, moral progress, the justice of institutions and even the happiness of human beings" (9). However, the positivist philosophies of universal progress, Cartesian rationalism, and technological and scientific dominion over the natural world were rendered impotent in the wake of the ignoble failure of secular humanism in the trenches. Modernity as a philosophical project was inescapably flawed by the conflicting interests of its utilitarian nature that obtained economic prosperity and modernisation only at the acute human cost of alienation and displacement. Thus, as famously argued by Adorno and Horkheimer in *Dialectic of Enlightenment,* the consequences of enlightened human activity reaped equal measures of destruction and construction in the inherently antagonistic nature of post-Enlightenment rationalism.[10] The secular, demythologising logic that constructed buildings and engineered empires transformed the same will to domination and assimilation of the unknown into mass slaughter and brutal social inequities. Elsewhere, Marshall Berman has viewed modernity as a profoundly ambivalent human project in which unity and profound disunity "pour[s] us all into a maelstrom of perpetual disintegration and renewal, of struggle and contradiction, of ambiguity and anguish" (15). As much as modernity was concerned with production of order and uniformity through social rationalisation, it was also in a constant state of anxiety as to how to maintain that order against the threat of the "outside."[11] The idea of the outside of course is of particular significance to my discussion of cultural primitivism and its aesthetic and political inscription.

As Adorno and Horkheimer have explained, the symbolic function of the notion of outside serves a dual purpose in the discourses of modernity: "Nothing at all may remain outside because the mere idea of outside is the very source of fear" (16). That archival or residual presence that remains outside of the rationalising forces of European modernity is construed as replete with both powers of terror and of enchantment that operate as a totemic text of difference against which the imagining (white) subject can narrate itself. From within the sense of ennui in the *entre-deux-guerres* the modern subject sought a remythologisation as a resolution to the anomies of the modern. The otherness of the primitive offered a means of reanimating the atrophied present through recourse to the past, in which "[t]he difference of another cultural or discursive regime" is mobilised in order "to disclose the contingency and the specificity of the present" (Thomas 21). This is may be as Andreas Huyssens says, a process of "Reason coming to terms with its mythical origins" (8). The racial other of modern primitivism offered a new mythology positing the possibility of an unsullied "elsewhere," a pristine space of the real in which life and art were fully integrated into the processes of subjectivity. Therefore, the figure of the other—in this case an imagined figure of blackness—performed a historically specific function within the postwar moments as both the affirmation and the opposition of Western modernity. Modern primitivism spoke to a desire for historical amnesia—forgetting the past by offering a flight from the nightmare of recent history—and simultaneously evoked a kind of nostalgia for the past, for a time that was premodern and not lacerated by the trauma of mass destruction. In *Minima Moralia,* Adorno has talked of the temporal and historical rupture and aporia produced by war:

> Just as the war lacks continuity, history, an "epic" element, but seems rather to start anew from the beginning in each phase, so it will leave behind no permanent, unconsciously preserved image in the memory. Everywhere, with each explosion, it has breached the barrier against stimuli beneath which experience . . . forms. But nothing, perhaps, is more ominous for the future than the fact that, quite literally, these things will soon be past thinking on, for each trauma of the returning combatants, each shock not inwardly absorbed, is a ferment of future destruction. (54)

Adorno points up here the effects of fractured time and space of war (in this case the Second World War) on the subject who must make an enormous effort of will to process the experience of trauma. The trope of the primitive seemed to offer a redemptive mythological space in which time was still whole and had escaped the alienation of modernity. Thus, the time and the space of the primitive other existed in an alternate historical continuum that was seen as real, or natural, time, uninterrupted by the shock of the modern. Johannes Fabian comments on the anthropological construction of the natural time of the other:

> It [anthropology] gave to politics and economics—both concerned with human time—a firm belief in "natural", ie evolutionary Time. It promoted a scheme in terms in which not only past cultures, but all living societies were irrevocably placed on a temporal slope, a stream of Time—Some upstream, others downstream. Civilization, evolution, development, acculturation, modernisation[. . .] are all terms whose conceptual content derives, in ways that can be specified, from evolutionary time. (17)

In this schema, the subject of modernity was wrenched out of time, "unable to return to its beginnings and thus recover its powers of renewal" and also "cut off from the past and continually hurtling forward at such a dizzy pace that it cannot take root [. . .]" (Paz 161–62). The activity of primitivism offered a conduit of reconnection with the past, while pointing out a path through to the future. Reviewing Josephine Baker's performance in *La Revue Nègre,* a critic noted that the *Revue* seemed to speak to the pressing concerns of the age and a desire for a flight from the "nightmare of history": "Our romanticism is desperate for renewal and escape. . . . We lean on our own unconscious and our dreams. . . . These blacks feed our double taste for exoticism and mystery. . . . We are charmed and upset by them, and most satisfied when they mix something upsetting in with their enchantments" (qtd. in Rose 48). The combination of a mysterious "upsetting" element of blackness mixed with an enchantment that could transport the viewer to another temporal and spatial locale where the present was made less solid. The primitive was a conductor of history that allowed a "practical critique of the imperatives of white civilisation" amidst "the maelstrom of modernity itself" (Schwartz 182).

A NEW PLASTICITY: DADA AND DIFFERENCE

My other brother is naïve and good, and laughs.

—Tristan Tzara, 1917

One afternoon whilst drinking in a bistro in Argentueil, the Fauvist painter Maurice de Vlaminck noticed that the proprietor had on display some statues from Dahomey and the Ivory Coast. It would scarcely be an overstatement to claim that this serendipitous experience marked a critical moment in the development of a new European visual aesthetic. Drawing upon primitive artefacts from Oceania and Iberia, Picasso painted a specifically inflected African form in *Les Demoiselles d'Avignon* that would come to encapsulate the new aesthetics of fracture and fragmentation. The new aesthetics redefined subject/object relations, temporal and spatial planes of art work, and reappraisal of line, perspective, and beauty. In his 1913 work *The Cubist Painters,* Guillaume Apollinaire has declared that a desire for a purity that rejects all attempts to duplicate nature or look for any "real resemblance" is central to the Cubist aesthetic programme (qtd. in Kolocotroni et al. 262). "Generally speaking," he has noted, "modern art repudiates most of the techniques of pleasing devised by the great artists of the past" (*Predicament* 264). Further, for the new art, "[T]he subject no longer counts," a fact reiterated by Habermas when he located the beginnings of this modernist sensibility in the nineteenth-century work of Baudelaire. Modernist art, Habermas has said, rejected the idea of realist reproduction: "Color, lines, sounds and movement ceased to serve primarily the cause of representation; the media of expression and the techniques of production themselves became the aesthetic object" (10). Vlaminck's purchase of African statues in the private sphere of social activity marked a decisive shift in the reception of the primitive artefact. Salvaged from the back rooms and curiosity cabinets of neglected state museums, masks and fetishes were dusted down and put on display in art galleries, salons, and national expositions. There was, as James Clifford has noted, a distinctive shift in the classification of the primitive artefact as it was installed into a circuit of exchange in which its aesthetic formal qualities, rather than its cultural contexts, became the focus of attention (199). At this moment we can say that the primitive artefact became central to and constitutive of the articulation of a radically new antirepresentational aesthetic.

In his "Note on Negro Art," Tristan Tzara, a Romanian emigré who fronted Zurich Dada during the last two years of the First World War, comments on this plastic art, which was centred on a new notion of purity: "The new art is first and foremost concentration . . . through purity we have first deformed and decomposed the object. . . . We want a clarity that is direct . . . " (281). Tzara's describes this new art as drawing on an essential harmony of form inherent in African art, what he refers to as the more "naïve and good" art of the "other brother." Thus, with the decomposition of the subject, the attraction of "Negro art" is its referent not to a real or material existence in the world but to its metaphorical possibilities of pure form. The real subject that has a visible existence in the world is precisely not what is being invoked here, but rather the energies of the formal medium. This is of course politically problematic, as postcolonial theory has pointed out. An understanding of African-ness set in opposition to Cartesian subject has been read by many critics as one saturated with a deep-rooted racism that, while claiming to act in a radically new way in Western aesthetics, only replicates the ideological manoeuvres of colonialism. Helen Carr suggests that modernist primitivism has been understood by some Marxist and postcolonial critiques, as simply an aesthetic extension of an imperial appetite for pillage, the "rifling of subordinated cultures for artefacts and inspiration, for exotic and dreams to bring a new vitality to a jaded West" (65). The question that needs to be answered here is one that addresses the ethics of an instrumental appropriation of the primitive artefact in order to express a rupture in European aesthetics. Is not this type of abstraction, however radically it disrupts received notions of time, space, and subject/object relations, simply a case of disavowal reminiscent of colonial discourse in which the native means exactly what you want it to mean for that precise moment? Is this avant-garde recuperation of difference simply a way of avoiding sinking into what Lévi-Strauss in *Tristes Tropiques* calls a homogenous Western monoculture? (27). These are central questions to which I will return throughout this book. But first it is necessary to look more closely at how the category of the primitive was actually used in the early European avant-garde and in particular Zurich Dada.

As war broke out in Europe, one group of artists reacted vociferously and controversially with now-famous nights of poetry, chanting, and burlesque theatre. A very significant part of Zurich Dada's "anti-everything" agenda was the construction of a certain text of primitiveness that seemed to voice the turbulence of the moment. The *Cabaret Voltaire,* set up by Hugo Ball and Emmy Hennings at Number One Spiegelasse in neutral Zurich, opposed the "utterly quixotic, unpurposeful, incomprehensible side of the world" (Ewen 74). Early Dadaist fascination with the limits of language and sound was played out in the *Cabaret,* a chaotic and defiantly ludic space where drumming, African chants, intricate non-narrative theatre, and discordant singing were the order of the day. Tzara, a regular participant in Dadaist evenings, was particularly interested in the idea of the primitive as a new terrain for the exploration of antirepresentational language and the *Cabaret* frequently featured primitive performance pieces called *chants nègres,* such as Richard Huelsenbeck's work "Chorus Sanctus":

> aao a ei iii oii
> ou ou o ou ou e ie a ai
> ha dzk drr br obu br bouss boum
> ha haha hi hi hi l i l l i li leiomen (*Memoirs* 20)

These *chants nègres,* mimicking the rhythms and tonalities of an imaginary African language, were performed against a background of enthusiastic "African" drumming and a display on stage of so-called tribal masks designed by Marcel Janco. For the Dadaists, the primitive represented a space still outside the reach of a totalising modernity—in which their energetic "anti-everything" agenda could operate. Thus, Huelsenbeck's 1917 Dada manifesto "The New Man" described Dada as closely identified with those unassimilated spaces of the "outcasts and the dehumanized beings of Europe, the Africans, the Polynesians, all kinds . . . " (*Memoirs* xxxi). To align oneself on the side of the primitive subject was a gesture of refusal of both political ontology and communicative responsibility.[12]

For Tzara the primitive functioned as a site of signification that could accommodate the weight of Dadaist nihilism (H. Lewis 3). Deeply scornful of the bourgeois world of moral decorum and rationality, Dada regarded the appropriation of the space of the primitive as an insurrectional gesture against the so-called civilised world as it seemed to be closer to a childlike refusal of signification in its apparent purity and spontaneity. In the primitive, Dada sought "[c]hildhood as a new word, and everything childlike and phantastic, everything childlike and symbolical in opposition to the senilities of the world of grown-ups" (Ball 52). The language play of sounds as signifiers and the insurrectionary use of bodily functions point to a desire for a freedom within the discursive limits of language, a way of communicating that has no real purpose beyond the immediacy of its own utterance. But more seriously, it represents a desire for the reintegration of the body and the intellect—an anti-Cartesian gesture—and thus for a rapprochement between art and life. As Peter Bürger notes:

> Avant garde artists were not just reacting to society with feelings of ennui, angst, weltschmerz, and a host of other pseudoexistential passions of the soul. Avant garde artists weren't merely reacting to society with last-ditch efforts at breaking up and dislodging prevalent styles. . . . Their effort was not to isolate themselves, but to reintegrate themselves and their art into life. (xxxvi)

This reintegrative possibility, or perhaps what can be more accurately called a desire for plenitude, was what Tristan Tzara discerned in the African poems that he was beginning to translate at this time. For Tzara the apparently symbolical purity of this language was a way of avoiding the mind-body split of the Cartesian subject. He sought an extralinguistic field of expression in which syntax and semantics were eschewed in favour of a more direct, less-mediated manifestation of bodily expression. Thus, for early Dada the notion of the primitive, in this case exemplified by "African" language, was a distinctly metaphorical, even allegorical, conduit for new forms of textuality: an expressive language grounded in the corporeal and the gestural and not an extension of the cerebral and the intellectual. The primitive operates not just as a banished enchantment or repressed instinctual residues of civilisation but as a "correlative of experiences and emotions which were felt to lie beyond representation" (Nicholls, *Modernisms* 118).

The *Cabaret* was a subversive, often physically chaotic space, which, as Hans Arp has recalled, performed against the "thunder of the batteries" that could frequently be heard rumbling in the distance on the battlefields (qtd. in Motherwell 52). Acutely sensitive to the insanity of the First World War, Dada's ostentatious evenings at the *Cabaret* were not, however, a simply nihilistic exercise in anarchic self-indulgence, as Bürger has pointed out above. At times, however, this certainly seemed to be the case, at least from the audience's point of view, as chairs and tables were hurled around the room in reaction to what seemed like an insult to their sensibilities. This early manifestation of Dada was an impassioned protest against what the movement saw as the entropic state of humanity and its wretched project of civilisation. The forward march of progress and of modernity placed more severe prohibitions on man's so-called natural impulses and increasingly enforced separation between science, art, religion, and morality.

For Tzara and Zurich Dada, primitivity was figured in terms of an allegorical Africanity in which the idea of racial otherness—always an imagined essence for the Dadaists—was deployed to explore the limits and negation of language itself. Tzara's 1917 Dada manifesto elucidated this position on what he has called "Negro art" and its apparent simplicity of bodily form and perspective. For Dadaists the presence of *art nègre* was simultaneously an invigorating and destructive influence in which the "drawers of the brain and of all social organisation" can be dismantled

(277). For early Dada, African-ness represented a return to forms of expression that were not the product of modernity. African art, in short, was seen as unbroken ritual expression that simultaneously signified wholeness and presence even while it served to metaphorise their very opposites. The Dadaist assault on verisimilitude and the figurative in the visual and performing arts was part of more complicated reaction to a pressing historical context and cannot be understood as analogous with a Conradian primitivism in which African-ness is set in a purely negative oppositional relationship to European identity. In *Heart of Darkness,* we see Africa functioning as an allegorical trope of repressed instinct, the Dark Continent literally shadowing the libidinal excesses prohibited by modern life in Europe. This is the primitive as the repository of the unassimilated residues of modernity, whereas in Dada the primitive functions as a way of thinking outside available language and its "semantic freight" (Williams, *Politics* 69). This does not assign "African-ness" with negative, destructive properties but as a means of testing new ways of seeing the fragmented present.

In interwar primitivism, the figure or text of the primitive functions simultaneously as the epitome of radical difference and yet speaks directly to the modern subject—in other words, the primitive appeals as a way of explaining the chaos of the present. This is a relationship described thus by Berman: "Chaos, the 'other of order,' is pure negativity. It is a denial of all that order strives to be. It is against that negativity that the positivity of order constitutes itself " (7). In a doubled process of identification and distantiation, the primitivised other is set up as both the negation and affirmation of the self and predicated upon a dis-order and difference as well as similarity and recognition. The familiar strangeness of the primitive offers the white gaze the promise of a return to an Edenic home—a site of premodern plenitude in which alienation does not exist. This raises, argues Hal Foster, questions of both otherness and relativism (193). Foster's conceptualisation of primitivism acknowledges the operation of the primitive as both an epistemological limit and a system of multiple beliefs, which is "projected both within and without," embracing a dialectic of fetishistic recognition and a simultaneous disavowal of difference (204). This concurs with Lévi-Strauss's theorisation of tribalism and difference in *Tristes Tropiques,* in which he suggests that for the West the idea of the primitive offers an imagined but finally unattainable solution to the teeming contradictions of the modern subject (196–97). In these ways primitivism fulfills a crucial function in that it posited "a realm of experience beyond the confines of a modernity that denies him the possibility of self-realization" (Bongie 10). The figure of the primitive other is both a reflection and a deflection of the self.

Functioning as both a figure of loss and of nostalgia for a premodern, natural past, the primitive also operated as the marker of a definitive sense of the modern—a dialectical pas de deux between the old and the new. This dialectic is succinctly represented in a short film called *Sur un Air d'un Charleston* (1926), in which the French filmmaker Jean Renoir shows a black spaceman descending to earth in the twenties to be taught to dance the Charleston by a white woman dancer. The setting is a bleak, unidentifiable, postapocalyptic Europe in which it seems that dominant ideologies have been replaced by an epistemological tabula rasa.[13] The black figure is a time-travelling astronaut in a reversal of temporal tables.[14] The nonwhite figure again functions here as both a bearer of the primitive past and of modernist futurism, showing the ways in which time could be spatialised—the primitive meets the modern in a juxtaposed collage (Harvey 21). Hence, in negrophile discourses, the figure of the other bears a double representative burden of the contradictions and antagonistic dynamics of the modern moment. Dancing naked for a German count and his aristocratic guests in Berlin in 1926, Josephine Baker haltingly performed a quasi-parody of a primitive dance ritual in which she slipped between "an ancient Egyptian relief frieze" and "one of George Grosz's mechanical dolls" (Kessler 284). The irruption of the ancient in an ultramodern text became a familiar modernist conceptual incongruity in which the erotic and aesthetic shock of the primitive disrupts the composed surfaces of naturalist representation.

The figure of the racial other thus functions as a metaphorical space in which anxieties over shifting apprehensions of the subject of modernity could be more easily contemplated. This contemplation entails a process of recognising the falsity of the unified surfaces of the self; Michel Leiris describes this civilised self as a thin layer forming on the surface of calm water until an "eddy comes to break it up" (*Brisées* 19). But it is also one whereby the "subject of a dominant culture can 'counter' that culture in the very process of returning to it" (Célestin 3). This act of returning to the self through the other (a reversal of the flow of ethnographic knowledge) involves the construction of the other as a conduit to channel dissident desire and unease into the imagining subject. This movement produces a "complex of desire and repression," a situation noted by Michael Taussig as a salient feature of all primitivisms (*Shamanism* 10). The imagined corporeal plenitude figured through the "excessive literalism or the excessive metaphoricity of the racial other" is crucial to this process (Suleri 163). The space, the time, and the body of the primitive are overdetermined in order to function as open-ended metonyms for the self as imagining subject. Thus, the primitive functions as a self-reflexive trope through which the imaginer can view himself or herself more clearly through the imagined.

For the modernist avant-garde, the idea of the primitive bridges the cognitive gulf between civic society and aesthetic practices that was separated into discrete entities by post-Enlightenment epistemology.[15] Susan

Sontag argues that "the man who submits himself to the exotic to conform to his own inner alienation as an urban intellectual ends by aiming to vanquish his subject by translating it into a purely formal code" (77). This implies a strongly solipsistic impulse characterised by an obsessive return to self-explanation, which requires an objectifying discourse like primitivism to construct truths about the magic of other cultures which in turn nourishes the etiolated poetics of the domestic subject.[16]

MICHEL LEIRIS'S PHANTOM AFRICAS

As France entered a fragile peacetime in 1918, it faced a range of new and shifting external political and social factors that affected all areas of the *entre-deux-guerres* period. The early fascination with the primitive in the visual and plastic arts of avant-garde modernism now began to rapidly shift ground. In 1934, Michel Leiris published his ambitious ethnographic work *L'Afrique fantôme.* Leiris's inscription of the primitive in this work is a complex one characteristic of the modernist avant-garde in its complicated engagement with both the instability of the subject and the realisation of the notion of outside. Ostensibly, an ethnographic account of the colonial Mission Dakar-Djibouti of 1931–33, which was organised to collect data on vast parts of Africa, the book is far from a coherent narrative of the mission. Rather, its oneiric textuality resists at every turn the authoritarian voice of the ethnographer and its unproblematic subject position. Textually, it is, in short, a modernist ethnography; an 833-page book, it is an ethnopoetic account of the minutiae of the ethnographic everyday, recording the experiences, both exhilarating and tedious, of the poet-ethnographer, who at all times rejects and subverts the objective voice of ethnographic accounts of Africa, phantom or otherwise (Clifford, *Predicament* 173). The book clearly demonstrates a refusal of the panoptical ethnographic gaze that observes, collects, and presents data in a linear rational narrative in order to yield up to its readers a clear and comprehensive portrait of the ethnographic other. Leiris disturbs the relationship between the writing self of the subject and the object under scrutiny. In fact, Leiris himself becomes the ethnographic subject—he is his own other. Marianna Torgovnick has said of Leiris's work, "The writing self becomes as much a phantom as the Africa under examination" (107–110). Typically, Leiris's writing privileges the uncertainty of visceral experience over a disassociated quasi-scientific process that claims to know through observation: "I'd rather be possessed than study possessed people, have carnal knowledge of a 'zarine', rather than scientifically know all about her. For me, abstract knowledge will never be anything but a second best" (*L'Afrique* 324). In saying this, he renounces the claim to objective truth that the social scientific discourses of anthropology and ethnography make and that he regards as an extension of the deadening tentacles of capitalism and "its increasing tendency to render all true human contacts impossible [. . .]" (*Brisées*, 1966 54). Thus, *L'Afrique fantôme* reveals as much, if not a great deal more, about the modernist writing subject from 1914 onwards and its precarious location of articulation as it does about Africa and its real and imaged spaces of otherness. In this work and in the later *L'Age de l'homme* (1939), Leiris is himself the object of intense examination as he goes about his everyday life in interwar Paris. Paris is depicted as a culturally exhausted space, choked by the bloodless abstractions of rationality and alienating modernity that diminishes the subjective processes of authentic self-hood. Leiris, whose obsession with Africa would increase over the years, finds a phantom Africa at home, in the bars and *bals nègres* of the working-class districts of Montmartre. Both *L'Age de l'homme* and *L'Afrique fantôme* recount his formative experiences in these nightspots during the immediate postwar period of the early 1920s. Leiris presents minutely detailed ethnographic descriptions of the spaces of otherness in the city. Describing the "abandonment to the animal joy of experiencing the influence of a modern rhythm" in these popular Montmartre bars, Leiris characterises the libidinal pleasures of the spaces of these *bars nègres* as inherently antithetical to a stultifying of European civilisation (*L'Afrique fantôme* 54). He describes these spaces of otherness as inherently erotic ones free of the atrophied intellectualism of the day. In *Brisées* (1966), Leiris sees this arid, theoretical tendency in popular and mass culture and the "all too insipid shows" that merely regurgitate the mechanical, bourgeois tastes of the public: "We've had enough of all that, which is why we would like to get closer to our primitive ancestry. [. . .] And so this music and this dancing doesn't stop at our skin but puts down deep organic roots in us, roots whose thousand ramifications penetrate us; and though this surgery is painful it gives us stronger blood" (*Brisées* [1966] 20).

The language of biology, penetration, infiltration, and suture is intriguing here. Leiris depicts the desire for the primitive as a process of cultural transfusion, a rendering up of the sterile Western body to the more vital lifelines of the primitive. Thus, in Leiris the primitive is construed as a variant of the Freudian id; the Dionysic energies repressed in order to construct a civilised veneer. The primitive exists in us, and if not permitted expression, it is transformed into the negative impulses of destruction that Leiris suggests are always ready to erupt through the surfaces of the everyday, cracking open this false front:

> All our moral practices and our polite customs, that radiantly colored cloak that hides the coarseness of our dangerous instincts, all those lovely forms of culture we are so proud of—since it is thanks to them that we call ourselves "civilized"—are ready to disappear at the slightest turbulence, to shatter at the slightest impact allowing our horrifying *primitiveness* to appear in the interstices, revealed by the fissures just as hell might be revealed by earthquakes. (*Brisées* [1989] 19)

This "'horrifying primitiveness" broke through in the turbulence of the years between 1914 and 1918. The Great War, marking a climacteric watershed for aesthetic cultural production in Europe and the possibility of humanity's destruction by itself, raised many questions about the idea of civilisation and society.

LA VOGUE NÈGRE

At the height of her popularity in France in the interwar decades, Josephine Baker, *La Bakaire,* was interviewed by a journalist for a local Marseilles newspaper who asked for her views on modern painting:

> I am so old fashioned, so stupid maybe because I think that when one looks at a painting one has to be able to see right away what it is supposed to mean. It used to be like that. But today! Take the other day, a rich woman, a bourgeois lady showed me with ostentatious enthusiasm a very small painting. She had paid an extraordinary amount . . . [she asked me] whether I thought it was great. It was by him, you know Pinarzo, or what is his name, the one everybody talks about? (Rudbeck)

Jokingly mistaking Picasso's name as Pinarzo, she claimed that her ability to decipher the new Cubist style was limited by her search for immediate meaning in the lines and the figures. She laughingly and playfully dismissed the small and valuable painting as an example of the emperor's new clothes, a simple deception of the wider public by the cunning of the individual modernist trickster. The irony here was that Baker not only knew Picasso extremely well (it was rumoured that the two had even been lovers at one point), but she was more than aware of her own influence on these apparently unreadable new forms of representation. As the playful *sauvage* shimmying through the jungle-scapes in only a skirt made from plush bananas, Baker knew perfectly well that she represented a kind of ur-typical symbol of modern primitivism for her eclectic Parisian audiences. As a music-hall star and later a *vedette,* she was positioned as racial icon across both popular and mass culture, but those she most conspicuously inspired, such as Picasso, Alexander Calder, and Constantin Brancusi, were from the higher echelons of cultural production. This crossover appeal of Baker and the *Revue Nègre* exemplified in many ways the dynamics of modern primitivism that drew its vitality from diverse areas of culture.

What had begun as *l'art nègre* in the visual arts gradually became less specifically *nègre* to incorporate a more general exhibition and apprehension of non-Western worlds. The other, loosely defined, became the subject of intense scrutiny, exhibition, spectacle, and debate in the postwar years. In 1919 the first official exhibition of *l'art nègre* in Paris was held at the Galérie Devambez, displaying Native American and Oceanic pieces along with objects from Africa and Indochina. This exhibition was complemented by the successful Exposition des Arts Décoratifs in 1925, which featured exotic and primitive artefacts from around the world. Following the sensual and controversial Fauvism of Stravinsky's *Sacré du Printemps* in 1913, Darius Milhaud, who had visited the jazz clubs and cabarets of Harlem in 1919, created a ballet for Les Ballets Suédois at the Théâtre Champs-Elysées in 1923. *La Création du Monde* presented Parisian audiences with a musical *métissage* of non-Western music and dance, featuring African cosmogonic rituals and masks from the Belgian Congo and the Ivory Coast.[17] Significantly, the text for the ballet was written by Blaise Cendrars, author of the popular *Anthologie nègre* (1921) and a series of collections of so-called exotic poems such as "Continent Noir" (1922) and "Les Grands fétiches" (1922).[18]

Gradually, the appeal of *les choses nègre* radiated out from the high culture of such works as Picasso's *Les Demoiselles d'Avignon,* André Schaeffner's *Le Jazz: La musique moderne* (1926), a detailed academic study of black musicology, and Tristan Tzara's Dadaist *chants nègres* to the popular music, dance, and fashion of everyday Parisian life. American jazz was extraordinarily popular and became *the* sound of 1920s Paris, with jazz clubs and *bals nègres* opening up all over the capital to cater to the enormous popularity of dances such as the mooch, the shimmy, the blackbottom, and the beguine.[19] Frequenting the clubs and cabarets of Montmartre and Montparnasse, the photographer Georges Brassaï took a series of photos of Parisian nightlife during the interwar period. Brassai was particularly struck by the hypersexualised atmosphere of the clubs. He described "a kind of hysterical sorcery" permeating black nightclubs such as *La Boule Blanche* and *La Cabane Cubaine,* which drew a large white clientele. "It was as though the carnage of war had inspired a sudden sexual frenzy," he said, "white women—drunk on their own bodies and forgetting that contact with a Negro had once been shocking—were irresistibly drawn to the Vth arrondissement, the Harlem of Paris" (23).

Several black American orchestras toured France from 1919 onwards, playing to sell-out houses across the country; the most popular of them was Will Marion Cook's Southern Syncopated Orchestra, which enjoyed a particularly successful run across European capitals. American jazz had become the musical leitmotif of all things modern in Paris, featuring heavily in visual representations of an undifferentiated text of blackness, as African Americanism and jazz music were unproblematically conflated into a homogeneous black identity in the totalising cultural sweep of early *négrophilie.* This conflation is most evident in works such as the 1920 production of *Le Boeuf sur le toit,* by Darius Milhaud and Jean Cocteau, set in a New York speakeasy with a black boxer as the main protagonist. Langston Hughes, who arrived in Paris in 1924 and worked briefly on the door of the Grand Duc cabaret, caught the atmosphere of the eclectic *négrophilie* of the day in his 1927 poem "Jazz Band in a Parisian Cabaret":

> Play that thing
> Jazz band!

LITERARY PRIMITIVISM

The primitivist theme extended into literary texts, continuing a long-standing fascination with the notion of cultural and racial otherness from Montaigne through Flaubert's *Salammbo* (1863) to the colonial novels, such as Pierre Loti's *Roman d'un Spahi* (1881) and Ernest Psichari's *Terres de soleil et de sommeil* (1908), which both enjoyed a renewed popularity between 1919 and 1926. Alongside the more renowned novels of confirmed negrophile writers such as Blaise Cendrars, Jean Paulhan, and Paul Morand, there was an upsurge in what were called *romans nègres,* for example, Gaston Joseph's *Koffi, Roman d'un vrai noir* (1922) and the Tharaud brothers' *La Randonée de Samba Diouf* (1926). The emergence of what has been called *la littérature coloniale* was clearly a manifestation of a widespread interest in the idea of Europe's cultural other.[20] Profiting from the public's excitement with this new genre of *romans nègres,* René Maran's 1921 novel *Batouala* was given the explanatory subtitle *un véritable roman nègre,* which promised an authentic African-ness rather than a white writer's observations from the outside. It won the prestigious Prix Goncourt despite its scathing indictment of French colonial practices in West Africa in the (in)famous preface. Maran was the first black writer to receive this literary accolade, although he paid the price for the bold preface when he was subsequently dismissed from his post as a colonial administrator. This dismissal marked the beginning of his political involvement in the journals and organisations that I look at in detail later. André Gide's *Voyage au Congo* and Albert Londres' *Terre d'ébène,* both published in 1928, also caused a stir in liberal literary circles for their damning indictments of the excesses of the French *mission civilisatrice.*[21]

There was also a deluge of exoticist films, colonial journals, and magazines depicting the colourful life of the *colons.* This was made possible by rapidly evolving reproduction and dissemination technologies in film and print media. A Citroen-sponsored auto race across continental Africa was captured in Léon Poirier's 1926 film *Croisière Noire.* The juxtaposition of the ultramodern French cars racing across the seemingly uninhabited and wind-swept plains of the Sahara was hugely popular, and the race was followed by a similar one across Asia, predictably entitled the *Croisière Jaune.* Cinema, as a new visual medium, was able to make full use of the primitive and the exotic locales of the empire. The most successful French film in 1921 was Jacques Feyder's film version of Pierre Benoit's novel

L'Atlantide (1919). The film, shot on location in Algeria, standing in for the Saharan Atlas region, was a lavishly illustrated tale of miscegenation, lust, and madness at the hands of the beautiful African princess Antinéa. It was heavily, and controversially, reminiscent of the hypercolonial style of Rider Haggard's earlier novel *She* (1887). The film set a trend for the new popular genre *cinéma colonial,* in which Josephine Baker would make a name for herself playing characters from all over the French colonies in the films *Zou Zou* (1934), directed by Marc Allégret, and *Princess Tam Tam* (1935), directed by Edmund Gréville.

Elsewhere, in the soon to be professionalised disciplines of the social sciences, the nineteenth-century concept of Africa as a blank slate lacking in civilisation was being slowly eroded by a series of ethnographic projects. These projects tentatively established paradigms of cultural relativism that would emerge more fully in the following decade.[22] In 1925 the Musée de Trocadéro reopened as L' Institut d'Ethnologie, formed by Marcel Mauss, Lucien Lévy-Bruhl, and Paul Rivet, all of whom had interests in the arts. Influential works such as Maurice Delafosse's *L'Âme Nègre* (1922), Lucien Lévy-Bruhl's *La mentalité primitive* (1922), Franz Boas' *Kwakiute Tales* (1911), and Leo Frobenius's *Das Sterbende Afrika* (1923) slowly engendered significant reconceptualisations in the methodologies of ethnographic and anthropological field work.[23] Gradually, *la vogue nègre* became a phenomenon in itself, constructing a category of blackness composed of an accumulation of cultural signifiers "about which syncretic statements could be made" (Clifford, *Predicament* 61).

I have discussed early avant-garde's fascination with the primitive as primarily one that allegorised difference as a countercultural tool. However, it is crucial here to talk about the *real* subject of difference, of the primitive and how it was positioned with this circuit of commodity exchange. *Négrophilie* occurred at a point in French history when its empire was at its *apogée,* not just in economic and strategic profitability but also in domestic support in a public hitherto largely indifferent to the fact of empire, unlike their imperial counterparts across the Channel. Colonial territories, cultural artefacts, and their imagined geographies of alterity had recently become increasingly accessible to Europeans through the cumulative processes of economic imperialism and colonial conquest and contact. Rapid technological advances in media and communications meant that knowledge of cultural difference could be mediated and disseminated as an exchangeable cultural commodity ready for metropolitan consumption. The nonwhite subject/figure in Europe was produced within a diverse set of cultural, political, and institutional discourses that constructed the notion of otherness in an ideological continuum informed at every turn by the ebullient ideological dynamics of imperialism and colonialism. Modern primitivism occurred at a point in French history when the colonies began to enter what Benita Parry has called the "cognitive landscape" of metropolitan culture ("Narrating Imperialism" 233), and thus was imbued with the ideological knowledge/power relations of a metropolitan colonial culture. At every turn the ideologies of French colonialism in its interwar *apogée* underpinned the discourses and representational practices of *négrophilie*, as colonial conquest brought home the cultural spoils of empire, both artefactually and textually. As Peter Hulme has rightly pointed out, colonialism constructed a discursive mode that ideologically *"produced"* the native for European consumption within a system of representation where the real presence of the colonial other is reduced to a generic unit of cultural exchange easily transferable from one geography to another, stripped of all but the most superficial specificity (2).

White negrophile interest in black cultural forms cannot be caricatured as either evidence of interwar metropolitan racism or liberal tolerance. It is not a question of distinguishing the good, or progressive, racial imagery of *négrophilie* from the bad, or retrogressive; rather the challenge is to recover some of the complicated inscriptions and uses of *négrophilie*. This critical position does not in any way ignore the underlying violence of the colonial encounter that ideologically and historically underpins the discourse of primitivism at this time. Rather, it is an approach that insists "patterns of domination and subordination" in the colonies must be read alongside those of "inter-dependence and mutuality" in the colonial culture of the metropolitan centre (C. Hall 69). This is not a plea for a brand of postcolonial theorising in which interstitial agency or the subtleties of hybridity and textuality define and even supersede material considerations. In other words, the inequities of the colonial situation itself do not account for nor precisely reproduce aesthetic and cultural engagements that may occur as a result of this underlying subjugation.

NOTES

1. See in particular Hulme and Carter on the new cartographies produced by the colonial encounter.

2. On the histories and representational practices of primitivism and exoticism, see Torgovnick; Price; Bongie; Laude; Pieterse; Frascina and Harris, and Archer Shaw. Attention to interwar primitivism in France has tended to remain in the disciplinary domain of art history; the most recent work is Jody Blake's *Le Tumulte Noir: Modernist Art and Popular Entertainment in Jazz-Age Paris 1900–1930* (University Park: Pennsylvania State University Press, 1999).

3. The category of primitivism has been extended to incorporate a more general allegory process of "othering," particularly in the case of class. There has been a considerable amount of work done on the ways in which the working class has been primitivised in both British and French contexts. See Lindsay Smith on Victorian street urchins and Gill Perry on representation of Breton peasants in visual arts in Frascina and Harris.

4. It is more difficult to place representations of First Nation peoples. Those of North America have generally straddled both categories, as have the aboriginal peoples of Central and South America and Australasia. See Nicholas Thomas for a very detailed and useful discussion of contemporary uses of primitivism in Hollywood cinema (170–95).

5. The novel is of course renowned for more than its depiction of a primitive otherness, but it is precisely this representation of the non-West that has been the subject of much of the most fervent critical commentary. For an example of the continuing political polarisation in recent critical work, see the dialogue between Caryll Phillips and Chinua Achebe in the *Guardian* 22 Feb. 2003.

6. For a detailed discussion of Gauguin's particular type of primitivism and the eroticised exoticism of his paintings, see Eisenman.

7. Baudeloire Charles *Les fleurs du mal*, ed. Jean Delabroy, Paris: Magnard, 1986.

8. See Chris Bongie's nuanced analysis of the variants within exoticism in *Exotic Memories* in which he examines exoticism as a variable generic category in the fin de siècle literature of Joseph Conrad, Victor Segalen, and Pier Paolo Pasolini.

9. See Paul Gilroy's seminal geo-cultural paradigm of the black diaspora in *The Black Atlantic.*

10. See specifically "The Concept of Enlightenment" 3–43.

11. See Bauman for a nuanced discussion of modernity and its ambivalent relationship to the notion of an outside (15–19).

12. The fascination with taboo-breaking, scatological, and grotesque gestures in avant-garde theatre was intimately linked to an earlier use of the primitive in Alfred Jarry's 1896 *Ubu Roi.* This was the prototype for an antirealist avant-garde theatre in which dialogue, plot, and characterisation were rejected in place of a parody of traditional realist theatre. The parody burlesqued the Oedipal dynamics of narrative in which the law of the father speaks the authority of the text. See Nicholls, "Anti-Oedipus?" 338. Elsewhere, Robert Nye notes that Tzara's first plays, such *as La Première Aventure celeste de M. Antipyine* (1916), were a complex refusal of bourgeois expectations and narrative expressed in his "non-discursive Dadaist poetics" ("Savage" 54).

13. The irony is that the Charleston was a black dance brought to France after the war by African American dancers who taught the dance to the French in the clubs and cabarets of Montmartre.

14. For a discussion on time, space, and the object of anthropological enquiry, see Fabian 26.

15. See Kuper 240.

16. See Taussig, *Shamanism* 7–11 and *Mimesis* 33–43. Taussig presents a suggestive set of arguments on mimesis, primitivism, and alterity, using Benjamin's constellative notion of history as flashes of recognition as its methodological framework. His idea of mimesis as the act of "becoming something else" (36) is of particular importance to a discussion of the relations between self and other in a modernist context.

17. See Clifford, *New History* 902–5.

18. See Blachère for an extremely valuable source book.

19. See Berliner.

20. See Jack.

21. Both of Gide's African novels condemned the brutality of French colonial tactics in central Africa. The novels are more ambiguous, however, on the underlying legitimacy of the principles of imperialism itself and merit a much closer reading as they are complex renditions of the conditions of contact between the metropole and the overseas colonies. See Hampton for a close reading of the colonialist novels of Gide, Maran, and Cèline.

22. See Kesteloot, *Ecrivains Noirs* 15.

23. See Manganaro 183–215.

CHAPTER 2

"I'll say it's getting darker and darker in Paris": Josephine Baker and *La Revue Nègre*

> The Negroes are conquering Paris. They are conquering Berlin. They have already filled the whole continent with their howls, with their laughter. *The Revue Nègre,* which is rousing the tired public in the *Théâtre Champs-Elysées* top thrills and madness as otherwise only a boxing match can do is symbolic.
>
> —Ivan Goll, January 15, 1926

INTRODUCTION

In 1985 the Paris metro ran an advertising campaign using an image of a young black woman dressed only in a skirt made of a fringe of yellow metro tickets. From a distance the tickets resemble bananas. The woman's hair is plastered down in a brilliantined Eton crop and her face is distorted by an exaggerated wide smile. The metro poster is a take on one of the many images of Josephine Baker that appeared around Paris in the 1920s to promote her appearances in *La Revue Nègre* and in *La Folie du jour.* The metro advertisement, framed by the caption "Tickets Folies 2ème Voiture le Plus Célèbre Spectacle de Paris," recalls a time in the interwar years in Paris when Josephine Baker was one of the most celebrated "exotic" spectacles, both on and off the music-hall stage. Although Baker went on to appear in a large number of shows, reinventing herself as a *grande chanteuse,* and although her wartime work in France's Resistance earned her the prestigious Croix de Guerre, this image of Baker, half naked, dancing frenetically in a suggestively phallic girdle of bananas, has persisted in popular cultural memory. The inclusion of three clips of Baker in François Mitterand's 1988 election video testified to the endurance of this primitivist myth. Baker was variously figured as the modern incarnation of Baudelaire's Jeanne Duval, the *danseuse de bananes* who brought the Charleston and the blackbottom to France, *La Petite Tonkinoise*, Princess Tam Tam, and the theatrical *grande vedette.* She performed all these roles against an interwar cosmopolitan hedonism and a spectacular *mise en scène* of the Second French Empire that had just entered its colonial golden age.

Baker came to Paris just as the city was about to experience the peak of *la vogue nègre.* In many ways, Baker's iconic figure represented the apex of *négrophilie* and forged explicit links between the modern and the archaic, already suggested in the high cultural domain of *l'art nègre,* in her stage performances and images. As I have already discussed, the cultural primitivism of interwar France was not simply a continuation of earlier exoticist or primitivist discourses, tracing a path from Montaigne through Henri "Douanier" Rousseau to Gauguin's Tahiti. Rather, it was specifically circumscribed by the national and political conditions of postwar France after "fifty two months of horror and deprivation," the ascendant rhetoric of the *apogée coloniale,* and the rapid expansion of popular and mass culture (Gates and Dalton 907). The phenomenal popularity of Josephine Baker in 1920s Paris occurred amidst a turbulent postwar cultural and political scene, where, in a general sense, as Jean Laude points out, "the West began to scrutinise everything that was not itself" (401).

This was a moment when concepts of race and cultural difference were articulated through a negrophile primitivism that venerated and celebrated particular rejuvenating aspects of black racial identity. Here, I trace the contexts in which a young black American woman became a national cultural phenomenon in France. What are we to make of the discrepancies between Baker's euphoric reception in cosmopolitan Paris and the simultaneous rise of xenophobic nationalism, a resurgence in theories of racial and cultural degeneration, the emergent radical "adversarial internationalization," and the beginning of political disquiet in the colonies (Said, *Culture* 295)? How are we to read Baker's success, culminating in her incongruous election as Queen of the Colonies in 1931, against a background of diverse French colonial practices overseas and their cultural manifestations in the metropole? Within the context of debates on race and difference and a growing preoccupation with documenting the figure of the colonial other, Josephine Baker's performances, literally, rehearsed a variety of texts of difference. She could appeal to the modernist artist as much as to the colonial lobbyist, the jazz lover, or the negrophile writer. Her performances provided a locale where colonial fantasy and ideological discrepancy could be played out yet contained. I argue here that textual representations of race in popular culture, high and avant-garde modernism, and academic texts were produced, consumed, and circulated in France in ways that both masked and revealed wider social and cultural anxieties. Baker's performances aestheticised racial myths and narratives into a safely commodified spectacle that could be fully contained while events in the colonies themselves began to shift. Nicholas Thomas's suggestion that "[c]olonial cultures are not simply ideologies that mask, mystify or rationalise forms of oppression that are external to them: they are also expressive and constitutive of colonial relationships themselves" has valuably pointed up the intricacies of racial representation and their relationship to dominant discourses of power (2). Within the specific colonial culture of cosmopolitan Paris, the racial spectacle of Baker's body as metonymic for all racial otherness reveals some of the complicated impulses of *négrophilie.* My analysis attempts to uncover some of the processes behind the rhetorical and spectacular devices that constructed Baker as racial icon and to suggest that the primitivist interests of both high and popular culture intersected in the figure of Baker's *petite sauvageonne.* Acknowledging these crucial historical determinants, I attempt to balance a reading of Baker's rendition as a cultural text with that of the real conditions of her life as a black woman in French society, a balancing act that Kadiatu Kanneh recognises when she says that

> black and female identities are not simply figurative or superficial sites of play and metaphor, but occupy very real political spaces of Diaspora, dispossession and resistance. What is complicated is the simultaneity of suffering and power, marginalisation and threat, submission and narcissism, which accrue to Black women's bodies and their representation in racist culture. (167)

Thus, the popularity of Josephine Baker in interwar Europe had as much to do with the Franco-Prussian War of the 1870s, the 1921–26 Guerre du Riff, and the enforcement of pro-natalist polices culminating in the 1920 anti-abortion act as with the dramatic erotic impact of American jazz and Baker's uninhibited, extraordinary nudity and participation in a prolific cultural consumption of difference. It also had much to do with Baker's own particular history as a performer in the United States and the kind of restrictions placed upon her as a young, black, working-class woman in the South. In order to properly contextualise the extraordinary trajectory of Baker's debut in Paris, let us first turn to Baker's working-class origins in an American society marked by violent racial unrest and social and economic segregation.

JOSEPHINE BAKER IN AMERICA: ORIGINS OF *LA REVUE NÈGRE*

Josephine Baker arrived in Paris in 1925 via Broadway and East St. Louis, Missouri, where she was born in 1906. She grew up in an entirely urban American environment in a city profoundly shaped by its historical connections to the French slave trade in the eighteenth century and then by violent race relations in the early twentieth century. These facts were to become almost completely forgotten when Baker arrived in Paris, where East St. Louis was routinely misconstrued as Louisiana in the press. The city became mythologised into a fictional new-world geography of plantations and slaves filtered through a nostalgic archive of New Orleans. In reality, St. Louis was far removed from this bucolic vision. The city was a sprawling network of factories, railway stockyards, and packing plants, with black ghettos forming a de facto segregated space in the downtown core (Hammond and O'Connor 2). The black population of East St. Louis had been increasing steadily since the mid-nineteenth century as part of migration that had been steadingly increasing since the end of the Civil War from the rural Southern states to Northern urban centres, where economic conditions promised a better standard of living. With this increase came a concomitant rise in racial violence that sharpened around 1916 in the midst of ever-worsening economic conditions for both black and white working classes. In her childhood, Baker witnessed considerable racial unrest in the city, the tension culminating on July 2, 1917, when a pitched battle occurred as mobs of an economically disgruntled white population invaded the black section of the downtown area. Baker recalled in a later interview that the city was "worse than the deep south" and described her family fleeing across the St. Louis bridge "to escape the red necks, the whites killing and beating them" (Rader 80).[1]

Born in 1907, Baker had a childhood of routine hardship and intermittent poverty, typical of black working-class communities in urban America in the early twentieth century. Baker's mother, separated from her father, supported the family of four children by taking in laundry. The children attended school only sporadically, as the need to send even very young children out to work was an unquestioned imperative for black working-class families in her East St. Louis neighbourhood. At the age of thirteen, Baker married, in common with many working-class black girls wishing to secure a viable economic future beyond the immediate family. Working from an early age as a domestic, a waitress, and then a street entertainer with a troupe of buskers, Baker quickly recognised that using her body as a performing spectacle gave her an immediate resource and a way of circumventing the traditional economic exploitation of black female labour.[2] As an uneducated working-class woman, she was locked into an oppressive racial and sexual economy of exchange that was the pressing material reality for the majority of black women outside of the "talented tenth," the intellectual élite of the Harlem Renaissance. Her background and her gender largely excluded her from W. E. B. DuBois's categorisation of black society. Her own path through Manhattan's black renaissance, for which she was later derided on her return to the States, was predicated on the cultural capital that she made of her body and its various performances of blackness. For many black American entertainers who performed in Harlem and in Europe in the 1920s and 1930s, there was an acutely pragmatic sense of capitalising on the "vogue for negroes" while it endured. In much of the literature documenting the Harlem Renaissance and African Americans in Paris at this time, there is a clear sense that this moment of black cultural renaissance in both Paris and Harlem was a precarious one and likely to pass, as dominant white cultural tastes moved on.[3] Langston Hughes commented on this in *The Ways of The White Folks* when he observed that those whites who "went in for the art of the Negroes" were primarily involved in a transient consumption and imitation of black art (18). Aimé Césaire also recognised the fickleness of the trend for negrophile primitivism when he wrote:

> Ou bientout simplement comme on nous aime!
> Obscènes gaiement, très doudous de jazz sur leur excès d'ennui. . . . (102–3)

Here, Césaire bitterly notes that if a black person could entertain the white crowd with an obscene pantomime of carefree spontaneity and free-form dancing, then derogatory racism can be temporarily allowed to become a fawning and condescending lionisation of *le nègre.*

Since the Civil War, St. Louis had had a thriving black vaudeville theatre and was a popular stopping-off point for many black entertainers and musicians on their way to New York.[4] Baker's first foray into show business was at the age of 13 when she discovered that she had a singular talent for making an audience laugh at her clowning, which was part of a blackface, "pickaninny" routine. She excelled in the role of the laughing black child, and that role, the infantile *bon sauvage,* would be incorporated in different ways into her early performances in the *Revue Nègre.* Baker, who had been singled out throughout her childhood as a light-skinned child, now found herself described as "too young, too thin, too dark by [American] producers who exploited the relative sexual appeal of the chorus girls' skin colour" (Hammond and O' Connor 8). Dressed in an oversize pickaninny cotton dress, Baker clowned her way through serious chorus routines in a parody of the explicit sexual spectacle of lighter-skinned chorus girls. These women, advertised as "sepia lovelies" and "high yallers," were marketed as intrinsically more sexually desirable, especially to a white audience. Baker's performance de-sexualised her role as erotic and exotic spectacle by an act of self-parodying pantomime. By distracting attention away from the currency of her black body to her comically expressive facial features, Baker was able to both overcome and subvert the role of the sexually overdetermined black woman. However subversive this may appear, I think it would be hasty to ascribe an unproblematically autonomous agency to Baker's performative life as both Lynn Haney in *Naked at the Feast* and Phyllis Rose in *Jazz Cleopatra* have done. The circumstances of Baker's apparently subversive minstrelsy for a young uneducated black woman was likely an act of show business survival, Too dark for true erotic appeal, she needed to distinguish herself somehow; she was not opposed in any way to the sexual commodification of black women; in fact, anything but. Her entire stage career would be based on a series of racial stereotypes. Baker's talent for racial burlesque and self-parody made her stand out from the run-of-the-mill black chorus girl in an act which was part comic mimicry of female minstrelsy and part natural comic talent. By virtue of her performative ingenuity, Baker distinguished herself from the massed ranks of the chorus line and, in doing so, realised a highly lucrative form of independence from impoverishment and oppression. Josephine Baker went on to become a millionaire at a time in history when career options for black working-class women were generally a choice between cleaning woman and prostitute. Her burlesque was a cartoon of black femininity that she seemed only too happy to repeatedly offer her public, even when, later in her career, her return to the States was greeted by derision and scorn for her Parisian version of Uncle Tom-ism.[5]

The black female body, bell hooks has suggested, is only interesting to white society "when it is sexually deviant" and when it is "synonymous with accessibility, availability" (*Black* 66). However, she goes on to claim that Josephine Baker had an agency over her performances of black female identity. Baker, hooks claims, was content in this commodification of the black body and moreover she was herself effectively exploiting the white eroticisation of black bodies (*Black* 66). This is close to Judith Butler's seminal work on the performative nature of gendered identity in which she argues for a notion of identity predicated on a "terrain of signification" that performs a particular identity on the world (*Gender* 136–48). This is useful here in an analysis of Baker's performances of a heavily racialised sexuality, but it tends to mask the importance of the particular historical context. Baker did not have the luxury of a selection of gender and racial positions from which to choose; rather, she nuanced the available stereotypes as much as possible given economic and cultural constraints. Baker's own self-definition as a star—a commodity amongst other commodities—must of course be taken into account. Acknowledging that Baker, as a modern music-hall and media star, was complicit in her own commodification does not, however, foreclose the wider debates around the representation of the nonwhite woman's body as one that has been denied historical presence and gravity through its exhaustive objectification as spectacle. Baker became a millionaire, as she says, through exploiting the intelligence of her body. This blackface pickaninny act, which the French critics called *la negrillone,* made Baker an outstanding comedy success, and she quickly became billed as "That Comedy Chorus Girl" wherever she appeared.

Early in 1925, just before she left for Europe, Baker worked as a dancer in the Plantation Club in Manhattan, where the main attraction was Ethel Waters. The show played around several variations of an Uncle Tom and

Aunt Jemima theme with the happy slave and the benevolent plantation master, and it included modern dance numbers, such as the Charleston, the messaround, and the blackbottom. The club was part of a select number of venues that were almost exclusively patronised by a wealthy white clientele, who came to Harlem to "slum it," dancing to jazz, drinking illegal alcohol, and mixing with "high yaller" chorus girls from the shows.[6] Baker went on to appear in *Shuffle Along* in New York, one of the first black musicals to appear on Broadway in 10 years. Produced by Noble Sissle and Eubie Blake, the show proved to be a tremendous success and could afford to pay Baker, still only 18 years old, around $125 dollars a week for her role. Although this was a considerable sum at the time, Baker would go on to receive more than twice that amount for her early performances in *La Revue Nègre*. By the age of 24, Josephine Baker was a millionaire twice over.

LA REVUE NÈGRE 1925–1927

> Joséphine Baker, . . . You symbolise youth for the whole world, you are the basis of life itself. . . . All the cities of the world bow down in front of you to learn of the secret that will prevent them from dying from under the weight of civilisation. "Le 'secret' de Joséphine Baker."
>
> —*Volonté*, December 10, 1929

> Negroes dance with their senses. (While Europeans can only dance with their minds). . . . Their revue is a bold challenge to moral Europe. There are eight beautiful girls whose figures conjure up a stylised purity . . . And at their head, the star, Josephine Baker. . . . But the leading role belongs to Negro blood. Its drops are slowly spreading over Europe, a long since dried-up land that can scarcely breathe. . . . The Negro question is an urgent one for our entire civilisation. It goes like this: Do the Negroes need us? Or are we not sooner in need of them?
>
> —Ivan Goll, January 15, 1926

Caroline Dudley Reagan, a wealthy white liberal entrepreneur who claimed that she had grown up at the knees of Booker T. Washington, astutely recognised the potential market for black American performers in a negrophile Paris.[7] In 1925, scouring America for an all-black musical troupe that could perform in Paris, she discovered Josephine Baker at the end of a Broadway chorus line, sticking out "like an exclamation point" (Haney 44). Dudley quickly saw Baker's appeal for a European audience and signed her up for the tour. In the cultural slump after the First World War, the Théâtre Champs-Elysées, in which the troupe was to appear, was losing money and had to attract new audiences whose jaded palates sought aesthetic novelty and spectacular innovation. Josephine Baker's startling repertoire of perpetual motion seemed to fit the bill. Thus, the 25-strong group of jazz musicians, singers, and dancers, including soprano saxophonist Sidney Bechet and Baker, sailed from New York to Cherbourg on September 16, 1925. This was a time in Paris when black Americans, such as Claude McKay, could earn substantial sums of money by transforming themselves into artist's models for the afternoon. James Clifford claims that the black body in Paris became an "ideological artefact," but perhaps it would be more accurate to say that it became an aesthetic commodity as the visual spectacle of blackness was in cultural demand (*Predicament* 197). Hence, even the least talented American jazz musicians were a valuable addition to the clubs and restaurants of Montmartre, where a *branché* clientele came to dance *le jazz hot*. When Langston Hughes arrived in Paris looking for work in 1924, he was given advice by a black doorman at the Grand Duc: "Less you can play or tap dance, you'd just as well go home" (Berry 45). As he could do neither, Hughes spent a brief period washing dishes in the Grand Duc, epicentre of the white expatriate community in Paris.[8]

Josephine Baker's Parisian stage debut was in *La Revue Nègre* on October 2, 1925, at the *Théâtre Champs-Elysées*. The site of the performance was itself replete with the recent history of cultural and aesthetic scandal as it was here that Diaghilev's Ballets Russes performed *Le Sacré du Printemps* to an outraged Parisian public on its first night. In 1919 Paul Guillaume, the celebrated art collector who would become a vociferous defender of *Revue Nègre,* had organised a *Fête Nègre* at the theatre after it had remained closed for the duration of the war. In addition, in August 1918 James Reese Europe and the Harlem Hellfighters, black American veterans from the war, played their first European concert at the same theatre. The theatrical managers, Rolf de Maré (a radical intellectual and member of the avant-garde group Les Six), André Daven, and the producer Jacques Charles, had all formerly worked at the Moulin Rouge. It was Charles who allegedly created the *danse sauvage* that was to become the phenomenal success of the *Revue*. Daven was friendly with the artist Fernand Léger, who had recently attended the exhibition of African sculpture at the Exposition des Arts Décoratifs (1925). Sensing the potential interest, and profit, in staging a spectacle of authentic *art nègre,* Léger advised Daven: "Give them Negroes. Only the Negroes can excite Paris" (qtd. in Haney 44). The first performances of the *Revue* were meticulously documented by the élite of Parisian modernists, such as Man Ray, who was on hand after the first night and took a series of photographs of the cast. Amongst the members of the audience were Jean Cocteau, who was later to dedicate some poetry to Baker, the surrealist painter Robert Desnos, the poet Blaise Cendrars, Francis Picabia, and the American writer and journalist Janet Flanner, whose review of Baker's debut in the *New Yorker* is worth quoting in full:

> She made her entry entirely nude except for a pink flamingo feather between her limbs; she was being carried upside down and doing the split on the shoulder of

> a black giant. Mid stage, he paused, and with his long fingers holding her basketwise around the waist, swung her in a slow cartwheel to the stage floor, where she stood like his magnificent discarded burden, in an instant of complete silence. She was an unforgettable female ebony statue. A scream of salutation spread through the theater. Whatever happened next was unimportant. The two specific elements had been established and were unforgettable—her magnificent dark body, a new model that to the French proved for the first time that black was beautiful, and the acute response of the white masculine public in the capital of hedonism of all Europe—Paris. Within half an hour of the final curtain on opening night, the news and meaning of her arrival had spread by grapevine up to the cafes on the Champs Elysées. . . . (xx–xxi)

Here, Flanner suggests the range of appeal that these overtly sexual performances would have on French popular culture. Her emphasis on Baker's statuesque presence with its embodiment of the "new model" and the sexual response of the "white masculine public" recognises the doubled appeal of Baker. She was a figure who could be read within a modernist visual aesthetic as her body took on the shapes and planes of the Cubist painting. But clearly a seminaked black woman appealed at another level. The white male audience is positioned as the colonial master, surveying, pursuing, and controlling this "genial, uninhibited savage," and engages in the eroticised colonial fantasy of power and seduction (Stovall 54). Flanner also suggested Baker as representative of "a new model" that articulated both the primitive and the modern; Baker was figured simultaneously as a nostalgic balm against the troubled modernity of postwar France and as emblematic of this very modernity. Speaking to this doubled appeal of the primitive in 1920s Paris, Jean Laude has commented: "Tantôt, cet intéret apparaît comme le signe d'un refus à l'égard de la vie moderne; tantôt il est effectué d'un indice positif, comme le signe d'une appartenance au mouvement moderniste" (10). Theatre critic Pierre Lazereff was effusive in his praise of the *Revue*, declaring, "After Josephine Baker, everything changed" (*Paris-Midi* n. pag.).

In the week before the *Revue* opened, members of the press and celebrities were invited to a preview. The mixture of the audience was eclectic: Paul Guillaume, celebrated music-hall star Mistinguett, artists Fernand Léger and Van Dongen, the redoubtable cultural critic of *Le Figaro* and member of the prestigious Académie Française Robert De Flers, along with an assortment of fashion designers, liberal academics, and cabaret performers. Such a cultural mix would become commonplace for the broad, crossover appeal that Baker enjoyed in Paris at this time, when the interests of the visual arts, literature, the social sciences, and the popular media coincided.[9] The original routines of the *Revue* were vastly different from those that normally enthralled Parisian audiences. The show was entirely transformed from a typical black chorus line set of song and dance routines to a set of tableaux on traditional black American life. The chorus was dressed in the theatrical Sunday-best style of costumes typical of earlier cakewalk revues in America, which were also extremely popular in Europe at the beginning of the century.[10] Jacques Charles thought the chorus rather inauthentic in their performances of "blackness." "Precision dancing," he said, "might be appropriate for German or English girls, but not for blacks, who, as everyone knew, were instinctive dancers, incapable of discipline" (qtd. in Rose 5). Baker's partner, Joe Alex, was from Martinique and, significantly, had much darker skin than Baker. The pairing of a light-skinned black woman and a much darker-skinned male partner was a sexual/racial combination routinely adhered to in Harlem nightclubs. Sensing the potential for this kind of erotic spectacle in Europe, the producers quickly dropped leading lady Maud De Forest's gospel and spiritual songs, as the producers found that they were depressing and suggested that the show lacked erotic appeal (Rose 5). The opening scene of the *Revue Nègre* had a backdrop of a Mississippi levee with steamboats interspersed with oversized watermelons set amid a Southern-style plantation, all designed by Miguel Covarrubias, the ubiquitous painter of the Harlem Renaissance. The revue consisted of a series of tableaux that offered the French audience so-called authentic set pieces on black life. These pieces were highly stylised renditions that seamlessly conflated Harlem and Africa in an imaginary and ahistorical exotic geography. Baker's entrance was in a piece set in a Harlem nightclub where she and her partner, Joe Alex, danced for a white audience. Thus the spectacle was doubled, a show within a show, where two sets of two white gazes surveyed the black performers. Baker's entrance into this scene was reminiscent of the earlier performances of her youth, in which she was renowned as the chorus girl at the end of the line who could bring the house down by a comic grimace or a gesture. Dressed in the traditional cut-off ragged shorts and a brightly checked shirt of the minstrel pickaninny character, Baker entered the stage on all fours singing a Spencer Williams scat. She was "bent double, slapping her palms of her hands against the boards of the stage" (Hammond and O' Connor 18), with her backside raised high up in the air. In this tableau, "The Mississippi Steam Boat Race," Baker's lips were painted white to exaggerate her mouth and her eyes were outlined in paint in the typical mask of minstrelsy.

But it was the final set of the "Danse Sauvage" that brought a "scream of salutation" throughout the Théâtre Champs-Elysées. The "Danse" perfectly encapsulated the primitivist zeitgeist and consolidated a visual racial vocabulary that would endure throughout Baker's early career. Baker and Alex appeared to be dressed only in feathers with primitive jewellery around their wrists and ankles. In fact, Baker was wearing a satin bikini that was covered by a skirt of feathers, a traditional music-hall adornment of playful artifice, used to exaggerate the appearance of naked female flesh. She also wore feather collars around her wrists, ankles, and neck in a pastiche of slave-girl chic—a look that she would exploit in numerous early photographs. The jungle setting of darkest Africa was an imagined geography of "paysages lointains" where "les hommes mangent des bananes et les femmes s'en habillent" (Brach 14). The dancing in the routine seemed spontaneously uninhibited in its depiction of an imaginary space of difference. This space was set in a conflated landscape of the jungle/Harlem/colonies, all replete with a manufactured aura of "noble savagery and primitive grace" in which the black body, carefully figured within this primitivist discourse, was positioned on the borders of human and animal (Mercer 113). She was, according to theatre critic Gérard Bauer, "Un être hybride" who "had come to Paris to give direction to its fascinations and to give a visual rhythm to the uncertainties of the time" (20). In a 1926 review for *Vanity Fair*, e. e. cummings was perplexed by exactly what Baker *was*. He described her as "a mysteriously unkillable something," uncertain where to place her mixture of erotic savagery and infantile parody (114). He had written an earlier review of *Chocolate Dandies* on Broadway in 1924 in which he had presciently summed up the particularly modern appeal of Baker's performances: "She resembled some tall, vital, incomparably fluid nightmare which crossed its eyes and warped its limbs in a purely unearthly manner—some vision which opened new avenues of fear, which suggested nothing but itself and which, consequently, was strictly aesthetic" (qtd. in Hammond and O'Connor 114).

THE "NEFERTITI OF THE NEW"

In 1925, Paul Brach, a well-known theatre critic for the *Comoedia*, describes Josephine Baker in ways that typified critical receptions of her in the French capital:

> And then she smiled, and her race offered up all its simplicity in this whiteness. You have come to breathe life into our grey and tired lives on the banks of the Seine. We are grateful to you for having distracted us with your grace and your naiveté. You parody our commotion, our insanity without malice, almost unconsciously and you cover up our worries with a blanket of noise. Who knows, perhaps your colourful feathers could save us from our time. (67)

The primitivist sentiments of this passage are obvious. Baker is positioned here as the signifier of an unspecified and transparent blackness; her "race" is offered to the troubled and exhausted West as a palliative balm to assuage the *tumulte* of modernity. What is also clear from the above is the sharp distinction between Baker as the figure from the outside or elsewhere and the *nous* of the speaking self, which is unproblematically and specifically located in a named geography. Baker's race, an imagined community of savagely playful natives, offers itself to the West as a resource that will both accentuate and soften what Berman calls the "possibilities and the perils" of modernity (15). The figure from elsewhere serves an instrumental function here, alternately engaged in both articulating and repairing the domestic disquiet of Western modernity. Audiences and critics received *La Revue Nègre* as both the primitive antithesis of European modernity trapped in "la vision antérieure, faite d'animalité, de sauvagerie, de barbarie" and as an inherently modern phenomenon (Dewitte 46). The sign of the primitive, therefore, becomes malleable in two opposing ways that render the category of the primitive epistemologically and aesthetically bifurcated. Ideas of the primitive are inscribed in a dualistic but not dialectical relationship. Baker's body stands for the non-Western body functions in a racial signifying process in which the timeless, placeless locale of the primitive is fixed in opposition to the West and civilisation. This opposition is clearly pointed up in Léon Poirier's 1926 *La Croisière Noire*, a documentary that follows the Citröen team crossing Saharan Africa in a gruelling car rally, as triumphant bearers of European technology set against a background of primitive landscapes and peoples.

As Raymond Williams has rightly pointed out, the cosmopolitan access to subordinate cultures that European modernism enjoyed after the First World War occurred at the same time as the concentration of capital in colonial territories. The relations between aesthetic modernism and imperial capitalism were thus drawn into the debate. Aesthetic modernism, with its emphasis on the innovative medium, stressed transience, fragmentation, displacement, and defamiliarisation, all of which were readily found in the "broken narrative" of the non-Western artefact and body, in all its putative "visual and linguistic strangeness" (Williams, *Politics* 169). For the modernist artist then, the expansive limits of the "significant form" of Baker's versatile signification were consonant with a quest for an innovative formalism. Consequently, artists such as Alexander Calder, Le Corbusier, and Adolf De Loos, all radical innovators of architectural form, were inspired by Baker's body as a model of a new human plasticity. She represented for them the perfect example of the denaturalised, unfamiliar human body: the modern(ist) and the primitive in aesthetic coincidence.

Thus, a striking contradiction was set up wherein Baker's perceived primitivism both affirmed and opposed a distinctly modern sensibility. Furthermore, there was the added complication that Josephine Baker was a black American who had minimal, if any, cultural contact with continental Africa or any of the French colonies. And yet her iconic personae were consistently framed as archetypal figures of blackness, whether an Ethiopian princess, a native of Haiti, or a dancing girl from Tonkin, as in her hit song "La Petite Tonkinoise." Baker was *la petit sauvageonne:* bearer of multiple racial guises. How did reviewers reconcile the manifest contradictions of a primitivist New World blackness in a modern metropolitan setting? The fact that Baker was American and very clearly not from Dahomey or Indochina or Algiers was a crucial factor in the success of her shows and her subsequent film career, in which she starred as the archetypal woman in all of the these locales. Verisimilitude was self-consciously not the aim. The spectacle that *La Revue Nègre* offered was a staged conflation of geographies and histories, scenarios that evacuated the category of race of any material history or specificity for a time and a public unwilling or unready to confront the actuality of colonial relations. The scenarios that Baker performed for a mostly white audience foregrounded the knowledge that she was precisely *not* from the French colonies, permitting her racial image to signify not just a retrogressive "African" primitivism but also a particularly modern (black) Americanism. Baker was framed as the archetypal *sauvage,* a figure of doubled alterity who was able to convey the acutely contemporary moment of postwar "horror and hypocrisy" (Rouverge n. pag.). The spectacular site of Baker's body—the body as text and spectacle—was necessarily emptied of its particular history and significance in its projection of a double set of possible meanings for her audiences.

The primitivist appeal of Baker and *La Revue Nègre* was that of a contained disorder. A spectacle of difference played out scenarios in which white society ostensibly rejected order and civilisation, and social and cultural amelioration, through a voyage into the spontaneous and natural geographies of black cultures. Thus, the primitivism of the *Revue* and of *négrophilie* fulfilled an impulse of both escapism and self-affirmation: a desire to enter into the imaginary spaces of the primitive as a self-affirming act that sought a definitive demarcation between the subject as beholder and the object as spectacle in order to negotiate a "crisis in identity" (Torgovnick 157). The primitive subject as objectified spectacle acted as the cultural conduit wherein the modern subject sought reconciliation with its alienated self. The fragile political and cultural climate of postwar France was particularly open to the romantic fiction of primitivism that might assuage the damage of historical decimation—1.38 million dead from the ravages of the war. In her performances Baker signified a staging of blackness that, in its simplicity, offered a naively redemptive vision to a life of drab, uniform exhaustion. This promise of regeneration and recuperation appealed to populist sentiments as well as to modernist artists and intellectuals. Bill Schwarz notes that this kind of voguish primitivism was the primary mode by which black subjects could be "conveniently accommodated in the imagination of those more self-consciously modernist European intellectuals as representatives of a pre-rational—or primitive—elan" (183). Thus, the appeal of these early shows of 1925–26 was a yearning for a moment of historical amnesia—a forgetting of the troubled present by a return to an imagined past of a premodern idyll. To return to this was to move away from the "nightmare of history" that had recently resulted in the slaughter of millions on the battlefields of Ypres and the Somme and to embrace a sensual, and erotic, escapism. As the imagined other of Western civilisation, Baker represented the unfettered frenzy of libidinal urges breaking through the nihilism of despair. For her Parisian audiences she portrayed an intoxicating deliverance from the fetters of administered rationality, embodying a nostalgic longing for the authentic, uncorrupted self of a mythical primitive past, a fantasmic space where the Western psyche could enjoy the erotic energy repressed by European civilisation. She was a savage Eros delivered from a people "who smile beautiful violet smiles and hammer metal with primitive instruments, while their swollen bellied children mill around them" (Rouverge n. pag.).

Baker's savagely erotic slave girl descending from a palm tree in the jungle-scape of the Folies-Bergère offered her Parisian audiences a "free and spontaneous" art through which, as one critic remarks, "our imagination can go in search of our dreams" (Rouverge 22). Similarly, Fernand Devoire testifies to the effect Baker had upon her Paris audiences: "Josephine Baker, our lives on the banks of the Seine were weary and depressing before you came along. In the eyes of Paris, you are the virgin forest. You bring to us a savage rejuvenation" (qtd. in Abatino 18). Other critics such as Pierre MacOrlan claim Baker's performance as a transformative moment in French cultural history in which the very foundations of perception are disrupted: "Josephine speaks to our unconscious. She turns upside down our way of seeing, displacing lives, calling to mind a primitive order" (qtd. in Haney 67). Figured as modernity's chaotic other, Baker represents "a pure cultural antidote" to the intellectualism of the West (Schwartz 191).

OTHER MUSIC

Baker's musical performances have been seen by musicologists and cultural critics such as Edouard Schneider as balms: "C'est le chant tout intime qui panse sans effort nos nerfs malades et tels de nos désirs indéfinis." Black music, Schneider suggests, is an almost infinitely elastic text into which the exhausted white subject can take refuge: the music "takes us so far away from ourselves that we don't ask why or how any longer" (qtd. in Abatino 11). The primitive subject is transparent and readable to its audience, who might know the truth of the black subject without the need for articulation at any linguistic level, a manoeuvre similar to that of the earlier *chants nègres* of Zurich Dada that I have discussed elsewhere. These critics describe Baker's voice as "strange" and "undefinable," the words unimportant in themselves as they are a sensual, aural antidote to moribund intellectualism: "Is it even useful to understand what she is saying?" Edouard Schneider asks. It is the sensation, the almost physicality of the words, rather than any inherent meaning, that offers her audience suggestions of a dream island-scape, articulating the secret desires of the modern subject and allowing the listener access to the uncorrupted prelapsarian paradise of the primitive subject:

> Nombre des heures à jamais mortes de nos désirs inassouvis, de nos musiques intérieures encore inattendues, la nostalgie des lointains fascinants que nous n'abordons jamais, ces mystérieuses nuances de notre concert intérieur où se prolonge l'accent de ce que nous pourrions nommer notre soif d'infini. (E. Schneider, qtd. in Abatino 12)

The "notre" of Schneider's writing is located in the white listener/viewer who desires to escape from the mundanity of daily life into the unnameable distance of the primitive other. Baker is the channel of these desires, a muse for the weary West who can turn to the ahistorical realm of nostalgia and infinite elsewheres to calm their "nerfs malades." Baker is always outside the realm of "we"; eternally framed as other, she is the essence of pure difference. Thus, progress and modernity are set in opposition to regression and antiquity, the classic Manichean binary, which finally asserts the authority of the West over the rest of the so-called uncivilised world. The West is positioned as the place and the history that can instrumentalise the terrains of racial and cultural difference to narrate its own systemic crises. The position of enunciation assumes an authoritative subject position of "I" or "We," which is, as Marianna Torgovnick observes, the "eye of the ethnographer, the privileged part of us," that is, an unambiguous, powerfully substantive norm from which difference can be observed and described (4).

However, Baker was equally held to be a personification of the modern esprit that turned its gaze to the future as much as to the past. She was the figure who symbolised excesses of both the already imagined primitive past and the yet to be imagined modern future: the living symbol of a modern primitivist aesthetic, simultaneously "a call back to nature, and a subway ticket to modernity" (Powell 42). In reality, Baker's voice was somewhat thin and unimpressive compared to those of other black singers who had come to perform in France. This was of little concern to her public, however, as they heard her voice, redolent with the history of black music and suggestive of the new polyrhythmic musical forms of American jazz, played on the polished metal and highly modern instruments like the saxophone. The modernist architect Le Corbusier considered Baker's voice, in her rendition of the song "Baby," as emblematic of a completely new aesthetic: "There is in this American Negro music a lyrical 'contemporary' mass so invincible that I could see the foundation of a new sentiment of music capable of being the expression of the new epoch and also capable of classifying its European origins as stone age . . . " (Jencks 102). Le Corbusier has identified something very important here when he depicts the music of the *Revue* as expressive not "of the absolute essence of the group that produced it," that is, of some essential black identity, but on what Paul Gilroy calls the "mutations produced during its contingent loops and fractal trajectories" (75–76). The music of the *Revue* was already a hybridised form of so-called black music that held the poles of modernity and antiquity together in the popular space of the music-hall song.

This bifurcated metaphoricity of the ancient/modern is perhaps nowhere more evident than in Baker's later performances in the role of Fatou in *La Folie du Jour* at the Folies-Bergère in 1926. In this role she wears the famous banana skirt. Baker's costume, which had begun as a skirt of feathers, then became one of plush bananas, perkily phallic in their movements on the stage, finally metamorphosing into menacing silver metallic spikes, echoing the gleaming metal lines of the saxophones of Sidney Bechet's band at the *Revue Nègre.* Many reviews of *La Revue Nègre* say that the modern music of jazz saxophones and percussion instruments seemed to emanate from the primitive body itself, a perfect doubled symbol of the modernist aesthetic of juxtaposition and incongruity. André Rouverge sees jazz music in the *Revue* as the equivalent of a certain cultural anarchy: "[C]'est l'abdication de la musique dans son office d'instrument de la culture traditionelle." He argues that the libidinal frenzy suggested by jazz music and dancing proved unquestionably Gobineau's theories on the natural proclivities of the *nègre* to music and dance: "Pour le nègre, la danse est, avec la musique, l'objet de la plus irréstible passion . . . " (*Mercure de France* n. pag.). For Rouverge, Josephine Baker personifies this essential "black" tendency:

> C'est d'elle, de son trémoussement forcené, de ses dislocations téméraires . . . qu'émane le rythme. Elle semble dicter au "drummer" en vouté, au saxophone ardemment tendu vers elle, syllabe par syllabe, le monologue fantasque de son corps en folie. . . . Les déchancements de la bataleuse cynique et bon enfant, le rictus qui fait grimacer la large bouche, font place subitement à des visions dont toute bonhommie est absente. . . . (n. pag.)

Baker's popularisation of the Charleston and jazz dancing further positions her as the bearer of both the new and the ancient. Michel Leiris, in *L'Age d'homme* (1939), recalls the "orgiastic tribute" that jazz music brought to "the colors of the moment" in Paris during the 1920s. "It functioned magically," he says, "to express quite completely the state of mind of that generation: a more or less conscious demoralisation born of the war . . . " (10). For Leiris, jazz also articulates the doubled notion of the modern primitive, which is "a naive fascination with the comfort and the latest inventions of progress . . . an abandonment to the animal joy of experiencing the influence of a modern rhythm, an underlying aspiration to a new life in which more room would be made for the impassioned frankness we inarticulately longed for . . ." (*L'Age* 10). Similarly, Pierre Lazereff, in *Paris-Midi,* describes Baker as "la petite sauvageonne" who had come to refresh "la vieille Europe à l'esprit de Charleston"(n.p.). Rouverge talks of the "éruption dionysiaque" of jazz and the vogue for "la sauvagerie," describing the Charleston as a kind of mechanical, loosely syncopated dance mocking the formalities of earlier European dances such as the waltz and the polka, or the mazurka. Jazz, he argues, is the "loosening of the instincts" full of "naivete and animalistic drunkenness" (143). The music of the modern moment is, he comments, "une musique révoltante, fulgurante, nihiliste, instinctive et puérile . . . comme violentée et déchirée, et brisée" (143). The combination of primal rhythmic and corporeal beats with the materials of modern technology, the steely metal of the saxophones and the drums, is a perfect modern–primitive fusion in which Baker's body is represented as another instrument of dark steel transmitting the uninhibited erotic vocabulary of the savage.

NOTES

1. The National Association for the Advancement of Colored People (NAACP) estimated that over a hundred black citizens were killed in the unrest and more than 1,500 were made homeless as they fled from East St. Louis to St. Louis, although this was barely reported in the mainstream press. The official congressional investigating committee later put the death toll at 39. See Hammond and O'Connor 1–13 and Rose 46–57 for detailed accounts of Baker's childhood in the United States.

2. After the formal end of slavery in the United States, there were many ways in which the physical resources of the black population were again coerced into a system of economic exploitation, primarily through poorly paid domestic work and arduous physical labour.

3. For detailed studies of the Harlem Renaissance, see Lewis *Harlem* and *Portable;* Huggins; Powell; J. Johnson 264–80.

4. The Chestnut Valley district in St. Louis was a renowned 12-block area of brothels and honky-tonk bars. Composers from Tin Pan Alley visited the city and spent time in these brothels writing songs that would become popular hits across America. Scott Joplin spent eight years composing in St. Louis before moving to Chicago. See Sampson; and Bogle *Brown Sugar* for comprehensive histories of black music in America.

5. Baker was almost universally castigated in America, where her shows were greeted with critical derision and charges of minstrelsy and Uncle Tom-ism. Her performances of the pickaninny and the sexy slave girl were not seen as either playful or empowering, as she was regarded as representing a degraded African American identity. When the news that Baker had been elected Queen of the Colonies reached the black presses in America, it was greeted with almost universal

contempt. The *New York World-Telegram* responded with an article entitled "Queen, Where is Yo' Kink?" March 4, 1931. See Papich.

6. Carl Van Vechten's novel *Nigger Heaven* (1926) describes the sexual promiscuity and illegal drug and alcohol clubs of 1920s Harlem.

7. Many other black American entertainers and musicians were in Paris at the beginning of the 1920s. These included Alberta Hunter, the jazz pianists Palmer Jones and Noble Sissle, and the singer Florence Mills Bricktop (Ada Smith), whose own fame rivalled Baker's at one point. See Fabre 114–46.

8. See Hughes *Big Sea*.

9. Both Lebovics and Clifford offer detailed and lucid accounts of the relations between the social sciences, visual arts, and politics in their shared cultural interests. In particular, Lebovics points out that after the war anthropology in France was crucially influential on the new cultural politics and questions of national identity in the ideological consolidation of the new republic (6–8). The founding of the Institut d'Ethnologie in 1925 by Paul Rivet, Marcel Mauss, Lucien Lévy-Bruhl, and Maurice Delafosse is the best example of cross-disciplinary projects at this time. During its brief time in power from 1934 to 1936, Léon Blum's Front Populaire gave serious consideration to some of the more radical ideas of the Institut.

10. In 1902 the first cakewalk troupes toured Europe on the crest of a vogue for this popular black dance. On the origins of black American dance and music, see Bogle *Brown Sugar* and Pieterse.

CHAPTER 3

Black Woman/Colonial Body

Almost immediately after her debut in *La Revue Nègre,* an 18-year-old black American woman became *the* metaphor of the negrophile moment: "the sound of jazz, the beauty of African art as interpreted by the Cubists, represented by decorative artists and symbolised for them in the angular movements of Josephine Baker" (Hammond and O' Connor 18). The combination of the modern and the ancient, or the primitive, offered a concretising moment of self-assurance for the French audience as the spectacle of both forged fragile links between the past, the present, and the future. Jean Laude calls this "la présentification du passé," in which the anxieties of the civilisation—the uncertain realignment of European nation-states, the growth of consumer capitalism, and mass culture, urbanisation, and social alienation—are sublimated into the immediacy of an exotic/primitive spectacle of "l'expression corporelle" (410, 417). The success of *La Revue Nègre* and Baker herself was, in part, predicated upon a collective desire for a fanstasmic geographical and temporal elsewhere. The blatant artifice of the music-hall stage was ideal for this particularly modern(ist) configuration of race and visual spectacle and the primitivist discourses that became commonplace in the numerous reviews of the *Revue* acknowledged the artifice of the shows but were nevertheless drawn into the "truth effects of the spectacle.

In 1926 postcards and posters bearing the image of Josephine Baker were among the fastest selling of the decade in France. This was the beginning of the marketing of *La Bakaire* phenomenon in France: publicity stickers on bananas for her film *Zou Zou* (1934), ads for driving schools, hair oil marketed as "Bakerfix," Josephine Baker shoes, and recipes for pancakes and corn beef hash. In 1927 posters appeared around Paris in a mass advertising campaign for Baker's first feature film, *La Sirène des Tropique.*[1] One of the most popular postcards featured Baker in the role of a "native" dressed in the famous skirt of bananas, jewellery strategically positioned over her bare breasts, and a glossy, slicked down Eton crop. It was arguably this single image, a highly stylised hybridisation of the modern and the primitive, that secured her reputation as "the perfect symbol of both sexuality and primitivism" (Stovall 54). To this day, this image, or a reinterpretation of its racial thematics, has been repeated more than any other. The scenes of a white clientele visiting so-called authentic black nightspots in Harlem were repeated throughout Paris for a time. But, as Georges Brassai notes, the negrophile craze seemed to disappear as suddenly as it arrived. The white clientele stopped frequenting these clubs as popular cultural *négrophilie* began to wane with the onset of the 1930s.

The ways in which Baker was produced as a racial, commodified spectacle mobilised a debate amongst critics and intellectuals on the actual meaning of the primitive subject. On the one hand, Baker was framed as the untouched primitive id, the living antithesis of the modern: a purely corporeal being seen as "a symbol of torrid, exotic black sexuality" who could expose the trammelled, hypocritical culture of the rational West, a position espoused by avant-garde artists, particularly the Dadaists, Surrealists, and German Expressionists (Stovall 53). However, Baker was simultaneously constructed as the living *apogée* of modernity itself; the elemental appeal of her blackness suggested an unruly challenge to bourgeois notions of domestic sexuality. To this end, Nancy Cunard has written of Baker's performances in *La Folie du Jour:* "The dancing could be compared to the purest of African plastic in motion—it was free, perfect and exact, it centred admirably in the spare gold banana fronds round the dynamic hips" (qtd. in Hammond and O'Connor 57). Baker's performances symbolised the esprit of *négrophilie* in the French capital, but this spirit, however intriguing, was fleeting. While Baker's success continued well into the 1960s, she would always be remembered as the half-naked *sauvage* with her banana skirt.

THE BLACK BODY

In "Danse Sauvage" Joe Alex is also strategically adorned with feathers around his hips and ankles. The aestheticised reinscription of slavery is obvious here, but it is dehistoricised in the spectacle of the *danse* that privileges a recognisable set of key racial signifiers: hair, skin, exotic body accessories, and Baker's undulating backside—all subsequently figure repeatedly in images of Baker. The reviewers of this first "Danse Sauvage" are enthralled by the corporeal abandon of Baker's performances. In his influential reviews of the show in *La danse d'aujourd'hui,* dance critic André Levinson emphasises Baker's "arched back" and "protruding haunches" and her "arms uplifted and entwined in a phallic symbol" and suggests that the appeal of Baker's performances is that she "possesses the compelling potency of the finest examples of African sculptures come to life" (qtd. in Abatino 37). Other reviewers are equally enthralled by the lithe physicality of the "Danse Sauvage," as Baker shimmied her way through the piece with an astounding dexterity and energy.

Interviews and articles in the popular press rave about Baker's exotic physical appearance. In various interviews with "la brune vedette," journalist André Viollis subjects Baker's features to a detailed scrutiny; her skin, her hair, her eyes, and her nails all become sites of racialised signification, subjected to the intense gaze of a critical ethnography. Baker's face and body are continually on display in photographs, posters, caricatures, and portraiture. Copious column inches are devoted to the physical minutiae of her body, her "cheveux ripolinés de noir" over a face that is a "masque égéen, tout doré, avec d'immenses yeux d'émail qui en font le tou." Her entire aspect is, Viollis suggests, "comme un fruit rouge et charnu au large noyau blanc, froncant la ligne pur de son nez, virnant des prunelles, louchant, grimacant. . . . " He continues his racial hagiography of her body: "Elle a le corps le plus harmonieux de statue grecque avec je ne sais quelle grâce hiératique et mystérieuse qui évoque à la fois l'Egypte et l'Inde. . . . " Just as Frantz Fanon commented on being "battered down by toms toms" (*Black Skin, White Masks* 112), Baker's body evokes a primeval race memory of "la forêt vierge où batifoliaient ses noirs ancêtres dès les premiers âges du monde" (*Peau noire, masques blancs* 91). He concludes by summing up Baker as both "affreuse" and "heureuse." She is the summation of the essence of *l'art nègre* in her intimation of both the grotesque and the beautiful. Similarly, Baker's skin becomes the focus of interviews and reviews; its dark tones, so reviled and devalorised in the negrophobic discourses of explicit racism, are now hypervalorised in the scopic fetishism of negrophile discourse (Mercer 183–87). Baker herself would later satirise the constant fetishistic attention that her dark skin received in France when she compared herself to dark-skinned French women on their return from their annual vacations on the Riviera. Although it is now well known that she used skin lighteners all her life, the precarious balance between "too dark" and "not dark enough" would be ever present for Josephine Baker.

Baker's body is overdetermined not simply by its racial markers but also by the intersection of these markers with racialised discourses of gender. Colette Guillaumin's work on the construction of gender and racial discourse includes her idea of the "natural marks" of the body and how these marks circumscribe the racialised (or gendered) subject into a regulatory field of apprehension by the dominant, unmarked group. Natural

Josephine Baker featured on the Paul Colin poster for *La Revue Nègre*, Paris, 1925, which launched her career. Courtesy of The Granger Collection, New York.

marks of race and gender "ascribe[s] the system of domination on the body of the individual, assigning to the individual his/her place as a dominated person: but it does not assign any place to the dominator. Membership in the dominant group, on the contrary, is legally marked by a convenient lack of interdiction, by unlimited possibilities" ("Race" 241). In *Peau noire, masques blancs* (1952), Fanon assigns these natural external marks a negative phenomenological existence, the racial-epidermal schema, that finally destroys the ontology of the black subject, who is crushed by the battery of archetypes and imperatives. Recognition for 'le noir' is involved in "une activité uniquement négatrice" that results in a position of absolute overdetermined racialisation (90, 93).

The interest generated in the *Revue Nègre* by the popular press was enormous and consequently the opening night was sold out. This interest was due in a large part to the advanced publicity that the *Revue* received in the form of a series of striking posters designed by the then little-known lithographic artist Paul Colin. Colin's collected works, titled *Dans le Tumulte Noir* (1926), produced for the *Revue Nègre,* revealed a particular set of scopic obsessions with racial characteristics that consolidated the foundations of a shorthand grammar of race and sexuality that developed around Baker's body in both written texts and visual image.[2] The drawings ranged from "caricature to near-abstract renditions of Joséphine's silhouette in images that are a synthesis of Cubist design and Fauve colouring . . . " (Hammond and O'Connor 51). These images of Baker's body foregrounded a corporeal dislocation, her limbs positioned at impossible angles to her torso reminiscent of the fractured perspectives of Cubism. The effect of her dance routines mediated by the camera or the artist's brush was one of visual dispersal that drew the eye away from the corporeal whole to its constituent racial parts. Images of Baker's body exaggerated the primary racial signifiers of her buttocks, hair, and breasts.[3] In the racial vocabulary around Baker's body, the repeated emphasis on her buttocks was the most visually striking.[4] Baker herself has said of the furore that broke out after her early performances in which she used her backside as part of her dance act: "The rear end exists. I see no reason to be ashamed of it. It's true that there are rear ends so stupid, so pretentious, so insignificant that they're good only for sitting on" (Sauvage 89). The over-racialised renditions of Baker's body and particularly her undulating derrière were claimed for and against modernity, at once primitive and savage and then modern and elemental.[5] Max Rheinhardt, the director of the Deutsches Theater in Berlin, where Baker performed in 1927, held up Baker's body as an aesthetic resource for a culturally depleted West. Her black skin and lissom torso were proclaimed as the fertile new sites of corporeal plenitude, hitherto unrealised by the moribund intellectualism of the West: "The expressive control of the whole body, the spontaneity of motion, the rhythm, the bright emotional color. These are your treasures. . . . " (Rose 85).

Just as the corporeal labour of the *indigène* functioned as a military resource for France during the war, the racially marked body of Josephine Baker functioned as a trope of cultural regeneration in the aftermath of the war. Baker's performances in the *Revue Négre* (1925) and the later *La Folie du Jour* (1926) offered the spectacle of the black female body as a site of hyperfecundity and replenishment. France's birthrate was stagnating after the war, which had reduced the male population by 10.5 percent.[6] A preoccupation with *natalité* was played out in metropolitan politics

Josephine Baker on a Paul Colin poster, 1927. Courtesy of The Granger Collection, New York.

throughout the 1920s and 1930s, as the notion of an expanding and fertile resource of *la plus grande France* began to enter into quotidian discourse. The colonies represented the promise of rejuvenation for metropolitan France and a decrepit Europe, both economically and demographically (Girardet 269).[7] But it would not be a literal cross-racial rejuvenation, as the labour and the image of the *indigène* were co-opted for *la mère patrie* in a formula that equated products from the colonies, such as palm oil and sugar, with the inexhaustible labour supply of indigenous peoples.[8] But the idea of regeneration also operated at a metaphorical level of an eroticised racial discourse. In *Paris Soir,* Paul Reboux's "Le Portrait du

Jour" has described Josephine Baker's conquest of Paris as being both artistic and sexual. In a comparison of the *Revue* with classical ballet, Reboux has stressed the sexual voyeurism that Baker offered her audience, urging them to a licentious sensual indulgence: "Live for the moment without looking back to yesterday or forward to tomorrow." Reboux emphasises the "baudelarien" pleasures of Baker's black skin as an inspirational spectacle for the uninspired white male while her "dark eyes" were the repository of desire—the essence of sexuality itself—"des yeux qu'elle nous dispense avec une indefatigable libéralité" (qtd. in Abatino 65).

THE EROTIC *INDIGÈNE*

In the summer of 1926, Baker appears in *La Folie du Jour,* donning the famous banana skirt for the first time to reprise her role of playful and uninhibited savage Fatou. This role is a pivotal staging of the Baudelarian black/white sexual desire and transgressive fantasies of mastery and seduction. Baker enters the stage down the trunk of a palm tree, limb by limb, until her seminaked body, adorned in strings of pearls and neck and wrist cuffs, is revealed in full to the spectator, a white colonial officer in a pith helmet. Baker begins to dance seductively in front of him in the midst of the jungle-scape and slowly leads him to his tent, as in the background two black men in loin cloths play tom-toms under a palm tree. The male gaze of the *colon* is the frame for the white spectator's transgression through the body of the racial other: "They claim the body of the colored other instrumentally, as unexplored terrain, a symbolic frontier that will be fertile ground for their reconstruction of the masculine norm, for asserting themselves as transgressive desiring machines" (hooks, *Black* 24). The colonial officer succumbs to the erotic chaos of Baker's seductive other, as he gives in to the "untutored sexuality just below the surface," one that is persistently "threatening to 'break out'" in the colonies (S. Hall, "Whites" 41). Clearly then, the "Dark Continent" of sexual otherness is invoked in Baker's early performances, a continent already familiar to her cosmopolitan Parisian audiences.[9] Edouard Schneider regards Baker as "one of the few human beings who could fulfil a symbolic function" that might include a "piquant distraction for our daily personal benefit" (qtd. in Abatino 14). The term *piquant* here is interesting and one echoed by bell hooks more recently when she describes this enduring fascination with the racial other as "the spice that can liven up the dull dish that is mainstream white culture." Baker's racial difference, marketed as a cultural commodity, is consumed like any other commodity in collective acts of consumer pleasure to be "found in the acknowledgement and enjoyment of racial difference" (*Black* 14, 21).[10] Paris at this time enjoys the outrageous spectacle of *La Bakaire,* both on and off the stage, as she fulfills her role as exotic star to the highest degree, reputedly strolling down the

Champs Elysées with her pet leopard Chiquita on a diamond-encrusted leash.

Phyllis Rose compares the colonial contexts of the *Revue Nègre* and Baker's earlier primitive personae to the popular erotic postcards of veiled, half-naked Algerian women in harems.[11] But there is a crucial difference between images of Baker in her topless performances in the 1920s and those of frozen, anonymous models in a harem or in rural Africa. It is true that the framing of Baker in numerous postcards, photographs, and cartoons from this period repeats the overdetermined racial vocabulary of the native woman as the site of excessive, lascivious desire. The non-white woman is figured as a blank repository for the white male gaze to fill, a sort of Gauginesque erotic ideal. However, Baker's role as the native girl is self-consciously performative in its figuration of colonial relations. The scene where Fatou seduces the colonial officer may have touched upon numerous truths about erotic life in the colonies or the fantasy of the native temptress, but finally it is knowingly performed by the black American Josephine Baker, Parisian music-hall star and media phenomenon. This knowingness about the performance does not have the same historical resonance as the images of young women in an Algerian harem posing for the "vivisector's gaze" of the camera (Alloula 92). While it is crucial to recognise Baker's performances as archives of these images, it is a performative archive removed from the actual historical subject of the colonial gaze, which she stood outside of by virtue of her African Americanism.

Throughout her career, Baker's performative roles shifted from the modern-primitive, the playful *indigène,* to finally the *grande chanteuse*—the blatant artifice of her medium constructed her as a one-size-fits-all racial metaphor. Her self-conscious figuration as a black American "star" permitted her some degree of distantiation from the cruder mechanics of racial and sexual exploitation. Relations between Baker and her audiences were predicated upon a shared fantasy of race and the erotic spectacle of difference that required a complicity on both the part of the public and Baker herself. The racial "truths" were performances of desire and repulsion, power and seduction, regeneration and degeneration.

Baker's performances offered an entirely fanstasmic racialised space untroubled by modernity or by any serious reference to colonial actualities but replete with the suggestive history of blackness that is glossed into one seductive fantasy of an unspecific blackness. Paul Archand's review in *Paris-Midi* points this up very clearly:

> We don't understand their language. We can't find a way to tie the scenes together but everything we've ever heard flashes across our enchanted minds: adventure novels, glimpses of enormous steamboats swallowing up clusters of Negroes who carry rich burdens, a caterwauling woman in an unknown port, stories of mis-

sionaries and travellers, Stanley, the Tharaud brothers, Batouala, sacred dances, the Sudan, plantation landscapes, the melancholy songs of Creole nurses, the Negro soul with its animal energy, its childish joys, the sad bygone time of slavery we had all that listening to the singer with the jungle voice. . . . (*Paris-Midi* n. pag.)

Archand's comments capture the multiple appeal of Baker's performances. The historical formations of the category of race are entirely occluded into an aestheticised, homogenised fantasy of otherness in which all difference is flattened out into a singular iconic spectacle of the exotic primitive. Mythology, fiction, colonial fantasy, geographies all blend into one space of thoroughly mediated otherness. The category of race, evacuated of any topographic precision or material location, is mediated as America's Deep South, Harlem nightclubs, Caribbean islands, all merging seamlessly into a singularity. The black female subject, throughout Baker's own career, metamorphisises from Fatou, into Nefertiti, Cleopatra, and Princess Tam Tam, La Petite Tonkinoise—an unproblematically flexible metaphor for *all* racial difference.

THE QUEEN OF THE COLONIES

Joséphine est le plus bel exemple de perfectionnement possible dans le façonnement intellectuel de la race noire par la civilisation europêene.
—Jean Sejournet, *Le Concours Medical*, February 8, 1931

La primitive danseuse aux bananes dont les mouvements de croupe avaient conquis . . . Paris, nous revient en vedette . . . en artiste. . . .
—Ruy Blas, October 15, 1930

In *Jazz Cleopatra*, Phyllis Rose remarks that "to read the reviews of *La Revue Nègre* is to immerse oneself in the fantasy life of the French male in the years between the wars." The spectators, she says, saw themselves as "white explorers voyaging on the edge of civilization, encountering the savage, incorporating it into themselves by making love with a savage woman" (22). She describes these erotic fantasies as colonialist rather than racist, and although the distinction here is unclear, her interpretation of these reviews quite correctly places them in a colonial context that sets civilisation in opposition to savagery, positioning the white European male as the agent of civilising transformation. (After he has explored and enjoyed the "dark continent" of black female sexuality, of course.) Between 1925 and 1932, Baker's performances can be read within a historical context inflected by a specific set of metropolitan discourses around colony, race, and the assimilationist logic of the *mission civilisatrice.* An examination of Baker's performance and imagery in the Folies-Bergère show *La Folie du Jour* in 1926, in which she appeared topless for the first time in the famous banana skirt, and in her later, comeback performances in 1930 at the Casino de Paris clearly reveals a trajectory of an idealised colonial narrative at work in these spectacles. Ignoring the realities of French colonial rule at this time and the attendant domestic anxieties in the metropole, this narrative of transformative *assimilation* presents a spectacle of the *mission civilisatrice.*

Germany's defeat in the First World War resulted in France's acquisition of additional territories, so that by 1919 the Third Republic ruled 12,500 square kilometres of foreign land. Thus began the era of Albert Sarraut's *mise en valeur* (rational development) of the Second French Empire, begun in 1830 with the conquest of Algeria and lasting until 1962, after the bloody Algerian independence war. The period immediately following the Allies' victory in 1918 was characterised by a tangible shift in attitude by the French public regarding their colonial possessions. This was mainly due to the conscription of massive numbers of colonial troops during the conflict, which had undoubtedly contributed to the victory but at a loss of 205,000 colonial soldiers on the fields of Ypres, Flanders, and the Somme. A school manual from 1925 makes France's sense of grudging gratitude explicit: "C'est en partie grâce à son empire colonial que la France a pu sortir victorieuses de la Grande Guerre, de même que l'Angleterre doit également à ses colonies d'avoir pu mener la lutte jusqu'au bout" (Girardet 118). The colonies had proved themselves a crucially important demographic resource during the war. Philippe Dewitte has noted that the shift in attitudes towards the colonies as a result of the conscripted colonial soldiers altered the ways in which race was subsequently represented in popular cultural discourses after the war: "La nouveau principale de l'après-guerre, c'est la naissance du mythe du 'Nègre enfant,' rieur et naif." This was a shift from the racism of the prewar period to a benign but paternalistic tolerance: "l'image du Nègre est pasée du stade de sauvage pur et simple à celui d'un 'grand enfant,' la chéchia du bonhomme Banania a remplacé l'os dans le nez au magasins des accessoires racistes" (45–46). Although the official metropolitan policy regarding the education and acculturation of colonial subjects was still one of *assimilation* (the creation of civilisable French *petits sujets* in the Republican ideal), the implementation of colonial policies in the colonies themselves differed greatly from one colony to another.[12] However, despite the economic and ideological consolidation of the colonial empire, the Third Republic had reason to feel anxious about the future internal stability of some colonies as the spectre of the Second International of the Communist Party began to make its presence felt on the international imperial scene and the Parti Communist Français (PCF) was gaining political ground in France. Unrest in West Africa, particularly the strikes and riots in Porto Nova in 1923, resulted in the enforcement of an 1881 law on freedom of association that prohibited any assemblies without express permission from the colonial administration. The Second Communist International promulgated specifically anti-imperialist views, linking the liberation of colonised nations to the proletarian revolution. The events in Russia of 1917 were still fresh in the minds of the politicians and colonial lobbyists who feared Leninist anti-imperialism might gain a serious foothold in their colonies. The French authorities were also extremely concerned about the spread of Marcus Garvey's Pan-Africanism through his United Negro Improvement Association (UNIA) in America.

On February 19–21, 1921, the first Pan-African Congress, organised by the NAACP, was held in Versailles, presided over by W. E. B. DuBois and Blaise Diagne. This was a worrying event for French colonial lobbyists and politicians because they regarded the growing internationalism of political and labour organisations as a potentially threatening development for the imperial status quo in France. The mostly untested theoretical Republican humanism of *égalité* and *fraternité,* the fulcrum of France's *mission civilisatrice,* would not hold up under any kind of real political scrutiny. Hence, the formation of the Association Panafricaine, in the wake of the second Pan-African Congress in 1921, provoked much consternation amongst the authorities who saw the network of influence between the colonies and African Americans as an extremely grave challenge to colonial rule. Their anxiety was well founded. In 1926 Messali al-Hajj formed the Étoile Nord-Africaine with the express aim of politically organising North African immigrant workers in France. Such developments were testament to the growing political activism in metropolitan France.[13] This emergent political activism was partially a result of the evident discrepancies between theory and practice in political and cultural assimilationism. These discrepancies were becoming ever clearer as hasty promises of political equality and full citizenship made during the war as part of *la dette du sang* began to crumble in the face of peacetime realities. After the end of the war, *assimilation* as a colonial policy began to be re-examined and became increasingly contradicted in metropolitan France. Laurent Bonnevay, deputy of the Rhône, unequivocally declared that France preferred European immigrant labour over that of the colonies as these groups were ethnographically "too different from the rest of the population which might lead to social problems" (Bonnet 121).

The ways in which the colonies were politically represented in the French assembly also began to provoke much debate.[14] After the war, colonial ex-soldiers from Governor-General William Ponty's Force Noire dating back to 1912 began to agitate for the promises of citizenship status promised before the war. These were the famous *tirailleurs sénégalais,* whose presence in France had made a significant impact on the visibility of the colonised in the metropole. In 1918 the recently elected deputy of the four communes of Senegal, Blaise Diagne, had worked tirelessly to persuade reluctant chiefs in West Africa to supply *tirailleurs* to the *mère patrie* in return for promises of greater political equality and assimilation with the French in the future.[15] But citizenship was to become an intensely debated issue throughout the interwar years, as was the subject of immigration from the colonies. At this time, only those in the *vieilles colonies* of the Antilles, Guyana, and La Réunion were full citizens of France dating back to the abolition of slavery in 1848. In Africa, only the four communes of Senegal—Dakar, Rufisque, Saint-Louis, and Gorée—were granted citizenship, while inhabitants of the other colonised territories remained *sujets.* As the assimilationist policies of the nineteenth century began to filter through the twentieth in the form of a growing number of metropolitan-based students, there was also the pressing question of how to evaluate the political and cultural positions of those élite *evolués* from Martinique, Madagascar, Sénégal, and Indochina who had reached the highest echelons of the French education system in the metropole. As I go on to discuss in detail later, these so-called assimilated groups nurtured a radical black political and cultural activism that would fully blossom in Paris in the years after the Second World War.

It was against this background of colonial economic consolidation and emergent political discontent that Josephine Baker performed for her Parisian audiences. Her spectacle of empire glossed the *l'age d'or* of French imperialism between 1918 and 1934 with a seamless narrative of first an unbridled primitivism followed by an unproblematic assimilation. In reality, Baker's complete assimilation into French life was perhaps possible only because she was a black American and was not circumscribed by the same restrictive discourses as the colonial *indigène.* Crucially, this points to the paradox in both the American (e.g., the Harlem Renaissance) and the French incidences of cultural primitivism that the widespread popularity of black entertainers did not impinge upon racism and colonial oppression at a macrosocial level. Speaking to this situation, Alice Conklin has observed that the interwar years in France were "amongst the most coercive in the colonial period" (247). The question follows then, how could Josephine Baker be lauded in Paris at a time when the French military suppressed indigenous resistance to colonial rule in West Africa and banned "seditious," anticolonial literature from America and the USSR? The reply to this lies in the performative function of many black entertainers and athletes, boxers in particular, who were not perceived as threatening to the racial status quo as they had a role that delivered a safely confined spectacle and sanctioned a scenario of racial voyeurism to a curious white audience. Thus, it was possible to have a situation where the populations of Senegal or Cameroon were made to participate in the *corvée* (forced labour) or be subjected to the makeshift judicial system of the *indigenat* (the colonial summary justice system) while black entertainers from America, and to a lesser extent from the colonies, found themselves racially in vogue in Paris. Clearly, there was an immense discrepancy between the theory and practice of assimilation. This discrepancy was nowhere more striking than in the Exposition Coloniale

Internationale, which was held at the same time as Josephine Baker's comeback shows, both articulating the same transformative narrative as spectacle.

Baker made her comeback performance, still only 24 years old, in September 1930 at the Casino de Paris with a "respectable" music-hall show called *Paris Qui Remue,* a collection of colonialist sexual fantasy skits. The show ran for a year and was an outstanding popular success. What distinguished this show from her earlier performances was the explicit disengagement from her *sauvage* persona into one that demonstrated a full assimilation of French cultural identity. She was, as Pierre Novy notes, transformed into "une grande vedette." "When she left she was a picturesque dancer. . . . And then she came back as an important artist. The little dancing girl is no longer content to twist her body into contortions. . . . She has become a moving, sensitive and magnificent star" (qtd. in Sauvage 12). In the *Petit Parisien,* Louis Léon-Martin likewise notes the metamorphosis of *la petite sauvageonne* into a "civilised" performer: "She is now not only sensual but sensitive, not only savage but childlike, not only frenetic but touching and moving." In a self-conscious, theoretical mirroring of the colonial civilising process, Baker has lost her "spontaneité sauvaugeonne" and been tutored in the ways of "civilisation occidentale" (Sauvage 56). Tyler Stovall also recognises this transformational trajectory when he says that the metamorphosis of "this black curiosity from Saint Louis" to "the mainstream of white French bourgeoisie society" represented the "civilizing mission's iconic example" (89). This culminated first in 1930, when she was elected Queen of the Colonies for the Exposition Coloniale amidst a storm of protest, and then in 1937, when she was granted the ultimate accolade of French citizenship (89). The 134,000 conscripted colonial soldiers who had fought for France and survived in the First World War as well as those brought in to work in munitions factories and on farms would have to wait many years before there was any question of citizenship for them. While Baker was elected Queen of the Colonies, many immigrant workers from the colonies were being actively deported from France in favour of a more assimilable Eastern European labour force. Further, on January 17, 1931, immediately prior to the opening of the Exposition, a right-wing newspaper, *Le Peuple,* published a scathing attack on Africans living in France. This indictment established *un discours d'exclusion,* setting the scene for the immigration controls of August 1932 that would actively promote the rights of a French workforce over an immigrant one (Bancel and Blanchard 21). The rise in a strident xenophobic nationalism in France at the beginning of the 1930s and the attendant regression to racial empiricism existed alongside a populist enthusiasm for colonial memorabilia in the wake of the Exposition. Likewise, critics and audiences could applaud Baker's transformation and assimilation into a full French citizen while newspapers like *Paris-Soir* carried articles such as "Des millions d'étrangers ont pénétré chez nous comme des rats."[16]

In *La Vie Parisienne* of October 18, 1930, an anonymous critic writes "La charmante Joséphine s'est bien transformée." She has learned the ways of the civilising centre who had begun to tire of her savage novelty: "Paris . . . avait rejeté ce jouet qui l'avait amusé un instant." Now, Baker is represented in her Poirier and Chanel gowns as the pinnacle of what French civilisation could fashion out of the raw materials of the *sauvage.* Described in the glowing, sentimental discourses reserved for the well-behaved, assimilated subject, Baker, as an archetypal racial subject, has been successfully transformed within the fictional trajectory of colonial assimilation and can now demonstrate a "nature non plus sauvage, non plus instinctive, mais sensible" (Louis Léon-Martin n. pag.). The native body, however seductive in its spontaneity, must be seen to be redeemed by the civilising centre, as Gérard Ruffy notes when he observes that "à côté de sa sensualité, de sa frénésie, des ses trémoussements, de sa puérilité, ells se révèle une meneuse de jeu extraordinaire tour à tour sensible, endiablée, touchante et même émouvante" (qtd. in Sauvage 24). This view of Baker's cultural metamorphosis is echoed by other critics who note that Baker's reappearance demonstrated her ability to civilise herself, to acculturate herself as a real French subject.[17]

No longer "une femme sauvage," Baker is credited with having transformed enough to effect a response on her audience that is more than physical: "Joséphine Baker ne s'est pas contentée de nous éblouir, de nous charmer, de nous faire sourire, mais encore elle a voulu nous émouvoir. . . ."[18] She has become "la nouvelle Joséphine Baker," no longer simply a "splendide statue de bronze doré" but a "grande artiste à l'âme douce, au coeur généreux." In her own performance of the *mission civilisatrice,* Baker has staged the progression from "l'étrange métisse désarticulée" and "idole nue" to "une grande vedette," whose sincerity, talent, and sensitivity have redeemed her from obscurity (Chabannes n. pag.). The language used to review these later, "more refined performances has changed from the superlatives of an overdetermined physicality and elemental vitality that greeted the *Revue Nègre.* Now, she is "émouvante," "sensible," and "tendre," and displays her knowledge of taste and elegance in Poirier gowns and Jean Dunand jewels; her choreography is undertaken by Georges Balanchine, the master of classical ballet. Moreover, she has worked hard, observes one critic, and can now speak French "avec un savoureux accent." Her comeback show is described as a "bien savoreux spectacle," performed with all the "tendresse délicatement féminine" of her renewed, civilised self (Sordet n. pag.). G. de Pawlowski notes that formerly Baker was "cet étrange et splendide animal sauvage," "un fauve," but now she even seems whiter, less black in fact than the native French women, the fashionable Parisiennes on their return from the Midi (qtd. in Abatino 35). Now, Baker sings romantic ballads in an assimilated "franco-anglais," entirely transformed from *une petite sauvage* to a star who has set her sights on playing at the Comédie Française. The critics notice, not without some disappointment, that she has "paled" as she has been "civilised by Western civilisation" (Archard 35).

In a 1932 show, *La Joie de Paris,* Baker sung what was to be, along with "J'ai deux amours," one of her most popular songs: "Si j'étais blanche." For this song, she donned a platinum blonde wig and white satin evening gown, and the lyrics of the song encapsulated the ways in which race can be trained out of the native body: "c'est mon coeur qui me donne du couleur." The transformation from *la petite sauvage* to *grande chanteuse* is complete, presented as the success of the civilising mission in its reformative cultural practices, welcoming the native subject into the national Republican fold. Thus, a picturesque racial narrative is achieved in which race is a malleable category in the service of a dominant colonial ideology, one that is seen to be working in favour of egalitarian transformation.

NOTES

1. Luis Buñuel was the assistant director.

2. For the full collection of Colin's posters for *Le Tumulte Noir,* see Rennert.

3. See Dalton and Gates on Paul Colin's lithographs of Baker in *Le Tumulte Noir.*

4. This kind of racialised scopic fetishisation did not, of course, begin with Josephine Baker's body. Erotic postcards from the Maghreb were popular in France in the first decades of the twentieth century. Veiled Arab women were set in a repetitive series of poses that emphasised the erotic contrast between the veil of Islam and the nakedness of the exposed breasts. See Alloula on the erotics of race and colonialism.

5. The visual emphasis on black women's buttocks can be traced throughout European and American popular culture, dating back to the Hottentot Venus, the "anthropo-erotic sensation" of the nineteenth century. See Pieterse 94; Gilman "Black Bodies"; and hooks, *Black* 62–64.

6. It was only 12.5 percent per 100 in 1919, an increase of 3 percent from 1916, and the lowest rate in modern French history.

7. The population of France as an imperial nation went from 40 million to 100 million as a result of modern colonisation, hence the catch phrase of the colonial propagandists "One hundred million Frenchmen." See M. Lewis.

8. See Ezra's discussion of colonial beauty contests, particularly the 1936 Concours du Meilleur Mariage Colonial that "pitted France against Germany in a battle of birthrates" (38–45).

9. See Doane for a discussion of the Freudian notion of the Dark Continent and its relationship to racial otherness, infantile sexuality, and nineteenth-century imperial discourse (209–11).

10. See Torgovnick 42–75 and Thomas 170–95 on the strategies of marketing cultural difference in Hollywood cinema in *Tarzan* and *Dances with Wolves.*

11. See Alloula for a detailed analysis of the popularity of erotic postcards from Algeria.

12. See Conklin for a history of *assimilation* and the judicial results of its implementation throughout the French colonies.

13. On Indochinese political activism at this time, see Hemery.

14. See Ayo Langley 70–79.

15. Conklin 150 and Dewitte 21.

16. Bancel and Blanchard 23.

17. See Rose 144–45.

18. From an anonymous press clipping in the *Collection Rondel,* October 8, 1930, n. pag.

CHAPTER 4

"Go to Harlem, it's sharper there": *Negro: An Anthology* (1934)

INTRODUCTION

> About six years old, my thoughts began to be drawn towards Africa . . . "The Dark Continent"—with Africans dancing and drumming around me, and I one of them, though still white, knowing, mysteriously enough, how to dance in their own manner. Everything was full of movement in these dreams; it was that which enabled me to escape in the end, going further, even further! And all of it was a mixture of apprehension that sometimes turned into joy, and even rapture.
>
> —Nancy Cunard, *Grand Man*

Nancy Cunard's *Negro: An Anthology*, published on February 15, 1934, is a monumental work in sheer size and presence alone. The original edition, weighing almost eight pounds in its final form, features the work of 150 contributors amongst its 900 pages, which include 385 illustrations and photographs. Even in its abridged form of 464 pages, *Negro* is a documentary work of unabashedly oversized proportions, making its near invisibility today even more puzzling. The anthology has been all but excised from studies of literary modernism and histories of early twentieth-century ethnography and anthropology and the Harlem Renaissance. Effectively written out of all but the marginalia of black cultural histories of the twentieth century, *Negro* has equally failed to make any serious impact on Anglo-American modernist studies and exists only as a contextual footnote to the period. Reedited by Hugh Ford in an abridged version in 1970, the original anthology comprises 250 separate pieces organised into eight broad sections: "America," "Negro Stars," "Music," "Poetry," "West Indies and South America," "Europe," "Africa," and "Negro Sculpture and Ethnology." In a lengthy introduction to the 1970 edition, Ford notes the final criteria adopted for the contributions: "historical importance," "value as commentary on contemporary racial developments," "relevancy to American race relations," and "quality and originality" of the individual pieces (xxix). Cunard began work on her "new book on COLOR" in 1929 and it was published five years later after repeated difficulties in securing a publisher. Her mission was to produce a collective work in which "all the indignities and injustices done to the race would have to be recorded too, and the beauty and ingenuity of African art would, for once, have to be elaborately illustrated" (Cunard, *Negro* xvi, xvii, xvi). Accordingly, the anthology has a lavish selection of photographs, maps, sketches, musical scripts, annotated diagrams, poetry, and music-hall lyrics, producing a generic eclecticism characteristic of political documentary work of the 1930s.

That such a massively proportioned work, with contributions from renowned figures in literature, politics, art history, and anthropology from France, Britain, and America holds only a marginal position in cultural and literary histories of the era is both puzzling and significant. The reasons for this exclusion are, I suggest, due in part to the portrayal of Nancy Cunard as an aristocratic modernist dilettante whose self-fashioning as a white negress has rendered her almost untouchable in a postcolonial era. Her idiosyncratic brand of political activism and her literary patronage have been largely overshadowed by accounts of her unorthodox private life. This depiction of Cunard, the disinherited heiress to the vast shipping fortunes of the Cunard line, has predominated in literary and intellectual histories of modernism and consequently has devalued her work as editor, writer, activist, and patron. Cunard's tendencies to mix the political with the personal, the worthy cause with the chance sexual encounter particularly in the arena of race politics, has led to a nonchalant dismissal of her as an influential figure in both literary modernism and radical politics. Her particular negrophile fascination with black culture provokes a certain degree of squeamishness amongst contemporary critics, particularly those involved in postcolonial critique, as it appears at times naively primitivist, even simply racist, in critical, and ethical, retrospect. However, I argue here that this combination of sentimental exoticism, which is affective and limiting, and racial essentialism with radical political goals represents a significant development of earlier *négrophilie* and that both strengths and weaknesses of the anthology contribute to the historical significance of the work as a whole. *Negro* remains a serious multidisciplinary intervention in internationalist anticolonial activism and an important model of transnational black Atlanticism of the 1930s.

The few critics who have worked on the *Negro* anthology to date have dismissed the work as a politically ambivalent polemic and a deeply flawed project in terms of its textual presentation and aesthetics. In *The*

Dialect of Modernism, Michael North unequivocally condemns *Negro* as a "miscellaneous, collective, disorganised, supergeneric sprawl of a book" and decries the anthology's limited political agenda: "For all the space it gave to responsible black commentary, the anthology still tended to represent African-Americans as objects of pity or comedy" (177, 191). He views Cunard's editorial presence as "simultaneously heavy handed and hopelessly lax," concluding that the work, which he characterises as "weirdly dissocative," makes points that are self-evident and, for the most part, incompatible with each other (191). Tyrus Miller has similarly criticised the work for its generic promiscuity, which he regards as belying the political intentions so carefully stated by Cunard in the anthology's introduction.[1] Emphasising the uneven nature, both structurally and ideologically, of the anthology, these critics view the work as one that finally falls short of a full engagement with its own progressive ideologies, avant-garde aesthetics and radical programmatic politics.[2] Elsewhere, however, Janet Montefiore more generously views *Negro*'s generic diversity as a precursor to the "multidisciplinary approach of Black studies by a generation," praising Cunard's skills as an editor, publisher, and translator (117). Similarly, Hugo Speck acknowledged the anthology as a "black manifesto" that, in addition to cataloguing the horrors of racial bigotry in America, provided a valuable survey of literary, artistic, and intellectual achievements from the black world (North 15). Indeed, Speck goes so far as to claim that *Negro* represented the most radical intellectual project on race and racism in America until the 1960s, when civil rights activists began to collate their own political and cultural histories. One of the anthology's contributors to the section on Africa, the South African poet William Plomer, described Cunard as "passionately serious" about her antiracist project and moreover that the anthology's "influence augmented other influences already at work. And ultimately [this was] of great political importance in the world" (qtd. in Ford 126). This is a view that Alain Locke, editor of the more prominent anthology of black culture, *The New Negro* (1925), has echoed, albeit equivocally, in his appraisal of the book:

> There is much of unique informational and critical value in these eight hundred pages which document both the wrongs and the achievements of the black man and capitalizes for the first time adequately the race problem as a world problem. But the capital "P" is for propaganda, not for poetry, and the book hurls a shell, a bomb, and shrapnel at the Citadel of Nordicism. (qtd. in Stuart 228–32)

The anthology does indeed make a bold incursion into the realm of documentary cultural studies in its methodology, producing an overly ambitious, unwieldy but valuable historical document. In undertaking its Herculean task of documenting "the whole complex history of Negro culture," Cunard's project attempts to forge a relationship between the social sciences, still in their institutional infancy, and the politicised aesthetics of the French avant-garde (Ford xvi). The results are certainly uneven, both aesthetically and politically, but nevertheless should continue to prove compelling to the modern reader. The anthology remains an important text for those interested in the history of American race relations, political internationalism in the 1930s, and the participation of the European avant-garde in anticolonialism.

I argue here for a reading of *Negro* that both recognises its value as a documentary text of its time while offering a sustained critique of its political impact. Considering a selection of pieces from the anthology, I examine the fraught relations between an affective negrophile aesthetic and a politically radical stance, a tension that oscillates throughout the anthology as a whole. Situating the work in the specific context of its production in France between 1931 and 1933, I suggest that parts of *Negro* demonstrate an important evolution of ideas from the earlier era of cultural primitivism circumscribed by a limited understanding of racial identity. Crucially, the *Negro* anthology attempts to reject these notions, dismissing them as bourgeois or weakly liberal, in order to produce models of racial and cultural difference that consider the political and economic as crucial factors in both the formation of racial identities and in racial oppression. Thus, the political agenda of the anthology, unequivocally stated by Cunard in the foreword, calls for a more responsible material contemplation of racial identity and economic oppression in the global circulation of labour and capital. A politically internationalist agenda is promulgated, specifically the Third International's espousal of contemporary Leninism, which viewed imperialism as the inevitable result of the forces of global capitalism within which race is understood as a socially constructed category and inextricably tied to systemic class relations. However, despite this radical political stance, many of the pieces in *Negro* continue to work from a model of racial essentialism in order to explicate the text's central political thesis. This essentialism tends towards a sentimental exoticism that authenticates certain essences of racial identity foregrounding spontaneity, corporeality, and cultural purity in a set of counterhegemonic constructions mediated as black culture. Cunard regarded her project as a radical departure from the earlier models of negrophile cultural primitivism, but despite this the anthology remains constricted by an affective racial aesthetic, articulated in varying degrees from an unreconstructed negrophile valorisation of black cultures to a more self-conscious avant-gardist primitivism. Consequently, despite a leftist politics seeking a genuine engagement with material and historical conditions of racial oppression, the work as a whole is frequently at odds with its own polemical intentions. However, in the contributions made by the Surrealist Group (to which Cunard was closely attached both personally and intellectually), an attempt is made to write against the grain of such metropolitan exoticism and to resolve the perennial friction between politics, praxis, and aesthetics. In Cunard's own writing in particular, this dilemma is presented as an unproblematic transition from a scopic appreciation of racial difference as an abstract aesthetic concept into an engaged politics of difference that addresses the material histories of race and racism in Europe and America. Thus, the text as a whole presents a substantial paradox: on the one hand, Cunard's editorial hand directs the pieces along the lines of radical political engagement, while on the other the work clings to the cruder aspects of negrophile primitivism.

I am not primarily concerned here with the complex theoretical debates surrounding racial essentialism versus constructionism, as this has been fruitfully rehearsed many times elsewhere.[3] Racial essentialism operates in the anthology within a series of complicated dialogues on racial identity and cultural difference that were taking place across disciplines in interwar France. What is significant then for my argument is the negotiation of these contexts and processes behind the articulation of race in the anthology. I argue that the anthology collates a set of debates and narratives that share a thematic continuity in a particular historical context. These debates were constitutive of a larger intellectual and cultural matrix in which ideas around race, cultural difference, and identity were contested by diverse voices. Significantly, the work of pre-négritude Francophone diasporic groups in Paris at this time frequently operated from a comparable model of racial essentialism that they subsequently complicated and qualified or dismissed and reformulated. Moreover, there are significant differences between Cunard's conceptualisations of race and difference in her own articles and those of some of the ethnographic pieces, as well as those by the Surrealist Group. In short, racial essentialism is employed as a broadly emancipatory paradigm of racial identity, but it is tempered throughout by the interventions of various contributors who point the way forward to a more sophisticated model of cultural relativism.

The anthology was produced at a time in France when there was a remarkable convergence between the social sciences, visual and written arts, aesthetic and political movements, and the ways in which race and cultural difference were conceptualised within these.[4] This convergence revealed, among other things, an ongoing tension between a romantic valorisation of racial difference in the cultural domain and the political responses to global imperialism and domestic racial oppression in Europe and America. The basis of this conflict is the incompatibility of a cultural primitivism that aestheticises black culture as essentialised difference with an engaged, radical politics that, while acknowledging the processes of objectification inherent in this essentialism, continues to construct black identity as an antidote to modernity and a rapacious Western capitalism.

Thus, the anthology produces a diverse range of enunciative positions and generic concerns that often rest uneasily against each other. This unease, however, does not deny *Negro* its historical relevance as a significant intervention into anti-imperialist and anti-colonialist debates and as an early twentieth-century multidisciplinary cultural project.

NANCY CUNARD: WHITE SLAVE GIRL/ AVANT-GARDE NEGROPHILE

> Maybe I was an African at one time.
>
> —Nancy Cunard, "Sonnet to Alfred Cruikshank"

Nancy Cunard (1896–1965) was the daughter of Sir Bache Cunard, grandson of Samuel Cunard, who founded the Cunard shipping line. In January 1920 she moved to Paris, where she began an extraordinary association with some of the most celebrated modern writers and intellectuals of the period. A poet in her own right, Cunard had begun writing under the guidance of Edith Sitwell and a group of writers and artists known to Cunard and her friends as the "corrupt coterie" because of their antiestablishment attitudes (Ford xiii). She began to publish poetry in 1921; her best-known works are the collection *Parallax* (1925) and *Sublunary* (1923), both minor critical successes in modernist circles. In addition to her writing, she was an experienced editor and a prolific publisher of avant-garde writers; an enthusiastic patron of experimental modernist work, she was involved with those who would become the most important literary figures in European modernism.[5] However, Cunard was familiar to the intellectual circles of modernist Paris and London not only for being an ardent patron and publisher of avant-garde literature but also for her own diverse self-representations in a variety of media.[6] Cunard's public image, which appeared frequently in magazines such as British *Vogue*, became inextricably linked to her cultural and intellectual pursuits. This close intermingling of Cunard's public and private personae has been cited by various critics as being responsible for the fact that she has been erased from all but the most anecdotal of literary history (Scott 63–64). Jane Marcus has argued that Cunard's highly public femme fatale reputation has been troubling for literary critics, who have written her off both intellectually and morally as an opportunist and a nymphomaniac, a "bad, bold body" of female sexual emancipation.[7] This characterisation of Cunard has been persistently reinforced by thinly disguised caricatures of her in Michael Arlen's *The Green Hat* (1924) and Aldous Huxley's *Point Counter Point* (1928), both of which depict her as a predatory socialite vamp, with left-wing views and a self-destructive bohemian streak. Whatever factual basis there may be for these suggestions, it is clear that Cunard's high public profile as an aristocratic rebel and sexually liberated woman was closely bound up with her various literary and political projects, a combination that has clearly not hindered male poets, painters, or patrons from success over the centuries, and it is conspicuous that these accusations, which smack of a deep misogyny, should be levelled at Cunard's work.

Cunard was an extremely wealthy and flamboyant socialite whose appetite for an eccentric, often scandalous, social life was well documented. Even after she moved to France in 1923, her various exploits, both artistic and sexual, were keenly followed by gossip columnists in the London papers.[8] Her image and reputation were iconically present throughout the 1920s; her angular, androgynous body, clad in the most modish outifits, captured the aesthetic zeitgeist of *les années folles*. Painted by Augustus John, Oscar Kokoschka, John Banting, and Wyndham Lewis, Cunard was also the subject of Constantin Brancusi's sculpture *Jeune Fille Sophistiquée* and was regularly photographed for fashion magazines by Cecil Beaton and Man Ray.

One of the most enduring images of Cunard in the 1920s is a photograph by Man Ray framing her as the white aristocratic mistress exhibiting the exotic accessories of an imaginary white slave girl. In this particular photograph, Cunard stages and exhibits herself as the perfect modern(ist) body. In an aesthetic suspension of disbelief, the viewer is invited to identify Cunard as almost black, her body strikingly covered in an armour of massive ivory bracelets and faux leopard skin. In this image, Cunard offers the camera an aestheticised blackness of the white flapper slave girl; fashionably short hair and kohl-rimmed blue eyes provide a striking visual contrast with the "savage" apparel that she wears for the shock of cultural juxtaposition. Cunard's defiant and unself-conscious gaze stares down the camera's eye in a composed and unquestioning authority over the visual irony of the pose. Here, the "dark continent" of primitivised blackness is inscribed on the white body and invested with a sartorial playfulness as a cultural accessory of the leisured cosmopolitan subject, who is free to play with ethnic and cultural signifiers with impunity. Cunard's self-representation as a white negrophile fetishises not only the primitive accessories but also her own aristocratic whiteness and her position as the knowing modern primitivist; the white body here operates as the normative centre—the unmarked subject—from which all other racial identities are deviations (Butler 171).[9] Another photographic image showing only Cunard's ivory braceleted arms visible around the head of Henry Crowder projects a strong sense of white narcissism. The blackness of Crowder's skin is objectified by the presence of her encircling (restricting) grasp, which renders him less a human subject with agency than an exhibited artefact, a metonymic fragment of an imaginary African aesthetic.[10] This kind of negrophile representation both deifies and reifies blackness as an aesthetic artefact in a process of racial scopic objectification. Thus, in the photograph of the two, Cunard's absent white body is powerfully present through her trademark armfuls of ivory bracelets (the precious white ivory of the bracelets lies on her aristocratic white skin as a set of beautiful African trophies); even in her partial absence, her presence around Crowder positions him as a racial foil.[11] However, it is crucial to recall here just how striking the image of intimacy between a black man and a white woman was to an audience of the 1930s. The avant-garde circles in which Cunard circulated may have accepted these images as part of a larger experiment in formal juxtaposition and moral experimentation, but outside of this small intellectual milieu the sexual implications of these images would have touched upon some deep-seated racial taboos both in Britain and France.

These images of Cunard are profoundly telling of her fascination with the exotic and erotic aesthetics of racial otherness and have direct bearings upon her later intellectual interest in black culture and society, an interest that was not uncommon among the avant-garde artists and intellectuals in which she moved at this time. Like many of her contemporaries, Cunard was initially interested in the notion of the primitive as a primarily visual device that formally marked out the spaces of alterity articulating the desolation of postwar Europe. As Georges Antheil has written in *Negro,* the "aesthetic of the Congo" reached Europe at "its most torrid, barren, smoking and psychological moment" and for a while seemed the only formal aesthetic that could articulate and assuage that moment (orig. ed. 348–49).[12] Cunard's representation of herself in these images was an effort to fetishise and display her own image as cultural rebel; the other of polite bourgeois society. Michael North has described this gesture as the modernist artist's self-figuration as cultural outsider, taking on an imagined and notional black identity in order to mount "an insurrectionary opposition to the known and the familiar . . . " (preface). As I have discussed in chapters 1 and 2, this aesthetic appropriation of a largely imaginary black identity formed part of a larger primitivist project of collection and display under the indiscriminate term *l'art nègre,* a catch-all term in interwar Paris for black culture. It is crucial to acknowledge Cunard's own specific position of cultural enunciation vis-à-vis cultural primitivism and to take seriously the residual effects that such self-representation had on her subsequent articulations of race in the *Negro* anthology. Her exhibition of herself as a white negress permits her to assume a racial guise of blackness—simultaneously rebellious and mystical—that allows her to shed the identity of a white, British, and upper-class subject to become a more fully authentic modernist image-maker. Crucially, though the normative authority of her whiteness remains intact under this appropriated mask of otherness, racial difference, assumed here as fashion accessory, becomes a commodity to be selected and consumed in the quest for self-definition of the alienated European subject adrift in the maelstrom of postwar Europe. The accessories of blackness in these images (clichéd exotic props familiar to a cosmopolitan white audience) suggest attributes of the primitive in which complicated processes of identification and disavowal permit the white subject to appropriate the signifiers of the black body. In the processes of aesthetic decontextualisation, the black body has been stripped of any material history through reification into visual accessory. Once again, as in the case of Josephine Baker, the black body "becomes burdened with the task of symbolizing the transgressive fantasies and desires" of the white subject regardless of its particular individuation or geohistoric specificities (Mercer 84). The black body fulfils a fetishistic, metaphorical function in all of this, while Cunard's fetishisation as the white/black modern primitive operates as a visual metaphor for her fascination with the relationship between black and white culture. Although this interest has been decried as being, at best, a paternalistic white patronage, the anthology has also been accused of displaying a deep racism.[13] It is more likely that Cunard's interest vacillates between an exoticist and erotic fascination with the aesthetics of formal alterity that she discerns in black culture (in particular black American culture) and a genuine political outrage at racial oppression that she was to discover initially through Henry Crowder. The vacillation between these two positions generates much of the momentum, and tedium, of the anthology.

Like many other white American and British expatriates, Cunard was a regular at clubs such as Boule Noir, Le Boeuf Sur le Toit, Le Bal Nègre, and Le Jockey in Montparnasse and Montmartre, the latter popularly known as the Harlem of Paris. It was at these clubs that she became infatuated with jazz, which had become widely popular with audiences in Paris since the mid-1920s.[14] Cunard's (very public) reaction to jazz, according to Daphne Fielding in her biography, was dramatic and impassioned: "its rhythm translating to her such artificial paradises as Baudelaire and de Quincey had found through opium" (58). In both her taste for African couture and sculpture and her visceral identification with jazz, Cunard typified a type of avant-garde cosmopolitanism. A loose collection of Dadaists, Surrealists, sous-realists, and ethnographers aligned themselves on the side of an imagined primitive subject who stood in opposition to the "bankrupt spirituality" of a rational, civilised, and modernised West and to the reactionary politics emerging in interwar Europe (Antheil, *Negro* orig. ed. 350). The affective nature of Cunard's primitivist disposition is clearly visible in the foreword to the anthology, in which she has stated that "it is high time that a separate book were made to do justice to a people so utterly rich in natural grace and beauty" and that "the Negro has a superb and individual sense of form and equal genius in his execution" (iv). These comments demonstrate how she responded to the immediate sensuous appeal of black music and art and are consonant with her subsequent interpretation of diasporic black cultures by presenting the transition from aesthetic appreciation to political affiliation as a largely uncomplicated manoeuvre.[15]

In 1926, Cunard, along with Louis Aragon, visited her cousin Edward Cunard in Venice, where she became fascinated with a group of black American musicians, Eddie South's Alabamians, who played at her hotel each night. She was especially interested in their pianist, Henry Crowder. Cunard's relationship with Crowder appears to have been a transformative moment in the development of a political consciousness on racial matters. Anne Chisholm has written: "In Henry Crowder she found more than a lover with a different colour skin; she found a cause, a symbol, a weapon, a victim. . . . Through Crowder she became something else: a woman who chose, deliberately, to cross the boundaries of convention, class and race in pursuit of a cause" (118). Similarly, in his introduction to the anthology, Hugh Ford has suggested that Crowder represented a turning point in Cunard's life, and through her relationship with him she was able to more fully comprehend the real, lived conditions of black American culture. This contrasted with her earlier, purely aesthetic response to African material culture that she sought out along with her modernist cohort. Her feeling for things African had started years earlier with sculpture, and something of those anonymous statues had now . . . materialised in the personality of Henry." Years later, Nancy herself wrote that Henry "was my revelation of it all . . . " (introduction xv). Her subsequent association with Crowder consolidated her long-standing cultural negrophilism, imbuing it with a political urgency that had hitherto been lacking in her intellectual life, their relationship revealing to Cunard her patent lack of knowledge about the realpolitik of race relations in the United States and in the colonised world. Thus, over the years from 1926 to 1933, Cunard became increasingly aware of the political limitations of a purely aesthetic appropriation of non-European cultures as one that privileged a restrictive primitivist ethos. This perspective on the primitive fetishised and commodified racial difference but was finally a position that Cunard found difficult to overcome, as demonstrated in the following readings. Crucially, then, in *Negro* Cunard both participated in and was critical of this commodification of the primitive, and despite the valid and bold political intentions of *Negro,* these two positions have been held in a fragile antagonism. Such an incompatibility has not been uncommon in a collaborative work of these proportions. In the following readings of selected pieces from the anthology, I intend to draw out the intricacies and the tensions inherent in the difficult relations between the aesthetic and the political, the historical documentation of black culture and an affective, sentimental negrophilia, and models of racial essentialism and cultural relativism.

ESSENTIALISM AND "RACE" IN *NEGRO*

The structural thematic in Cunard's own contributions to the *Negro* anthology points up the uneasy relation between the appreciation of formal beauty and cultural novelty in an exclusively aesthetic domain and the exposition of a harder-edged, material reality. There is, then, a palpable tension between Cunard's appreciation of artefacts from an imagined Africa (source of an unsullied humanity) and the documentary investigation of the material, lived experiences of race relations in the United States; this tension produces an uneasy dynamic between sentimental aestheticism and political indignation. For example, in the foreword to the original edition, Cunard writes that the reader of *Negro* will find "first in this panorama the full violence of the oppression of the 14 million Negroes in America . . . who are in the grip of a bloody white supremacist culture" in which they continue to be forced into "the dumbest and most terrorised form of subjection" (iii). Later, her outrage over the subjugation of Africa—"a continent in the iron grip of its several imperialist oppressors" (iv)—is accompanied by her evaluation of African society as "a people so utterly rich in natural grace and beauty" (iii). This conflation of the lived conditions of imperial oppression with a vaguer, more subjective apprehension of racial and cultural difference tends to characterise much of her work in the anthology. She goes on:

> At one time labelled en bloc "cannibals", "savages", who have never produced anything, etc., it is now the fashion to say that the white man is in Africa for the black man's *good*. Reader, had you never heard of or seen any African sculpture I think the reproductions in this part would suggest to you that the Negro has a superb and individual sense of form and equal genius in his execution. The writings of Michelet and Feuilloley will demonstrate that the African has an adequate enough soul (somewhat different from your own though it may be) and had also (though that too was different from yours) a social organisation perfectly adapted to the conditions of his own continent. (iv)

The implied reader here is a white, metropolitan, and cosmopolitan subject, to whom Cunard appeals through an assumption of shared aesthetic taste that in turn, she hopes, will be transformed into political awareness and activism. What is suggested here is an unproblematic equivalence between the aesthetic experience of the primitive artefact as spectacle (here, the entire African continent) and a heightened political understanding of the material conditions of its production, establishing a relationship wherein the white reader/viewer is drawn into a "political allegiance forged between white aesthetic subjectivity and black material reality" (T. Miller 6). This alliance is a fragile one as it privileges a position of leisured metropolitan consumption in which the consumer scrutinises the object on display for evidence of an "adequate enough soul" and a competent "social organisation" (Cunard, *Negro* iv). These will reveal the object's worth beyond that of novel formalism. Thus, racial and cultural differences are rendered immediately transparent through the reader/viewer's aesthetic response to the formal qualities of the artefact—the thing in itself. This commingling of the aesthetic and the material, of the "economic, inter-racial, social and political systems implanted by the different imperial masters" is partially reminiscent of what James Clifford has called modernist ethnography (iv). This interdisciplinary methodology, embraced by sections of the avant-garde and radical left intellectuals, blurs the demarcations between the political and the aesthetic and argues that these are artificial divisions imposed by a super-rational Cartesian dualism held by the Surrealists to be the "curse of Western thought" (Nicholls, *Modernisms* 282). Indeed, the *Negro* anthology was a forerunner of the ethnographic surrealist projects of the art journals *Documents, Minotaure,* and *Cahiers d'art* and the later work of Georges Bataille, Michel Leiris, and Roger Callois in the *Collège de Sociologie* in 1938.[16]

Cunard's agenda was to produce a work that challenged racism by assembling a collage of voices and texts from a diverse range of sources around the world. Contributions to *Negro* were to demonstrate the false logic of racism and to show support for the racially oppressed by European intellectuals and writers. However, consider the following extract from William Carlos Williams's essay entitled "The Colored Girls of Passenack": "The colored girls today have learned the trick of dress very ably. . . . And the vivacity, the awareness of manner is like nothing the white can offer. The American white girl today is shop-worn toady compared to the Negro girl" (Cunard, *Negro* 72). This crudely essentialist, and sexist, paradigm that pits the liveliness of the "Negro" against that of the white girl is a central model for some parts of the anthology. It is most strongly iterated in one of Cunard's own essays, "Harlem Reviewed," which I will look at in detail later. Clearly, this is simply a reversal of racist paradigms in the service of an antiracist, emancipatory polemic; a laudable but unsophisticated negrophile intention that dogs the anthology throughout with its black = good, white = bad equations. Stuart Hall, amongst others, has cautioned against antiracist theorising that advocates a "strategy of a simple set of reversals," which results in an inversion rather than a displacement of the Manichean aesthetic. Such a reversal of terms, Hall claims, succeeds only in "putting in place of the bad old essential white subject, the new essentially good black subject" ("New" 27–30). Hall invokes Fanon's seminal arguments in *Black Skin, White Masks* as an antidote to this reinscription, as they seek to avoid this simple inversion of terms. Fanon points to the doubling and splitting on both sides of the Manichean racial divide, a theory of colonial self/other relations that has been taken up by several postcolonial critics but is perhaps most notable in the more postmodernist camps within postcolonial critical theory.[17] Unlike these more refined postcolonial theoretical models of self/other relations, much of the work in *Negro* does not recognise the complicated processes of identification and disavowal between racialised subjects or the notion of a normative white centre from which cultural authority emanates and defines the other's authenticity. The anthology frequently resorts to the paradigms of cultural primitivism in which the emphasis is on the construction of a blanded-out "good black subject" who is both a source of vitality and colour and the repository of an antimodernity.

Racial essentialism posits ethnic identity with an invariable and fixed set of meanings and markers that are transhistorical and universally applicable. As I have discussed earlier, Fanon asserts that the emptying out of the black subject takes place first and foremost in the visual sphere. Fetished and denigrated in equal measures, the black subject is "battered down" by the weight of the stereotypes that shift only according to the whims of the unmarked white centre of domination. For Fanon, the weight of racial essentialism is a purely negative one and for the African it is always echoing with associations of "intellectual deficiency" and "racial defects" (*Black Skin* 190). Stuart Hall has correctly described the "essentializing moment" as a fundamentally weak one, as it "naturalizes and dehistoricizes difference, mistaking what is historical and cultural for what is natural, biological, and genetic." Consequently, essentialism, he says, ignores the "dialogic strategies and hybrid forms essential to the diaspora aesthetic" ("Black" 29). However, as Diana Fuss points out, the slippery discourses of essentialism have been "deployed effectively in the service of both idealist and materialist, progressive, and reactionary, mythologizing and resistive discourses" (xii). In other words, the anthology's essentialism is a reversal of Fanon's negative neurotic position of blackness by an inversion of the terms, just as negritude would do a few years later. This demonstrates, as Stephen Heath has famously pointed out, that, somewhat paradoxically, sometimes "the risk of essence has to be taken" (99). The inherent risk, of course, in the strategic deployment of racial essentialism is that it draws on a historically static paradigm of racial identity. Such a paradigm renders any movement outside of this inauthentic and politically dubious and it thus incurs the danger of fixing blackness as a signifier that is both ahistorical and without agency.[18]

RAYMOND MICHELET: "PRIMITIVE LIFE AND MENTALITY"

Raymond Michelet's essay in the anthology constructs a Manichean relationship between the "atrophied sensuality" of the "white rationalist," the Cartesian subject, and the African (unspecified by either geography or history) who enjoys "a more profound, ample and precise perception of reality" because the African mentality is "more elastic and in closer contact with nature" (orig. ed. 740). The spectre of Joseph Arthur Comte de Gobineau (1816–82) is never far from these typological inversions.[19] However, Michelet's article deserves attention for its curious refutation of Lucien Lévy-Bruhl's seminal work *La Mentalité Primitive* (1922), a crucially influential text for social and cultural anthropology in Britain, France, and Germany. In refuting Lévy-Bruhl's theory of native prelogicism, Michelet asserts that "the black mentality, like that of all primitives in general, is absolutely impervious to experience and to European modes of thought" (orig. ed. 739). Michelet offers a sustained critique of these theories, rebuking Lévy-Bruhl for simply reformulating the "old legend" of typological essentialism, which he has merely "dressed up to the latest nines" (orig. ed. 739). Michelet argues that the weakness of Lévy-Bruhl's arguments lies in the fact that "in this system no single reference is made to the desirability of understanding the native, his acts and thoughts, and how his mode of life, tribal organisations and other circumstances, explain and even justify the beliefs he holds" (orig. ed. 740). Michelet stresses the importance of the political economy of imperialism in the perpetuation of these mythologies of the "native mentality," which, he says, "very soon creates its own ideology" of a degraded African identity (orig. ed. 739). He further claims that it is evidently in the economic interest of the European coloniser to construct the native as a subject governed by irrational mysticism and an "arrested mentality," as this justifies and condones the systematic theft and violence of colonial conquest:

> Thus our tradesmen and gentry enjoy the satisfaction of being able to elicit from the perusal of M. Lévy-Bruhl the obligation that is laid upon the white man to relieve, on no authority but his own, the Negroes of their responsibilities, take over their land which they are clearly unable to work themselves, and instruct them in the healthy methods of European labour and Christian morality so that they may emerge from their vale of folly and ignorance into the light of pure reason. (orig. ed. 740)

Michelet adroitly traces a relationship between the development of this notion in the economic domain and its subsequent spectacular dissemination in "the capitalistic studios of Hollywood and Joinville," which churn out images of the "howling and cannibal nigger," as well as in the popular press and by the "bourgeois writers of liberal reputation."[20] He adds that the exhibitionary equivalent of this dissemination is the Paris Colonial Exhibition or the English Wembley (orig. ed. 739).

The tone is thus set for a trenchant critique of the fundamental notion of prelogical primitive mentality. However, rather than developing his argument around the ways in which the West has subdued and coerced the native other within the global manoeuvres of capital and labour in

European imperialism, Michelet himself reverts to the absolutes of racial typologies and the immovable doctrines of racial essence, by selecting the identical terms of description that he has singled out for criticism in Lévy Bruhl's methodology. The over-rational and mechanical world of the "white" is placed in opposition to the magical and natural world of the "African." White society, with its exclusive emphasis on material activity, "has concentrated all its powers of development on labour and the most tawdry enjoyment and reduced aesthetic exaltation, religious, social or sensual to a repertory of superannuated, artificial and *dishonoured* gestures": Africa, he claims, "is more elastic and in closer contact with nature than the atrophied sensuality of the 'white rationalist.'" In contrast to the "narrow cocksure brain of the European (or American) positivist," he praises the "unrivalled natural endowments of the African's complete civilisation which have escaped the stultifying processes of modernity in all their rationalising sophistry which have constructed a false archive of the real" (orig. ed. 740–41). This description of the essence of a sensually etiolated white identity is set against the hyperbolic physical simplicity of the African:

> It is now time to consider a sphere of native activity distinguished by a more profound, ample and precise perception of reality. It should be noted in the first place that this perception is undoubtedly promoted by senses and a physical and nervous organisation much more delicately receptive than ours and which, while atrophied or inoperative in white men, have been highly developed in the Negroes by the mere fact of their mode of life. (orig. ed. 740)

Michelet's argument develops his theory of the "Negro" who is possessed of an "amazingly delicate nervous sensibility" and a personality that is inherently "more sensitive to mysterious 'vibrations'" (orig. ed. 741–42). The intention of the article, made explicit in the opening, is to take issue with Lévy-Bruhl's theories of "native mentality," but the argument reaches the same fundamental conclusion, albeit within a more loosely comparative paradigm. Criticising Lévy-Bruhl for the demonstration of the "black mentality" as operating on "an entirely different plane" of prelogicism, Michelet constructs a similar, if not identical, picture of a society entirely driven by the twin pulses of mystical intuition and instinct (orig. ed. 739). This repeated insistence on instinctual physicality externally determines, and fixes, black identity at a purely biological level, where the assumptions of physiological difference are transformed into a static binary that reinforces the fixity of positive or negative racial essences.[21] The negative term unproblematically becomes the positive one, with little consideration given to the legitimacy or mechanics of the transformative process. This is a movement typical of much of the writing in the *Negro* anthology, but it is most clearly discernible in Cunard's own contributions in which, as in the essay "Harlem Reviewed," she venerates black culture and denigrates white society through a visual or scopic aesthetic of racial difference.

"HARLEM REVIEWED": THE VISUAL PLEASURES OF RACIAL DIFFERENCE

In this long essay, Cunard meticulously describes the atmosphere in the streets of Harlem: "[I]t is the zest that the Negroes put in, and the enjoyment they get out of, things that causes one more envy in the ofay. Notice how many of the whites are unreal in America; they are *dim*. But the Negro is very real; he is *there*" (Ford 49). The paradigm of racial identity constructed here is consonant with her larger polemical project to describe, valorise—almost deify—so-called authentic black culture and establishes a relationship between the enjoyment of racial difference as scopic pleasure and the political consequences of aesthetic appreciation. Accordingly, she begins by asking, "Is it possible to give any kind of visual idea of a place by description?" (Ford 47). An authentic black identity and culture are privileged as long as they conform to an order in which black societies, whether in America or Africa, constitute an "enclave in the modern world," a place where "magic predominated over reason and the libido over the work discipline" (Schwartz 182).[22] For Cunard, Harlem functions as the "other" cultural space par excellence: an edgy, modernist geography of social and cultural juxtaposition. Cunard is careful, though, to exonerate herself from any charges of white paternalism or racial voyeurism in this essay, asserting that she is entirely distinct from the legions of white liberals who go "slumming" in the "coloured dives" of Harlem (Ford 50). In this way, she excludes herself from the degraded, voyeuristic gaze of whiteness, positioning herself as an omnipotent observer—the objective ethnographic eye—with the ability to transcend race, gender, and class in order to give a true account of contemporary race relations in America. Insisting upon the immutable essences that constitute the racial identities of black Americans, she observes that they are "very real" and culturally "there," whilst in the same paragraph she deplores whites who come to Harlem "out of curiosity and jealousy and don't know why" (Ford 49). Later in the essay, she describes a spiritual "revival meeting" on 7th Avenue, presided over by a minister who was Countee Cullen's foster father. Clearly, she is transported by the immediately visceral excitement of difference that she encounters. Consider the following description of the religious service in Harlem:

> These services, really superb concerts, are the gorgeous manifestations of *the emotion* of the race. . . . A manifestation of this kind by white people would have been utterly revolting. But with the negro race it is on another plane, it seems positively

another thing, not connected with Christ or the Bible, the pure outpouring of themselves, a nature rite. (Ford 51)

Again positioning herself as urban participant-ethnographer, Cunard figures the assembly in the church and the rituals as constitutive of a "natural" black soul, thus subduing the importance of organised religion, which had played such a crucial role in diasporic black culture since slavery, to a biologist and ahistorical expression of "natural" essence in which the "Christianity is only accidental" to the "fervour, intensity, stupendous rhythm" of the worship. The meeting, notes Cunard, was *"aesthetically* speaking, so moving" (Ford 51). Harlem becomes a site of ethnographic curiosity for Cunard, as it has for many others before her; a fact remarked upon by Langston Hughes in his autobiography, *The Big Sea*, in which he clearly identifies the modish voyeurism inherent in the cultural spectacles of the Harlem Renaissance. White audiences "were given the best ringside tables to sit and stare at the Negro customers—like amusing animals in a zoo. . . . " He continues, "It was a period when Charleston preachers opened up shouting churches as side-shows for white tourists. . . . It was a period when white writers wrote about Negroes more successfully than they wrote about themselves . . . " (224–25, 227–28). Cunard's own position of enunciation is, of course, in many ways similar to that of the "ofays" (whites) whom she denigrates for their prurient interest in Harlem nightlife: "They want entertainment," she says, emphatically placing a measured distance between herself and the white masses (50). Elsewhere, she makes a point, which, in its careful distantiation from other whites could almost be read ironically:

Go to Harlem. It's sharper there. And it doesn't upset their conviction of the Negro's social status. For all the time that the Negro has entertained the whites, but has never been thought of by this type as possibly a social equal. There are, however, thousands of artists, writers, musicians, intellectuals etc., who have good friends in the dark race, and a good knowledge of Harlem life. . . . (Ford 50)

Whereas Cunard's intention in this article was to demonstrate the diversity of black American culture, she fails to disengage her own voice from the multitude of white patrons of Harlem's clubs and cabarets whose paternalism she consistently and vehemently decries. Her search for authentic blackness tends to recapitulate the more politically naive positions prevalent in the classic primitivist works of Paul Morand, whom she calls "another profiteer in coloured " and Carl Van Vechten, "the spirit of vulgarity" (Ford 73). These writers are, according to Cunard, examples of crass white commercial interests in black culture producing a "revolting and cheap lithograph" of Harlem life (73).[23] There is, however, a crucial difference in intentionality between the lurid prurience in Van Vechten's

Nigger Heaven and Morand's reactionary primitivist *contes*, on the one hand, and Cunard's polemical interventions in *Negro* on the other. While the three may share a thematic continuity, Cunard's work, while employing a similar, if not identical, model of essentialism to point up the contrasts between black and white culture, seeks to extend this inverted paradigm into the domain of the political and transformative internationalist activism.

However, for all the political rhetoric of Third Internationale communism that underlines the article, Cunard falls short of delivering a rigorous class analysis of culture and race in American society. Whiteness simply becomes homogenised into a debased and brutish mass, positioned in opposition to the "negro race," which is applauded as possessing authentic identity simply by its very existence. She then turns to deliver a scathing indictment of the inauthentic "Negro bourgeoisie" and their subservience to white American money (Ford 52). Decrying the liberal black press (in particular, the NAACP's *Crisis*) as behaving "worse than the black imperialist lackeys in colonial countries," she concludes, "The Negro race in America has no worse enemy than its own press" (Ford 53). Her attack on the black middle class is stinging, but it remains on shaky ideological ground as there is no sustained analysis of the interactions between race and class other than an a priori assumption that there are good and bad ways to be politically active. This is a position that leaves the historical complexities of the black middle class in America unaccounted for. Observing that a "number of the younger writers are race-conscious in the wrong way, they make of this a sort of forced, self-conscious thing, give the feeling that they are looking for obstacles," Cunard rejects the possibility of individuation within a larger political collective as racial false consciousness writ large (Ford 53). As valid as this comment may be in light of the explicit Communist remit of the anthology, the essay lambastes the black bourgeoisie in America, disregarding the manifest historical and geographical differences between the formation of white and black classes in Europe and in the United States.[24] The revolutionary internationalism of the Second and the Third Communist Internationale, borne out of a particularly European political tradition, is directly transplanted onto an American scene where the particular and local nuances of black history, ongoing racial segregation, and brutal lynch laws in the South are subsumed into the class struggle between capital and labour.[25] She conflates the complexities of the social (re)production of race with those of class that results in a limited political analysis of American racial issues. This is evident in the following observation on the elitism of a black middle class in New York:

> If treachery and lying are its main attributes [the Negro press] so is snobbery flourishing in certain parts of Harlem. 'Strivers Row'; that is what 139th Street has

been called. . . . There are near-white cliques, mulatto groups, dark-skinned sets who will not invite each other to their houses; some would not let a white cross their threshold. . . . The snobbery around skin colour is terrifying. (Ford 53)

For a work that makes repeated and vociferous claims to progressive racial politics, there are some uneasy assumptions made here: the bourgeois ideology of the black middle class is characterised as having "no horizon, and possessing no philosophical link with life"; in other words, they are inauthentic black subjects (Ford 53). The black bourgeois subject, identified by income and skin colour, is by default a failed racial subject bereft of the authenticity of the race as a whole. This position, however consonant with the polemical intentions of the anthology, is an ideologically precarious one as it confines the black subject to a notion of the political determined by debilitating, primitivist concepts of racial identity. For example, describing the solidarity of the black and white working-class Harlemites under threat of eviction, Cunard writes, "There is no finer relationship than that of knowing that the black and white proletariat is getting more and more together now on the only real basis that must be established and consolidated forever: the equal rights of both under the Communist programme" (Ford 54). This plea for the erasure of racial discrimination through class solidarity is, however, immediately tempered by a retrenchment to an unreconstructed scopic primitivism. Harlem's "gorgeous children" with "their magnificent strength and lustiness" represent for her the visual metonym of the authenticity of black community as whole (Ford 56). The scopic pleasure, derived from the apprehension of visible difference, operates as a utopian exotic symbol representative of an imagined premodern life force. Here, Cunard's voice shifts into a sentimentalising aesthetic approval that rests uneasily with her earlier revolutionary polemic. The documentary tone softens at the sight of the physical beauty of racial difference that is "so *aesthetically* moving." Cunard resorts to the inverted essentialism typical of white negrophilia: "an aesthetic idealisation of racial difference" that does not displace the old racist values but "merely inverts and reverts the binary axis of colonial discourse" (Mercer 99).

It is perhaps significant that a large section in the original edition dealing with the "scale of colouring" in Harlem's population has been edited out of the revised anthology. Cunard's unabashed aesthetic admiration for the "rhiney," the "all too rare" red-haired African-American, is palpable and in her words we can read traces of the ethnographer/anthropologist (even scientist) who has discovered a rare example of a species:

I only saw one in Harlem—an entrancing girl of eleven or so, in the street. I became aware of a very exciting new colour, way off: and as I came into range I marvelled at the superb suffusion of skin colour and hair colour . . . the perfect blend . . . of a rich, dry, gingery sand and an old mature brandy. (orig. ed. 77)

Cunard's comments, couched in the objectifying language of ethnographic observation, reveal the tension between aesthetic excitement and political commentary—something the Surrealist Group also attempts to address elsewhere in the anthology. Here, she positions her observations within a discourse of urban ethnography in which the entity under scrutiny is at once recognisable. The racial whole of working-class Harlem seems to be entirely knowable, standing in this essay "as the referent for a certain kind of truth" (Thomas 85).

From the vantage point of a privileged white viewer, Cunard narrates the Harlem that is really "there"; she is a tourist from the decrepit Old World of Europe in search of the authentically beautiful and real in New World blackness.[26] Again Cunard attempts to fuse the material and the social with a visual aesthetic, suggesting that to *see* Harlem as phenomenological experience is to comprehend the "strength of a race, its beauty":

> For in Harlem one can make an appreciation of a race. Walk down 7th Avenue—the different types are uncountable. Every diversity of bone structure, of head shape, of skin colour. . . . Red Indians and negroes (a particularly beautiful blend, with the high cheek bone always, and the sometimes straight black hair) . . . and, exquisitely fine, the Spanish and Negro blends; the Negro bone and the Negro fat too, are a joy to the eye . . . there is a great satisfaction in seeing that the white American features are absorbed in the mulatto, and that the mulatto is not, as is so often in England, a coloured man with a white man's features and often expression as well. (Ford 54)

Here, the complexities of racial *métissage* are glossed to a purely aesthetic set of scopic racial typologies in which an authentic/nonauthentic paradigm of black identity allows for little hybridity or difference except at a purely physiological level. However, this paradigm is not consistently applied throughout. While Josephine Baker ostensibly lost her authentic black identity by assimilation into white, French culture, Cunard suggests that the simple presence of black performers in blackface shows on the American music-hall stage merits an unproblematic celebration in the anthology. Despite the fact that there were many voices raised in opposition to the spectacle of blackface, these are conspicuously absent from the pages of *Negro.* Michael North has spoken of this contradiction in the anthology. In acting outside of the politically sanctioned scope of international communism, black culture, as Cunard depicts it, stands accused of "virtual race treason," but on the other hand, "if they became self-conscious and left their primitive and sun-burnt arts behind, African-Americans also became unreal" (193). This encapsulates the double bind of negrophile primitivism. Cunard's efforts to construct a political aesthetic around racial oppression in the United States and incipient anticolonial movements are only partially successful. Her discourse remains unaware of its own ideological limitations, marked as it is by the benign intentionality of white negrophilia. This was the challenge of self-interrogation taken up by the Surrealist Group in *Negro.*

NOTES

1. From an unpublished paper given to the convention of the Modern Language Association, December 1996, Washington, DC.

2. Henry Crowder, Cunard's collaborator on the project, disliked the final version of *Negro,* calling it a "big drum that has little inside," "hollow and empty" (Ford 183).

3. For discussions on the operation of essentialism in terms of both gender and race, see Fuss; S. Hall "New"; and Gilroy 31–36. The most recent works on race and essentialism by French theorists include Colette Guillaumin's *Racism, Sexism, Power, Ideology* (1995) and Etienne Balibar and Emmanuel Wallerstein's *Race, Nation, Classe: identités ambigues* (1991).

4. See Clifford *Predicament* for a detailed definition of "ethnographic surrealism" 117–52. His piece on Michel Leiris and *L'Afrique Fantôme* is particularly suggestive on the relations between cultural movements and academic institutional projects (165–75).

5. In 1923, Cunard purchased a printing press from William Bird, founding the Hours Press in 1928, which published Ezra Pound's *XXX Cantos* and Samuel Beckett's *Whoroscope* in 1930. Beckett had submitted the piece to the Hours Press as part of a poetry competition. Cunard printed 300 copies of the poem, which were sold for a shilling each. She also printed and published Louis Aragon's French translation of Lewis Carroll's *Hunting of the Snark.* See Ford xv–xvii.

6. In accounts and biographies of the 1920s in Paris, Cunard's name repeatedly features amongst an international roll call of a white expatriate bohemian circle that included Peggy Guggenheim, Sylvia Beach, and Caresse Crosby. See Scott 63–67.

7. From a paper given to the Modernism Research Seminar, University of London, March 23, 1994.

8. The perhaps apocryphal anecdote that appears most frequently in descriptions of Cunard's life is one in which her mother, Lady Emerald Cunard, was lunching with Margot Asquith, the wife of the former prime minister, at an aristocratic London gathering. In the course of conversation, Lady Asquith inquired about Nancy's latest activities: "Well Maud, what's Nancy up to now? Is it dope, drink, or niggers?" (Ford xvi) Cunard would later write what Hugh Ford described as the "vitriolic pamphlet" *Black Man and White Ladyship* (1930), in which she delivered a caustic indictment of the hypocrisy and racism of the British aristocracy, in particular that of her mother, who had publicly attacked her daughter's interracial sexual liaisons, suggesting that she should be tarred and feathered for her relationship with Crowder.

9. See Torgovnick and Clifford *Predicament* for detailed analyses of the notion of the modern primitive. See also Foster.

10. Crowder was frequently heard to complain that Cunard would strenuously berate him for not being "African enough" (Chisholm 85).

11. Cunard's reputation as a negrophile was well known during the 1920s. Consider the following description of Nancy Cunard:

> Aristocratic and British, like the heroine of a novel, she moved with the self-assurance of women who are used to receiving and being received. . . . Nancy almost always wore huge golden jewelry; she had a weakness for bracelets, which, squeezed around her forearms, looked like a piece of armor. The loveliest and strangest ones were enormous bracelets of ivory, from Africa or Asia. Her taste for them had been acquired from Aragon, who had given her most of them. . . . Nancy often drank too much. She would become nasty, aggressive, and brutal, slapping men with the back of her forearm, crushing their faces with the ivory or metal that squeezed her in from her wrists to her elbows. . . . More than anything she loved men. (Thirion 128–29).

12. The anthology was republished in 1970 with significant changes made to the overall work by editor Hugh Ford. I have used both editions where necessary. The original edition is indicated by the abbreviation orig. ed.

13. See North 191–94 on the question of racism in the anthology.

14. See George Brassaï's account of Le Bal Nègre on the rue Blomet (65–68).

15. *Le culte des nègres* formed an exotic backdrop for white café society at this time, as Richard Aldington's (ex-husband of H.D. [Hilda Doolittle]) letter to Bridget Patmore illustrates:

> went off to Montmartre and went to a most amusing nigger cabaret. (Between ourselves, I deduce that Nancy has now passed to the *Culte des nègres,* and is no longer interested in poor white trash) the dancing room was decorated in Style Moderne . . . there was an alcove with a large picture of a Mississippi steam boat . . . the walls had a number of black panels . . . with very clever sketches of Negroes in white outline. . . . The nigger orchestra was good. . . . There were some turns, a nigger songstress whom Nancy thought marvellous and I thought rather bad; a nigger lady, clothed only in a red and silver cache sexe and silver breast containers, who dances with remarkable undulations of her lumbar regions. (qtd. in Chisholm 129)

16. See Clifford, *Predicament* 141–48 and Jamin, "Un sacré collège" 16.

17. See particularly R. Young 29–55.

18. For example, in the original edition of *Negro,* Cunard harshly criticises Josephine Baker's success in France as that of an inauthentic black subject. It is significant perhaps that this article was edited out of the abridged edition (39).

19. Gobineau's racial typologies would, of course, be deployed again for the strategic essentialism of *négritude.*

20. Michelet cites André Gide's *Voyage au Congo* (1927) here as an example of bourgeois misunderstandings of African society. This is a rather misguided opinion in many ways as Gide's novel is a subtly complex but damning indictment of colonialism. Gide was later active in hosting salons in Paris for black writers and artists in the 1930s.

21. See Mercer 172.

22. The most notable exception to this is her campaigns for the nine black youths from Alabama who were set up as scapegoats for the alleged rape of two white women in a train on March 25, 1931. The women did not bring any charges against the boys, who ranged in age from 13 to 20, and defence called no witnesses. The nine, who became known as the Scottsboro Boys, were sentenced to death on April 10, 1932. The international political community, with unwavering participation by Cunard herself, intervened, and the sentence was eventually commuted. In *Negro* "Scottsboro—and Other Scottsboros," Cunard vehemently attacks the NAACP for their "astoundingly hypocritical and treacherous bearing" throughout the case

and consistently scorns the NAACP's reliance on "white liberal money" as the reason for their moral and political discreditation (*Negro*, ab. ed. 161–62).

23. Morand's collection of popular primitivist stories *Magie Noire* met with great success in France.

24. It seems fair to recall here that Cunard consistently refused to become a member of the Communist Party, preferring to be identified as an anarchist.

25. This is not to suggest, however, that communism failed wholesale in America in the 1930s. There are several articles in *Negro* that document the important role that leftist organisations such as the International Labor Defense played in high-profile civil rights cases, including the Scottsboro trial.

26. See Moynagh 71–75.

CHAPTER 5

"A Conceptual Swindle": Surrealism, Race, and Anticolonialism

Tu marches vers Auteil tu veux aller chez toi à pied
Dormir parmi tes fétiches d'Océanie et de Guinée
Ils sont des Christ d'un autre forme et d'une autre croyance
Ce sont des Christ inférieures des obscures espérances

—Apollinaire, "Zone" (1912)

A number of important surrealists and avant-garde writers contributed pieces to the *Negro* anthology, all of which were translated by Nancy Cunard's literary protegé Samuel Beckett. The pieces included George Sadoul's "Sambo without Tears" (orig. ed. 570–73); Réné Crevel's "Negress in the Brothel" (Ford 354–59); and an article entitled "Murderous Humanitarianism," jointly signed by the Surrealist Group (orig. ed. 574–84). The composer George Antheil wrote a piece called "The Negro on the Spiral" or "A Method of Negro Music" (Ford 214–19).[1] The Surrealist writers appear in the section entitled "Europe" and it is the European, specifically French, intellectual contexts of *Negro* that will be considered here. The earlier wave of cultural primitivism continued in the momentous spectacle of the Exposition Coloniale of 1931. It was crucially modified, however, by some major historical changes that had taken place since *les années folles*, when the Charleston and *La Revue Nègre* momentarily distracted Parisian audiences from their postwar *ennui*. I look here at the efforts of a politicised avant-garde to move beyond the Manichean binaries of cultural primitivism to a more politically engaged understanding of racial and cultural difference. The Surrealist Group were arguably the most dominant within many diverse avant-gardisms in the 1930s, although by the beginning of the decade had splintered into a number of subgroups.[2] The Group's anticolonialist activities in France, catalysed by the Guerre du Rif, represented a gesture of committed intellectual praxis against the general injustices of European imperialism and the particular hypocrisies of France's *mission civilisatrice.* I am not primarily concerned here with the distinctions between avant-garde Surrealism and the broader category of literary modernism. However, there is a crucial distinction between the increasingly politicised aesthetics of the Surrealist avant-garde in the 1930s and an earlier, more abstract modernism that emphasised the formal over the material. This observation is one recognised by Raymond Williams when he says that although modernism in general "proposed a new kind of art for a new kind of social and perceptual world," the avant-garde went further than mere experimental formalism: "aggressive from the beginning, [the avant garde] saw itself as the breakthrough to the future; its members were not the bearers of a progress already repetitiously defined, but the militants of a creativity which would revive and liberate humanity." This rightly characterises parts of the Surrealist avant-garde as bearers of a countercultural politics that sought to regenerate human relations through a deliberate and often violent repulsion of tradition and "a clean break with the past" (*Politics* 3, 51). This search for cultural revitalisation produced an intellectual trajectory from Dadaism's rejection of the signifying power of language through the Cubist search for new painterly forms in the art of Oceania and Africa, avant-garde composers such as Darius Milhaud through to George Antheil's research in musicology from the Orient, South America, and Africa, to the European sculptors who took Benin masks or Côte d'Ivoire fetishes as their models. Through their later affiliation with both the Soviet Communist Party and the Parti Communiste Français (PCF), the Group tried to unite text and context, reconciling aestheticism with a grounded social and material praxis. Thus, in the *Negro* anthology the Surrealist Group attempted to move beyond pure formalism to a more sober contemplation of the material conditions of production behind the construction of the primitive as a transculturated artefact. Their contributions to the anthology were part of a wider collaboration between anticolonialist activism, in which writers such as Daniel Thaly, Léon Damas, Aimé Césaire and Léopold Senghor, were already active and the increasingly politicised aesthetic practices of the avant-garde in the 1930s. Furthermore, while grounded in an exclusively Marxist-Leninist anti-imperialism, the Group's collaborative projects with ethnologists, anthropologists, and dissident intellectuals around issues of race, imperialism, and cultural difference moved beyond those of the PCF at this time. The involvement of the Surrealists in the colonial counter-Exposition of 1931, the publication of anticolonial tracts, and their work in the *Negro* anthology all demonstrated a movement away from negrophile primitivism to a political engagement challenging the insidious cultural essentialism that had recently re-entered the French political arena in the reactionary discourses of the extreme right.[3]

It is important here to distinguish between the two decades of the inter-war years. The popular liberalism of *négrophilie* in the immediate postwar period did not translate into progressive mainstream political projects in the following decade. On the contrary, the 1930s in France saw the emergence of a reactionary conservatism and xenophobia in the form of a *volkish* regressive nationalism. The political situation of France in the 1930s was one that severely tried the racial tolerance of the population: "La xénophobie monte au sein de la fraction de la population française la plus touchée par la crise mondiale et les ligues d'extrême-droite remettant en question la présence des étrangers sur le sol de France."[4] In particular, Dewitte points out that although there still existed a strong Left interest in the *idea* of cultural alterity and the abuses of France's colonial *mission civilisatrice,* in general anticolonialist sentiments remained firmly restricted to a marginalised intellectualism and diasporic groups active in trade unions (253). However, the situation was not as simple as an outright rejection of popular negrophilia of the 1920s, which had visibly waned by the early 1930s, with the singular notable exception of the Exposition Coloniale, and been replaced by or, more accurately, developed into increasing academic attention produced in liberal metropolitan institutions in France. These institutional dialogues, however marginal they were to French society in the 1930s, ran alongside those of even more peripheral political and cultural movements such as the Union des Travailleurs Nègres, short-lived journals, and student organisations, discussed in detail in chapter 4. As France became increasingly fractured by internal political dissent and encroaching economic pressures, the ideological climate became less conducive to any consideration of the morality of colonial policies or the complexities of cultural relativism. On the contrary, this was a decade of keenly contested ideological manoeuvres around notions of nation and national identity, tensions erupting primarily around debates between the Catholic, conservative right and a liberal, cosmopolitan left.[5]

Cunard's association with the Surrealist Group began in 1923 when she first met Tristan Tzara, who had fronted Zurich Dada during the last two years of the First World War. A regular participant in Dadaist evenings at the Cabaret Voltaire, Tzara was particularly interested in the idea of the primitive as a conduit for new forms of language and utterance. As I discussed earlier, for the Dadaists, the primitive represented a space unpolluted by the reach of modernity in which their "anti-everything" agenda could operate. To align oneself on the side of the primitive subject was a deliberate gesture of cultural nihilism that rejected both political ontology and communicative responsibility, and was a desire to tap into "the 'primitive' structures of affective life" (Nye, "Savage Crowds" 54).

For Tzara, the primitive functioned as both a negative and a positive site of signification, and could accommodate the insurrectional weight of Dadaist nihilism. Postwar Dada, scornful of the bourgeois world of rationality, memory, and history, regarded the appropriation of the antithetical space of the primitive as a confrontational gesture of negation against the so-called civilised world. The 1917 Dada manifesto described this position of the group as "saturated, stuffed full to the point of disgust with the experience of all outcasts, the dehumanized beings of Europe, the Africans, the Polynesians, all kinds of outcasts . . . " (Huelsenbeck, *Memoirs* xxi).[6] Thus, for these "polyglot cosmopolitans," Africa and Oceania functioned as both siphon and screen for the avant-garde's intellectual malaise; in a refracted economy of negative equivalence, the primitive was precisely what Europe was not.

By the time Tzara met Cunard in Paris, the Dadaist movement had faltered and splintered, producing a breakaway group of young writers who sought a more a politicised notion of cultural practice.[7] Disenchanted with certain nihilistic tendencies of Dadaism and the magazine *Littérature*, André Breton, Paul Éluard, and Louis Aragon left to form a group of their own that would eventually become the Surrealist Group. By 1924 the Surrealists had established a new review called *La Révolution Surréaliste*, which was significantly more politically engaged than their previous work in Dada. Through Tzara, Cunard met Aragon in 1926 and the two soon became regulars at the Café Cyrano in La Place Blanche, where the group, with Max Ernst, René Crevel, Éluard, Breton, and Phillippe Soupault at its core, met twice a day.[8] Like many of their contemporaries, Aragon and Cunard had a common interest in non-Western artefacts. In England and France, they scoured dockside curio shops for what Cunard described as "African and Oceanic things"; these artefacts, "ivory, gods, masks, fetishes," she claimed, were "the most recent and now a very large interest in my life" (Chisholm 101).[9] The relationship between Cunard and Tzara and Aragon attracted her to the politics of the Surrealist Group, in which she recognised the possibilities of a radical leftist politics that could accommodate both art and doctrine in revolutionary praxis. Although in 1932 the Surrealist Group would irrevocably split over the question of their affiliation with the Communist Party, in the middle years of the 1920s there seemed to be a natural, if stormy, affinity between surrealism and communism.[10]

ANTICOLONIALISM AND THE SURREALIST GROUP

The rhetoric of Albert Sarraut's colonial *mise en valeur* and its resources of a "hundred million Frenchmen" worked tirelessly in the interwar period to promote the idea of an economically viable and picturesque French

Empire. This was actively instrumentalised in projects such as the military schools at Joinville and Fréjus, which trained *bloc noir* colonial soldiers for the express purpose of exhibiting them at colonial exhibitions. Sarraut's notion of *la plus grande France* was gaining ground with the general public, millions of whom flocked to the Exposition Coloniale Internationale in 1931 in the Bois de Vincennes. There were a handful of student protests against the Exposition and its blatant exoticist hypocrisies, but these were systematically quashed by the Service de Contrôle et d'Assistance en France des Indigènes des colonies (CAI) and those involved either deported, gaoled, or fined.[11] Apart from these students, the Surrealist Group was one of the few dissenting voices raised against this spectacular staging of French colonialism that presented paternal, Republican France as the global donor of civilising modernity and technological progress. The Exposition, an exercise in paving over the ideological and ethical cracks in France's colonial *mission civilisatrice*, offered the populace the *fait accompli* of the "beauty and riches of the colonies," which could nurture the nationalist sentiments of *la plus grande France* (Lebovics 18). Accordingly, in the *Guide Officiel* to the Exposition, André Demaison's opening statements have expressed an explicit, unabashed nationalism: "You have sensed that today this great human collectivity that is France has horizons wider than those you have been accustomed to see on the map of Europe." The triumphalist note continues with the affirmation of France as a global imperial power and warns that as a modern nation state it could not afford to "remain indifferent to the colonial activities of our neighbours . . . " (20). However, in the guide's "Addresse au visiteur," Demaison has taken pains to point out that the Exposition is a sober contemplation of France's extended empire and not a frivolous sideshow of exotic curiosities: "Mais vous ne trouverez pas ici une exploitation des bas instincts d'un public vulgaire. . . . Point de ces bamboulas, de ces danses du ventre, de ses étalages de bazar, qui ont discrédité bien d'autres manifestations coloniales" (20). Thus, the ideological agenda of the Exposition officially distanced itself from the gaudy, raucous primitivism of the 1920s in favour of an ostensibly more serious consideration of cultural difference under a paternalistic Republicanism.

Against this background of colonialist and Republican nationalist fervour, a group of artists and intellectuals mounted a counterexhibition to the Vincennes fair in the former Soviet pavilion used in the 1925 Exposition des Arts Décoratifs.[12] The anti-Exposition was organised and designed by Yves Tanguy, André Breton, Georges Sadoul, André Thirion, and Louis Aragon and ran from July 1931 to February 1932. The group, under Alfred Kurella, formed a political organization called the Ligue Anti-imperialiste, and a large number of prominent Surrealists were active in it. Aghast at the PCF's apathetic response to the Exposition and to the suppression of anti-colonial and anti-imperial demonstrations, Kurella saw the Surrealists as the only group capable of mounting any kind of effective opposition to the monstrous spectacle of imperial rule: "The Surrealists are practically the only ones who have demonstrated an intelligent hostility against that enterprise and shown their disgust through specific action" (Thirion 289). Accordingly, in the pamphlet *La Véritable Guide de L'Exposition Coloniale,* the Group reeled off lists of economic and social atrocities that successive French administrations had inflicted upon the colonies in the name of the *mission civilisatrice,* an anticolonial gesture that was rare, if not unique, amongst the avant-garde at this time.

The Group's opposition to the colonial question was not solely due to their political alliance with the Communist Third Internationale. They also balked at an ontology that described Christian civilisation as the epitome of absolute progress. As a group, they were interested in the "customs and traditions of savages" and believed that "the myths of native peoples were better than those of Christianity"(Lebovics 252). For the Surrealists, modernity as a philosophical project had failed to acknowledge the value of difference and had systematically attempted to rationalise and erase this difference in the utilitarianism of imperialism. In the journal *Le surréalisme au service de la révolution,* which had replaced *La Révolution surréaliste,* similar anticolonial images and tracts were collected as a response to what the Surrealists regarded as the crimes of colonial conquests. The group subsequently produced a broadsheet entitled *Ne visitez pas l'Exposition Coloniale* (1931), signed by André Breton, Paul Éluard, Louis Aragon, Benjamin Peret, Georges Sadoul, Pierre Unik, André Thirion, René Crevel, René Char, Maxime Alexandre, Yves Tanguy, and Georges Malkine. Attacking the gross fiction of *la plus grande France* as a "concept-escroquerie" that had been constructed in the Bois de Vincennes, they proclaimed:

> Il s'agit de donner aux citoyens de la métropole la conscience de propriétaire qu'il leur faudra pour entendre sans broncher l'echo de fusillades lointaines. Il s'agit d'annexer au fin de paysage de France, déjà très relevé avant-guerre par une chanson sur la cabane-bambou, une perspective de minarets et de pagodes. (Breton 5)

This "conceptual swindle" of the Exposition Coloniale was, the Group argued, simply a logical extension of an unself-conscious metropolitan primitivism that unscrupulously appealed to only the most superficial conceptualisations of racial and cultural difference in a propaganda exercise for French imperial expansionism. Crucially, the Group recognised the powerfully organising role of culture as a domestic palliative for the rawer imperial ideologies still kept at a distance from the mother country.[13] The kinds of nineteenth-century politics of exhibition employed in the Exposition were mocked and subverted by the Surrealists at their own anti-Exposition pavilion. Their display punctured the racialised taxonomic hierarchies of colonial discourse by de-centering the authoritarian ethnographic gaze. In the Surrealist pavilion, the rooms teemed with a chaotic jumble of material objects taken from their own salons and collections and jostled cheek by jowl with European fetishes such as plaster-of-Paris Madonnas and *images d'Epinal.* The categorisation, display, and mastery of colonial objects, including human exhibits, presented in the Exposition Coloniale reinforced the rigid self/other Manichean structures of colonial discourse. In the Surrealist pavilion, these structures were humorously undone by the "make do" techniques of the *bricoleur* that deflated the panoptical colonial eye. The Group showed up the idea of exotic authenticity as an empty gimmick and tried to reverse the flow of objects, as Jean Jamin has deftly summarised:

> The notions of distantiation, exoticism, representation of the other, and difference are inflected, reworked, readjusted as a function of criteria no longer geographical and cultural but methodological and even epistemological in nature: to make foreign what appears to be familiar; to study the rituals and sacred sites of contemporary institutions with the minute attention of the "exotic" ethnographer, and using his methods; to become observers observing those others who are ourselves—and at the limit. This other who is oneself. . . . (Jamin, "Un sacré collège" 16)

In a lecture entitled "What Is Surrealism?" given to an audience of Belgian surrealists on June 1, 1934, in Brussels, André Breton outlined the Surrealist doctrines that proposed a working alliance between art, culture and political commitment. He opened by establishing the quotidian relevance of surrealism that constitutes "a desire to deepen the foundations of the real" and "to bring about an ever clearer and at the same time ever more passionate consciousness of the world perceived by the senses" (115). Rejecting the notion of the autonomous work of art as outmoded and essentially irrelevant to the contemporary situation, Breton suggested that art and culture must be capable in all its endeavour to "face the *breath of the street*" and to "present interior reality and exterior reality as two elements in process of unification, of finally becoming one. This final unification being the supreme aim of surrealism" (116). Defining the aim of surrealism as the "*liberation of the mind* and the *liberation of man,*" Breton concluded by saying, "we must struggle against our fetters with all the energy of despair" (115). The confrontational spirit of Dada lingered on in this declaration but was tempered by a more sober impulse to social change drawing its energies from the urgency of the European political situation. In the face of the accumulating forces of fascism, Breton invoked the names of Hitler, Dolfuss, and Mussolini as proof that art cannot turn in upon itself in textual hermeticism; rather there must be a recoil from text as the source of definitive authoritative meaning to matter as "a *living* movement" (118). He identified the Moroccan War of 1925, in which France spent a year and deployed 150,000 allied French and Spanish troops putting down the rebels' claims for independence, as a crucial turning point in Surrealism from absolute idealism to dialectical materialism (117).

> No coherent political or social attitude made its appearance until 1925, that is to say (and it is important to stress this), until the outbreak of the Moroccan war which, re-arousing in us our particular hostility to armed conflicts. . . . Surrealism . . . suddenly perceived the necessity of . . . dialectical materialism, insisting on the supremacy of matter over mind. (35)

The Guerre du Rif was also the provocation for the publication of the polemical tract *La Révolution d'abord et toujours* (1925) and for a document denouncing the imperial "war," *Les Intellectuels contre la guerre du Maroc.*[14]

Concluding his Brussels lecture, Breton stated unequivocally the crucial importance of the Surrealist project: "In 1934, more than ever, surrealism owes it to itself to defend the postulate of the necessity of change" (118). Accordingly, then, in the last issue of *La Révolution surréaliste,* René Crevel's article "Le Patriotisme de l'inconscient" demonstrated an unambiguous anticolonial position and the Group subsequently declared intellectual war on imperialism in the first issue of *Le Surréalisme au service de la Révolution* in July 1930.

The following articles selected from the *Negro* anthology show the Surrealist Group's commitment to a radical critique of imperialism, which began with their opposition to the Guerre du Rif, and their desire to puncture the enduring metropolitan myth of the *mission civilisatrice,* with its seductive rhetorical gloss of liberal humanism. In the following readings, I show that in their contributions to *Negro,* the Group offer the most rigorous and sustained critique of the complexities of modern colonialism in the anthology as a whole. The convergence of aesthetics and activism, politics, and culture in these pieces distinguishes them from the straightforward ethnographic pieces and political polemic in the anthology. Furthermore, these pieces are more politically and culturally self-conscious than Cunard's own work, which tends towards an affective formalism—with race as the mutable text of alterity—which the Group attempts to qualify.

POLITICS AND AESTHETICS IN THE NEGRO ANTHOLOGY

In "Sambo without Tears," Georges Sadoul takes on the myth of French liberalism and racial tolerance that "proclaims that democratic France makes no distinction between black and white" (orig. ed. 570). The short essay uses the example of children's magazines and reads them as emblematic of the cultural dissemination of France's *mission civilisatrice.* In his readings of a variety of children's comic books, Sadoul offers a satirical perspective on French colonial attitudes both in the continental mother country and in the colonies, a distinction often overlooked by contemporary commentary and critics. His acerbic irony is targeted at the stock racial stereotypes found everywhere in French colonial literature: the cross-Sahara trek in a "caterpillar car," and the "ferocious maiden of Sudan" (orig. ed. 571). Africa exists as a scenic backdrop, he suggests, to the infantile exploits of *colons,* whose actual colonial practices amount to little more than a series of ludicrous "boys' own" style capers. This debunking of the colonial mythology of exploration and conquest challenges the twin ideologies of improvement and generosity of the *mission civilisatrice,* which extended its reach most effectively in metropolitan France into the cultural domain, for it was there that the picturesque site of Africa as scenic other was most successfully employed as political currency. The proliferation after 1931 of illustrated colonial magazines, journals, and even films was testament to this reification of colonised space as a consumer commodity.

Sadoul's piece is relentlessly polemical in its Communist pronouncements that "[t]he whole colour question becomes a question of class." A coruscating antibourgeois stance is sustained throughout, concluding with a song sung to Sadoul by "Negroes" in Finland as he was en route to the Soviet Union: "Black and white we stand united . . . / All the workers are united" (orig. ed. 572–73). The underlying thesis is one of class solidarity, specifically the solidarity of the colonised proletariat against both the mediocrity of the uninspired bourgeois colonial officials and the imperial proprietors of capital and property.[15] Linking this thematic to the domestic situation, Sadoul notes that in France the tradition of migrant labour is not restricted to unskilled black workers in the ports and brothels and that class rivalry is actively promoted by the French authorities in impoverished communities. Migrant workers—Poles, Italians, and Arabs—are employed at starvation wages and "segregated from the French proletariat"; scapegoats for all social ills from unemployment to moral decline and nationwide economic inflation, these "lousy foreigners" are France's "niggers." Sweated labour, whether denoted by language or skin colour, meets with the same treatment at the hands of both French and American industrial capitalism: racial difference is merely invoked as a means of disuniting the proletariat (orig. ed. 572). Sadoul reaffirms Cunard's position on race and labour unrest in the United States. In "Harlem Reviewed," Cunard says that "the black and white proletariat is getting more and more together now on the only real basis that must be established and consolidated for ever: the equal rights of both under the Communist programme" (Ford 54). Thus, in his conclusion Sadoul insists that race and class are inextricably linked on an international scale: "a Pole in

France receives the same treatment as a Negro in the States" (orig. ed. 572). The article sets in place a programmatic political internationalism in which specific examples of racism and imperial aggression are positioned within the larger, global contexts of the early stages of late Western capitalism.

However, despite Sadoul's claims that political revolution in the Soviet Union has produced a society in which racial prejudice is unknown or regarded as the inevitable cultural result of free-market economic competition, he obfuscates the multifarious complexities of race and history. For example, he ignores the fundamental differences between diasporic experiences and conditions in the United States, France, and Britain. In particular, the differences between the American and European diaspora are studiously avoided in a meticulously polemical reading that exhaustively attributes *all* racial prejudices and exploitation to the inevitable systematic effects of capitalism. Although valid as a description of the construction of the category of race within industrial modernity, this reading is consistently undertheorised in its geohistoric particularities.

In contrast, the Surrealist Group's collaborative essay, "Murderous Humanitarianism," written by leading surrealist writers (André Breton, Roger Caillois, René Char, René Crevel, Paul Eluard, J.-M. Monnerot, Benjamin Péret, Yves Tanguy, André Thirion, Pierre Unik, and Pierre Yoyotte), nuances Sadoul's overhomogenised analysis of race and imperialism. There is a complexity to their argument that attempts to unmask the ostensible humanitarian mission of imperialism, so seductively constructed during the Exposition Coloniale. The writers allude to the sentiments of regressive nationalism in contemporary reactionary political and cultural discourses:

> Our gallant sailors, policemen and agents of imperialistic thought, in labour with opium and literature, have swamped us with their irretentions of nostalgia; the function of all these idyllic alarums among the dead and gone being to distract our thoughts from the present, the abominations of the present. (orig. ed. 575)

The present in Western Europe, fraught with internal dissension, is appeased by the construction of nostalgic utopian fictions of *la plus grande France* and the *mission civilisatrice*, in which the racial other is invoked as a repository of recuperative difference and diversity always in the service of a hegemonic imperial authority.

The economic crisis that had begun in America with the crash of 1929 was beginning to be felt in Europe and the mounting anxieties of France's right-wing government led to an increase in state judicial power to swiftly put down any potentially subversive political activities. André Thirion has noted this fact when he observes: "In the colonies, the least attempt at emancipation, even within the legal framework of the empire, was drowned in blood." It was time, Thirion continues, that the Surrealists publicly opposed the official ideology of the colonial question in France, despite the fact that in the face of a "meddlesome, vexing and often racist law . . . the masses generally remained attached to the tricolor, Bastille Day, and the vague ideal of Republican glory and liberty" (252). In contrast, the Group spiritedly wrote against the Republican myth of *assimilation,* challenging its universalist liberalism as a self-interested rhetorical manoeuvre that effectively suppressed dissent through its appearance of tolerant egalitarianism. The anthology was an outlet for this mounting anticolonialism on an internationalist scale, collating the dispersed interests and activities of those seeking a way to breathe praxis into their aesthetic stances, at a time in Europe when art began to respond to an increasingly polarised political scene.

Sadoul attacks the overgeneralisations of non-Western peoples when he looks at the way in which the "Negro" is made to stand metonymically for "colonial peoples of every shade of colour," a position typical of "the average French bourgeois" image of a colonised subject. The magazines and comic strips present the "Negro" as a "dangerous ruffian," requiring the rigours of European colonisation in order to be transformed into the civilised ways of the colonial masters (orig. ed. 570). The public project of the *mission civilisatrice* is satirised through the magazine *Puerto,* a "Roman Catholic organ" that represents the white *colon* as kind and altruistically interested in the group of "good fellows" who simply want to offer Africa the benefits of European life: "This silly people seems to imagine that we come to Africa to conquer, whereas of course we come as benefactors . . . " (orig. ed. 570). Sadoul savagely mimics the pompously disingenuous voice of the "brilliant officer" of the French military: "We have organised a campaign against all social ills; we have created schools with medical instruction . . . " (orig. ed. 50). But the introduction of modern medicine and Republican judicial systems is starkly set against the real methods of violent colonialism: "Won over by the oration he soars into the blue on his mission of mercy, which takes the form of spraying the bold black Berbers with bombs" (orig. ed. 570). Political rhetoric merges into violence as the final, coercive logic of imperialism is exposed.[16]

Significantly, in both "Murderous Humanitarianism" and in Thirion's later accounts of Surrealist anticolonialist activism, the writers are at pains not to underestimate the potential benefits of a European presence in their colonies in a blanket condemnation. Speaking to these mutually dynamic, although always uneven, power relations between the colonisers and the colonised, Thirion uses the example of the *vieilles colonies,* where "a certain freedom, of speech, and the practice of elections brought forth gifted individuals, set up a local intellectual life, and enriched the French universities, the theater, and the army" (252). Similarly, in the *Negro* anthology, the Surrealist Group deride the liberal Left who decry all cultural contact between France and its colonies: "A Holy-Saint faced international of hypocrites deprecates the material progress foisted on the blacks, protests, courteously, against the importation not only of alcohol, syphilis and field-artillery, but also of railways and printing" (orig. ed. 575). The Group's analysis of modern colonialism does not dismiss out of hand the civilising mission as wholesale destructive coercion. Rather they offer an account of the mutually constitutive, but again never equal, processes of coloniser/colonised, which is nuanced with the recognition of a necessarily dialectical relationship between the two, a condition more fully recognised five years later by Césaire in his *Cahier d'un retour au pays natal* (1939), which depicts colonial contact as violent, callous, and rapacious but also as the source of creative energy and political internationalism.

What is also striking about the Surrealist Group's contributions to *Negro* is the fact that these are the only writings in which the liberalism of cultural *négrophilie* is rigorously challenged. "Murderous Humanitarianism" offers the following perspicacious indictment of modern primitivism:

> Those blacks who have been merely compelled to distort in terms of fashionable jazz the natural expression of their joy at finding themselves partakers of a universe from which western peoples have wilfully withdrawn may consider themselves lucky to have suffered no worse thing than degradation. The 18th century derived nothing from China except a repertory of frivolities to grace the alcove. In the same way the whole object of romantic exoticism and modern travel-lust is of use only in entertaining that class of blasé client sly enough to see an interest in deflecting to his own advantage the torrent of those energies which soon, much sooner than he thinks, will close over his head. (orig. ed. 575)

This clearly identifies earlier periods of exoticism and primitivism (here eighteenth-century Orientalism), in which economic and strategic contexts are culturally translated into a booty of collectable knick-knacks to adorn the bourgeois domestic space of the French home. In other words, an aesthetic appreciation of non-Western culture as artefactual domestic commodity does not produce an equivalent political tolerance. While recognising that the appropriation of the exotic into a domestic aesthetic commodity has existed throughout imperial history, the writers stress that primitivisms are products of their own specific historical conditions of production; *négrophilie* is no exception. The article astutely points up the ways in which intellectuals have been duped by the liberal veneer of *négrophilie*, just as much as the unsuspecting French populace who queued to see the Exposition Coloniale; both lack a sense of self-critique, the Group suggests, which finally negates the agency of the colonised by constructing them as reflections, both positive and negative, of the metropolitan centre. In a move similar to their 1929 map of the world, "Surrealist Geography," in which they realigned the cartographic proportions of the globe to predominantly position the subordinated geographies of Polynesia, Ireland, Mexico, and Alaska over Britain, America, and France, the Group raise the question of epistemological as well as material aggression of imperialism into the intellectual arena that had long been dominated by an idealised fetishisation of the primitive other.

In "Sambo without Tears," Sadoul points up the ways in which the metropolitan cosmopolitanism of interwar primitivism mirrored the economic project of colonialism that turned every colonised body to the economic advantage of the mother country. This process, observes Sadoul, is reconfigured in the metropolitan space as a reification of racial difference. He demonstrates this by the inclusion of several images showing the ways in which an undifferentiated trope of blackness was co-opted in order to sell products and goods such as tobacco, the flavoured milk drink Banania and the Papillons Noirs (orig. ed. 568). The poster of the African woman's head in silhouette is typical of many advertisements for the Exposition that recognised the scopic appeal of the exotic figure as emblematic of the modernising forces of the colonial mission as well as the rich economic resources that the colonies themselves offered the *mère patrie*.[17] Crucially, Sadoul insists that commodification of the black body and image takes place at wider cultural levels. He comments that the "Negro is elevated into the more rarefied spheres of French society, as groom or purveyor of jazz to the 'quality' " and further that the black man can also be fashioned into a "buffoon created by special request for the entertainment of the white man" (orig. ed. 570). Just as the "Negro" has been praised as a "soldier or a cop," the *tirailleurs* of Senegal are much admired by a wide French public for their "innate" fighting skills and redoubtable ferocity on the battlefields of the Sommes and Flanders. The reification of the nonwhite body into marketable cultural images begins with the brute forces of economic colonisation that construct the colonised body as "capital which had to be safeguarded just like any other capital" (orig. ed. 574). This capital may take the form of outright slavery—as in the case of the notoriously brutal *travaux forcés* or, as suggested in René Crevel's "The Negress in the Brothel," of metropolitan sexual relations between black and white that "cannot rise above the simple notion of an act of annexation." (I). The economic motives for annexation are repeatedly stressed in "Murderous Humanitarianism," described as the relation between "the colonial machinery that extracts every last penny from natural advantages . . . " and the "universe from which western peoples have wilfully withdrawn," one where rationalism has failed to deliver social or economic equality. Such a society callously transforms surplus black bodies in the colonies into cultural distraction and spectacle for exhausted appetites in the metropole. The process is, the Group claims, one of shamelessly exploitative commodification that demonstrates a "counterfeit liberalism" (orig. ed. 574), typical of those French bourgeoisie who organise human resources in the colonies in order to transform them into domestic commodities:

> But even when for one reason or another he is obliged to remain at home he demands to be entertained and debauched by the exotic curiosity that lifts him clear of the national fact into an illusion of renewal. Hence the popularity of Martinique jazz, Cuban melodies, Harlem bands and the entire tam-tam of the Colonial Exhibition. (orig. ed. III)

The notion of remaining at home is an important observation here, as *négrophilie* is depicted as a thoroughly metropolitan phenomenon rehearsing wider patterns of colonial relations and bringing them back to the *mère patrie* as a safely domesticated commodity of racial and cultural difference, a fact that René Crevel picks up and develops in his essay "The Negress in the Brothel."

Of all the Surrealist pieces in the anthology, René Crevel's article is the most characteristically surrealist in texture and tone. A torrential flow of intricately convoluted prose, layered mosaics of ideas, sharp aphorisms, idiosyncratic outbursts, and spirited accusations, Crevel's argument centres on the sexual exchanges between black women and white men in the urban French brothel, where the "average Frenchman who is not interested in depravities, who is merely seeking the picturesque, can go to the brothel and meet a thoroughbred Negress" (III). Crevel suggests that the phenomenon of *négrophilie* in Paris, symbolised here as the metropolitan brothel, recapitulates the hypocrisies of religion, commerce, and colonial coercion, offering the less adventurous French citizen the metropolitan version of Martinique, Harlem, Cuba, and Africa in the safely domesticated domain of the mother country and the "scenic organisation of venal love" (orig. ed. III). This reading of sexual exoticism is appropriate, of course, to the phenomenon of Josephine Baker and *La Revue Nègre* that staged this voyeuristic and libidinal relationship as cultural spectacle. In addressing the psychosexual dynamics of race in a colonial context, Crevel effectively sums up the limited horizons of cultural *négrophilie.* Cultural primitivism, he suggests, is a process of self-delusion in which the troubled present is assuaged by recourse to an imaginary other, a space untouched by capitalist relations, a position that blithely ignores the will to mastery of imperial colonialism that has delivered this racial other to the metropolitan centre. Crevel suggests a transhistorical connection, comparing twentieth-century imperial France to imperial Rome: "Nowadays the white man regards the man of colour precisely as the wealthy Romans of the Late Empire regarded their slaves—as a means of entertainment" (orig. ed. III). Here, he is historicising the imperial present by realigning it with the varied but similar patterns of exploitation in the name of empire, all driven by the impulses of economic utilitarianism. Thus, the liberal narratives of a Republican civilising mission and the project of *assimilation* are systematically debunked. As Léon Pierre Quint later observes: "Today the entire colonial system is represented as a cultural dispensation . . . and yet there is scarcely any difference between this system and that of the early slave traders" (orig. ed. 576–77). At base, modern colonial tactics, glossed by the liberal discourses of the *mission civilisatrice* and *assimilation*, simply reiterate earlier coercive methods of conquest and subjugation.

Crevel begins by presenting the versions of France's nationalist myth that operate within the contemporary political and moral discourses of the nation, concluding that "[i]t is natural enough that a nation whose practical ethics never lost sight of at least one transcendental proposition: Un sou est un sou (a penny's a penny) . . . " (I). Every moral and religious path, he continues, leads to the same end of annexation and corruption based on brute capitalist exploitation of the colonies' human and natural resources: "So much then for our ideas, our Christian ideas, whose faculty of arbitrary restriction twenty centuries have not exhausted . . . and that still claim the right to direct a world that they have so completely trampled to death" (orig. ed. I). The moral hypocrisy that Crevel identifies has resulted in what he calls the "pernicious literary antithesis between soul and epidermis" and the "holy and divided kinesis" of spirituality and sexuality, a denouncement enshrined in the doctrines of positivism, traditional foe of the Surrealists (II–III). Attacking the patriarchal misconduct of Enlightenment figures like Rousseau and Diderot, Crevel forges a genealogy through the centuries of literature and high French culture, as well as the "infected settlers and cut-throat Jesuits" of France's colonies, that has produced little more than a transient exoticist interest in other cultures (orig. ed. II-III). As the most recent variant of this exoticism, *négrophilie* has simply reiterated the endless drive to consume difference as exotic cultural capital, this time positioning the black woman as the newest object of fascination in the "décor of desires" (orig. ed. III). For all its lofty visions of moral and cultural benevolence, the *mission civilisatrice* remains complicit in the exploitation of Europe's colonised populations, here reformulated within an economy of sexual exchange that mirrors the fundamental inequities of imperial capitalism through the prostitute/client dynamic. Baudelaire's vision of Jeanne Duval—"Charme inattendu d'un bijou rose et noir"—is used as the paradigmatic model of black/white sexual relationships, just as her name was repeatedly invoked in reviews of *La Joséphine*. Black women, says Crevel, are positioned as exotic and rare commodities in the brothel, a metaphorical space for all unequal exchange:

Now, if, instead of appropriating the value of his money with the traditional member of his nauseating person, he could be persuaded to approach those hired nymphae not merely as the exquisite negation of the regrettably proliferous article on tap, so to speak, at home, but rather as the shell that imprisons the music of the sea, it is just possible that he might be favoured, for all his cloacal labyrinth, with the inexorable vibrations of a distant wave that hastens to engulf every capitalistic fortress, from brothel to cathedral. (orig. ed. III)

Crevel posits the possibility of revolutionary change, not just at the level of the political economy and the class system but also at the libidinal level of the colonial psyche, where white men are complacent in their sexual annexation of the black prostitute. After all, Crevel contends, "For what are they doing, governors, generals and even the Imperial Roman marshall himself? Playing with the piccaninnies . . . " (orig. ed. III). He concludes that *négrophilie* was simply an exercise in erotic tourism and that it reinforced beyond a doubt the unequal power relations between metropole and colony by reducing race to a spectacle of alterity to be haphazardly consumed by a public increasingly attuned to the endless innovations of consumer capitalism promoted by the burgeoning mass culture industry. Such a cultural consumption effaces any traces of the material or ideological conditions behind the construction of difference and refuses to recognise either agency or resistance on the part of the colonised.

The lukewarm reception of the *Negro* anthology in America, France, and Britain revealed what Tyrus Miller calls the work's "heavy sign of double failure" in terms of both its political impact and its own aesthetic organisation (3). However, Alain Locke, editor of *The New Negro* (1928), wrote to Cunard congratulating her on "the finest anthology in every sense of the word ever compiled on the Negro" and one that he regarded as "a subtle accumulative force of enlightenment which is beyond all contradiction and evasion" (Marcus 8). However, Locke's views were not shared by the black presses in America, which either ignored the publication of the anthology or mentioned it only in passing. The *Amsterdam News* referred to it in passing simply as a work exhibiting a "definite Communist bias" (Ford xxxiii). Cunard's scathing indictments of W. E. B. DuBois and the NAACP doubtless did little to smooth the anthology's reception in the United States, where it was duly shunned by major black intellectuals and publications such as *The Crisis* and *New Masses.* In addition to Cunard's coruscating attacks on the bourgeois liberalism of the NAACP, particularly over the Scottsboro incident, the work lacked political impact in American debates on race because of the unfeasibility of an effective radical Left politics. Leftism continued to be regarded as a particularly European response to socioeconomic crisis that occupied only a very marginalised place in North American liberal politics. The histrionic nature of the Red Scare in 1917 never fully dissipated and revolutionary communism became the spectre that haunted American liberalism.[18]

More recently, the academy has been reluctant to critically evaluate a work, such as the *Negro* anthology, that slips in and out of theoretical positions on race, difference, and essence. Given the often stringent requisites of the paradigms of identity politicking, particularly in a certain postmodernist inflected brand of postcolonial theory, the work now seems naive, paternalistic, and even racist in its essentialism and is therefore easily written off as another example of white, modernist dilletantism. However, that an activist critic like C. L. R. James (a long-time advocate of Gramscian organic intellectualism whose own *American Civilization* (1950) was in many ways an heir to the multidisciplinary approach of *Negro*) used the anthology as part of his teaching in Britain and in America is testament to the enduring value of Cunard's documentary project. James recognised the value of the work both as an historical document and as an example of the possibilities and limitations of the often difficult rapprochement between cultural innovation and political intervention.

The challenge for the *Negro* anthology, then, was one of grasping and documenting the particular historical moment and rendering it accessible as an emancipatory, progressive text, while attending to the aesthetic of an avant-garde whose energies distrusted the signifiying power of language itself, preferring an interrogation of the unconscious and desire to the codified reality of positivist truth (Nicholls, *Modernisms* 287). As Breton pronounced in "La force d'attendre": "I would like to believe that there is no true work of the mind that is not shaped by the desire for the real amelioration of the conditions of existence of the world" (12–13). Accordingly, the anthology tends to vacillate between these two poles, attempting to weld an affective, moral outrage against social and economic injustice in Breton's "vulgar universe" with a set of aesthetic concerns that potentially rejects the tenets of that very universe. While these goals are not consistently achieved throughout the work as a whole, the anthology's immense diversity and range of contributions provide an invaluable insight into the political documentary culture of France in the 1930s.

NOTES

1. The decision here to focus on a limited selection of European contributions to the anthology should not overshadow the importance of other sections that have an impressive inventory of contributors, including Langston Hughes, Zora Neale Hurston, Arthur Schomburg, Jacques Roumain, George Padmore, W. E. B. DuBois, Alain J. Locke, William Carlos Williams, Theodore Dreiser, and Arna Bontemps.

2. On the diversity of modernisms and avant-gardisms from 1914, see Nicholls, *Modernisms*. See also Bürger for a detailed analysis of the differences between modernism as a general periodisation and specific avant-garde movements.

3. The legacy of cultural pluralism and political internationalism that the Sur-

realists championed was systematically eroded by the Vichy administration after the fall of the Front Populaire in 1936. See Lebovics 98–134 on the uses that the Right in France made of racial and cultural essentialism in the 1930s.

4. See Girardet 154.

5. Perhaps the most spectacular example of this cultural tension was the violent reaction to the Surrealist film *L'Age d'Or* (1930). The ultra-right-wing Ligue des Patriotes interrupted the film's showing at Studio 28 on December 3, throwing stink bombs and slashing Surrealist paintings to shreds as they chanted anti-Semitic abuse at the audience. The press came out on the side of the protesters and castigated Luis Buñuel and Salvador Dali as "gentlemen of the synagogue" and "Jewish Bolsheviks." See Alexandre 6 and H. Lewis 90–93 for a full account of this incident. Cunard later arranged a private showing of the film in London to raise money for her political projects in America.

6. Marinetti's Italian Futurism made use of another version of the primitive in his ideas of "body-madness" and nondiscursive crowd energy. See the 1920 manifesto "Beyond Communism" and "Technical Manifesto of Futurist Literature" (1912) for his ideas on primal energy in Fillipo Tommaso Marinetti, *Marinetti: Selected Writings*, trans. R. W. Flint (London: Secker and Warburg, 1972). See also Nicholls, *Modernisms* 84–111.

7. However, among the Berlin Dadaists, John Heartfield, George Grosz, and Wieland Herzfelde were all members of the Communist Party.

8. Cunard's position in the avant-garde milieu was redoubtable: for instance, she counted Jean Cocteau, René Crevel, Phillipe Soupault, André Derain, Marie Laurencin, Louis Aragon, and André Breton among her closer friends. Tzara wrote a play called *Mouchoir des Nuages* for Cunard. Constantin Brancusi made a sculpture of Cunard, *Jeune Fille Sophistiquée*. See Chisholm 97–99.

9. Anne Chisholm notes that Cunard's interest in African art began around 1926—when *l'art nègre* was already in vogue in cosmopolitan circles in Paris: "She and Aragon shared an interest in primitive art, which still seemed crude and ugly to most people. . . . They would visit the docks in the east End of London, and bars where French sailors could be found in seacoast towns, searching for pieces to add to Nancy's growing collection" (97).

10. The Surrealist Group was founded in 1924. But it was not until 1929, in Breton's *Sécond Manifesto*, that the Group aligned itself with the Communist Party (CP) and dialectical materialism, although Breton, Éluard, and Aragon had belonged to the CP since 1927. After 1933, in an increasingly polarised Surrealist group with Dali and Aragon at the two opposite political poles, *Minotaure* replaced *Le Surréalisme au Service de la Révolution* and focussed more heavily on arts at the expense of politics.

11. Protests came from the Association Indochinoise d'Enseignement Mutuel and the Ligue de Défense de la race Nègre. The CAI found plans of a Comité de Lutte Contre l'Exposition, and on May 22, 1931, Nguyen Van Tao, a student, was arrested and deported back to Vietnam. The only other effective opposition noted was that of Léopold Senghor, who urged students to boycott the exposition. See Dewitte 101–3 and Langley, *Pan-Africanism and Nationalism* and "Pan-Africanism in Paris," for valuable studies of anticolonial protests at this time.

12. Despite the fact that the Service de Contrôle et d'Assistance en France des Indigènes des Colonies (CAI) discovered make-shift entrance tickets to the anti-

Exposition being sold for one franc apiece, there was very little publicity for the event. This lack of publicity was due to the fact that the PCF was not involved to any significant extent and not one official member of the PCF attended the exhibition. The unofficial figure for attendance was put at 5,000. See Lebovics 105–10.

13. The Group published a second anticolonial pamphlet in 1931, *Premier bilan de l'exposition coloniale.* See H. Lewis 95–96.

14. This document was written in partial response to another document, *Les Intellectuels aux côtés de la patrie,* published by the "intellectual establishment," expressing unequivocal support for the war.

15. See Lenin on imperialism.

16. The ideals behind France's *mission civilisatrice* were further tarnished by later revelations in the metropole of the infamous *indigenat* in the colonies, which set up a dual system of trial and punishment that gave the indigenous population little or no recourse to basic civil or human rights.

17. Many advertising images around the time of the Exposition combined the visual extremes of the modern and the primitive, seen in earlier images of Josephine Baker in the 1920s. Here, the juxtaposition of the "primitive" woman and the cigarette, symbol of affluence and European sophistication, suggested the productive relations that could be possible between the colonies and the metropole.

18. Between November 1919 and January 1920 thousands of people suspected of being Communists or Anarchists were arrested in the United States in what became known as the Palmer raids, after Woodrow Wilson's attorney general, A. Mitchell Palmer. Among those arrested were Jane Addams, social reformer, pacifist, and member of N.A.A.C.P.; as well as Emma Goldmann, a political activist who was deported to Russia after the Palmer raids.

CHAPTER 6

Diaspora and Resistance: A French Black Atlantic and Counterprimitivism

> [R]acism is perpetuated when blackness is associated solely with concrete gut level experience conceived as either opposing or having no connection to abstract thinking and the production of critical theory. The idea that there is no meaningful connection between black experience and critical thinking about aesthetics or culture must be continually interrogated.
>
> —bell hooks, *Yearning*

> Most histories of European aesthetic modernism leave out the massive infusions of non-European cultures to the metropolitan heartland during the early years of this century. . . .
>
> —Edward Said, *Culture and Imperialism*

INTRODUCTION

It is commonplace to read in literary histories of modernism that interwar Paris was a space of exile for writers and artists from Europe and the United States. From Hemingway, Stein, Joyce, and Beckett to Tzara, Janco, and Arp, Paris offered a particular set of expressive freedoms for the modernist innovator. The presence of African American and Caribbean writers and artists in Paris has tended to be a secondary narrative to this notion of modernist exile and one more focussed on a later phase, between 1945 and 1960, when writers such as Richard Wright, Chester Himes, and Gordon Parks made Paris their temporary home. Black cultural activity in the interwar era has been a much less explored area, limited in the main to studies of individual writers like Langston Hughes or Claude McKay. Recently, however, there has been a notable upsurge in critical attention to what has been dubbed Paris Noir and a more general consideration of the colonial and racial contexts of interwar Paris.[1] In general, though, while black cultural production in early twentieth-century France is now beginning to be narrated as the prehistories of negritude, it has not been considered as integral to the histories of modernism, even in studies that give race a central place in their critiques, as noted above by Edward Said. Consider Raymond Williams's characterisation of the modernist metropolis: "The most important general element of the innovations in form is the fact of immigration to the metropolis, and it cannot too often be emphasised how many of the major innovators were in this precise sense, immigrants" (*Politics* 45). If we consider a French-speaking black diaspora, a very particular historical and political diasporic formation, as part of this formula and conjoin it to existing modernist narratives of exile and innovation, then we have quite a different picture of the modernist metropolis. Said has talked of the "voyages in" of the colonised, or the "dissenting native," as examples of "hybrid cultural work" that was testament to an emergent "adversarial internationalization in an age of continuing imperial structures" (*Culture* 295).

These voyages in of the black diaspora occurred as a result of a handful of factors: the ex-soldiers from the colonies who had remained in France after the end of the war; the journeys of the colonial *évolués* to the mother country, and black Americans who left behind the oppressive conditions of their homeland. The writer Jessie Fauset described the black writer's dilemma thus: "I am colored and wish to be known as colored, but sometimes I have felt that my growth as a writer has been hampered by my own country" (*Paris Tribune* 1 Feb. 1925: n. pag.). To complete the discussion around the place of race in modernist aesthetics, we must take seriously the contribution of a transatlantic black diasporic presence in Paris and its construction of a counterprimitivism and a "new historical poetics of modernism as sustaining narrative of anti-colonial struggle" (Zavala 3). This was a delicate manoeuvre, as Kumkum Sangari points out: "Ironically, the 'liberating' possibilities of an international, oppositional, and revolutionary modernism came into being at a time when modernism was itself recuperating the cultural products of non-western countries largely within an aesthetics of the fragment" (182).

During the interwar years various black groups found the city space of Paris a fertile site for these discussions. Students from Guadeloupe, Martinique, Réunion, Senegal, Guyana, Indo-China, and Haiti were influenced in various ways by black Americans whom they had encountered in Paris and by the transnational crosspollination of intellectual ideas and political activism. These debates taking shape in the 1930s were not in themselves new but belonged to a tradition of diasporic political activism that had been occurring in Paris since the immediate postwar years. Since the end of the First World War, publications like *Le Paria*, official organ of the

Union Inter-Coloniale (begun in 1921), *Les Continents, Le Liberé, L'Action Coloniale* (1918), and *Le Messager Dahoméen* (1920) circulated in Paris and the colonies, albeit initially in sparse numbers. They represented the first attempts to address issues of exploitation and injustice in the French colonies. These publications and their attendant political affiliations were the predecessors of the later journals examined here: *La Dépêche Africaine, La Revue du Monde Noir,* and *Légitime Défense.* The three journals that I have chosen differed from earlier publications in that they devoted considerable space to the notion of the politics of cultural representation as well as to the political economy of colonialism.[2] The genealogy of influence from previous diasporic publications in the 1920s is clear: *La Revue du Monde Noir* emerged out of René Maran's moderate liberalism in *Les Continents* and *La Dépêche Africaine,* to which the Nardal sisters contributed. *Légitime Défense* developed the radical ideologies of earlier Communist-influenced, anti-assimilationist writing in *Le Cri des Nègres* and *La Race Nègre* into the cultural domain.[3] The journals point to the ways in which diasporic groups articulated new conceptions of racial and cultural *métissage,* which considered the importance of the colonised subject's presence in metropolitan space as much as in the colony—a distinction that has hitherto been overlooked. The journals had an energetic internationalist outlook, addressing the Harlem Renaissance and the New Negro movement of Alain Locke, French colonial policies and economics, indigenist and nationalist movements in the colonies, and the conditions of workers under French-owned colonial capital enterprises. This dynamic black Atlantic internationalism encompassed all points on the political spectrum and engendered a range of oppositional, anticolonialist activities.[4]

The founders of *La Revue du Monde Noir,* sisters Jane and Paulette Nardal, came to France in 1928 from a middle-class *mulâtre* background in Fort-de-France, Martinique. Their political formation was nurtured by the colonial policy of *assimilation,* characteristic of the majority of the *mulâtre* bourgeoisie on the island; they were amongst Martinique's élite *évolués* who had the opportunity to journey to France. On their arrival in Paris, they met René Maran, through whom they became involved in regular literary salons. Maran, also from Fort-de-France, had been active in the literary and political scene since the beginning of the 1920s and in 1921 his controversial preface to *Batouala* won the Prix Goncourt.[5] Although the rest of Maran's novel did not sustain this confrontational tone, it was nonetheless a significant moment of a literary *discours anti-colonialiste,* and its reception acted as an important point of cultural liaison between black French-speaking writers and those of the Harlem Renaissance. From 1923 to 1925, Maran and Alain Locke corresponded regularly and subsequent meetings between American, Antillian, and African writers and intellectuals established Paris as the centre of a vigorous black Atlanticism.[6]

In 1924 René Maran, along with Kojo Tovalou Houénou, founded the journal *Les Continents;* both had contributed to the earlier journal *L'Action Coloniale. Les Continents* was the publication of the Ligue universelle de défense de la race noire (LUDRN), run by Maran, Tovalou, Ouanilou Behanzon, and Sosthène Mortenol. The journal was the political and cultural forerunner of *La Revue du Monde Noir,* as it was one of the first diasporic publications to examine cultural issues. The remit for *Les Continents,* however, was not one of revolutionary anticolonialism, unlike that for Ho Chi Minh's publication *Le Paria,* which stated its radical political aims as an explicit denunciation of "les abus politiques, l'arbitraire admininistratif, l'exploitation économique dont sont les victimes les populations des vastes territoires d'outre-mer" (*Le Paria* 1 Apr. 1922 n. pag.).[7] *Les Continents* did not call for political independence from France; rather, it denounced specific colonial practices such as "l'indigenat" and "le travail forcé" within a larger framework that clearly admired the ideals of assimilation and France's Republican humanism. Advocating a consistent programme of political and cultural assimilation, both in the colonies and in the metropole, as a solution to the fermenting discontent of colonised subjects, *Les Continents* turned its attentions to a pragmatic notion of *assimilation* as a means of constructing colonial subjects who would be faithful to *la mère patrie* and its overarching humanist civilising mission, rather than to the political radicalism of communism or to the separatism of Garveyism. Maran duly noted these latter possibilities in the first edition: "Les races opprimées laissent sourdre leur mécontentement. Et ce mécontentement gagne. Et peut-être, grâce à la rapacité aveugle des races européenes, sommes-nous au seuil des guerres raciales" (*Les Continents* 1 Dec. 1924 n. pag.). Despite its diverse and rich selection of contributors, *Les Continents* was not destined to be a long-lived journal. It merged with *Le Liberé* in 1925 after a disastrous legal action taken by Blaise Diagne. It was not until 1928 that *La Dépêche Africaine* took up and elaborated upon the issues that *Les Continents* had begun to address.[8]

LA DÉPÊCHE AFRICAINE

La Dépêche Africaine, founded in 1928 by Maurice Satineau, espoused a politically moderate agenda that advocated the continuation of *assimilation* as a colonial policy. The political agenda of the paper was largely derived from the Comité de défense des intérêts de la race noire (CDRN), the paper's attendant political organisation, which had succeeded the LUDRN in 1926.[9] The CDRN promoted a moderate politics that distanced itself from the strongly Communist sympathies of the earlier LUDRN. In October 1927 a tract signed by Satineau as head of the CDRN and circulated in the colonies of A.O.F. (Afrique occidentale française) characterised the Comité's admiration for France's assimilationist project:

> Elle (la politique du Comité) tend à faire disparaître les préjugés de race, à combattre les injustices et les erreurs qui se commettent aux colonies et à rayonner le vrai visage de la France qui est fait d'équité, de justice, de bonté et d'amour. Elle s'inspire . . . des principes immortels de la glorieuse révolution française, selon les hommes naissent libres et égaux en droit. (Dossier du CDRN n.d n. pag.)

The implicit superiority of French culture and civilisation was unchallenged and remained uppermost in the journal's agenda, which reiterated the dominant ideological view that the colonies were an indispensable economic resource for France. The assumption here was that France needed its colonies in order to retain its position in the global imperium, and for their docility colonised subjects would eventually be rewarded by French citizenship or by material benefits for the territories themselves. However, under the policy rules of *assimilation,* the gift of French citizenship would be limited to those who had proved themselves capable of a transformative "évolution économique et sociale"; in other words, the acquisition of French identity was the reward for passivity and resignation to the colonial system.

Although the journal often offered a platform for a diverse range of political positions on empire, assimilation, and racial identity, its final political position was an accommodationist stance on French colonial rule and a qualified pragmatism towards the principles of *assimilation.* In his regular editorial, Maran set the political tone for the contributors with his careful condemnation of some unscrupulous colonial practices. However, he shied away from an outright denunciation of the ideological project of colonialism itself because he regarded France's colonial policies as humanistic in the tradition of 1789, in which empire enabled the global construction of a "plus large humanité." There was some admission of the weaknesses of "la tyrannie d'administration sans scrupules et sans conscience," but these were attributed to individual administrative failures rather than any political shortcomings of the *mission civilisatrice* per se (*DA* 1 Feb. 1928 n. pag.). Although *La Dépêche Africaine* took a moderate line on the legitimacy of colonialism itself, it was in the arena of cultural critique that its work broke new ground for diasporic cultural politics.

CONTESTING *LA VOGUE NÈGRE*

The first edition of *La Dépêche Africaine* clearly explains its goal of expanding the debates surrounding the meaning and significance of *la vogue nègre* that were up to now the exclusive domain of white intellectuals and artists: "Notre but est de faire connaître en Europe, l'évolution de la Race Noire, dans le domaine artistique" (*DA* 1 Feb. 1928: n. pag.). In an essay "Pantins Exotiques," Jane Nardal examines the fetishising narratives of *la vogue nègre* that were exploited to the full by writers such as Paul Morand

and Carl Van Vechten. Morand famously claimed at the height of the negrophile 1920s: "Le Nègre, c'est notre ombre," thus establishing a normative whiteness as the marker against which all other possibilities of cultural alterity were to be measured. Paulette Nardal notes that Morand's fiction, particularly *Magie Noire* (1928), represents the hyperbolic excesses of the primitivist vogue and argues that writers like Morand position themselves at the normative centre of the European *notre* against which the atavism of the black subject is perpetually fixed in debilitating cultural stereotypes. Earlier, the novel was severely criticised in *La Race Nègre* by Tiemoko Garan Kouyaté as an example of the European cultural ignorance about African societies that constructed a sensationalist fantasy of an imagined primitive subject: "Tous ces personnages sont repris par les instincts ataviques de la race nègre, incapable de progrès, et ne prisant que la force brutale" (*La Race Nègre* 3 1928 n. pag.). Nardal concurs with this critique but goes further by placing Morand's novel within a longer exoticist tradition in French literature. Citing as examples Victor Hugo, Alphonse de Lamartine, Jules Michelet, and Harriet Beecher Stowe's *Uncle Tom's Cabin*, she argues that *Magie Noire* was continuing a long tradition of white fascination with black culture. The primitive black subject is represented, she says, through two main literary metaphors. Either through the geographical topographies of blackness, which reverberate with a primeval eroticism in which "tout est vibrant et enflammé," or through an allegorical representation of the black body in which the exotic environment segues into the hyperbolic corporeality of blackness, "l'air, les coeurs, les corps" dissolve to construct the primitive/exotic subject (*DA* 1928 n. pag.). She calls this repertoire of racial stereotypes "la bôite des accessoires exotiques," which writers employ to create stock racial figures in their work (*DA* 1928 n. pag.). She succinctly explains the enduring popularity of the exotic novel in France, noting that the exotic, or primitive, black subject is constructed as pure essence for the white subject who wants to reclaim an innocence and wholeness from their metropolitan *ennui.* The novels of Morand and Van Vechten, in particular the latter's *Nigger Heaven,* are simplistic fabulations, she argues, that resound to the coda of "la puissance de l'atavisme des nègres," thrilling and repelling its white readers in equal measures while masking the desire for and fear of the black subject (*DA* 1928 n. pag.). Koyauté has similarly identified what he saw as the psychodrama underpinning white negrophilia: "Le parti pris dans la *Magie Noire* est tout bien considéré, M. Morand a horreur du Nègre" (*DA* 1928 n. pag.). Such a deeply concealed negrophobic disavowal articulated as a love of black culture results in a solipsistic narrative that speaks only of the white writer's own context while reducing the other to an all-purpose, self-reflexive metaphor. Koyauté and Nardal's analyses are the first published castigations of negrophilia by black writers in France and lay down important foundations for later writers. One can detect in these critiques some of Fanon's later, more astringent attacks on white negrophilia in *Peau noire, masques blancs*.

Significantly, both Koyauté and Nardal suggest that negrophile fiction is not to be confused with those texts that have black characters at their centre. Negrophile fiction effectively evacuates the text of any specific cultural dimension by rendering the black subject as a timelessly hypostasised figure who, despite living in Harlem or Paris or New Orleans, remains close to an ancient African past, untouched by modernity. Thus, nation, ethnicity, class, gender, and finally individual subjectivity become reduced to a homogenous primitivist fetished object. Nardal regards Morand's *Magie Noire* as the archetypal negrophile text; a fantasy of blackness that always turns the scrutinising gaze, putatively about black culture, back onto Europe itself as the only real subject of significance. Such cultural ignorance is hardly surprising given that the research Morand undertook for his novel was conspicuously removed from his subjects. Nardal reveals that he gained his knowledge of Africans from the ethnographic work of Lucien Lévy-Bruhl, in particular *La Mentalité primitive* (1922) and that he borrowed Alain Locke's depictions of African Americans from the *New Negro* (1925). For depictions of the French-speaking black characters, Nardal says, he visited *Le Bal Blomet* several times (*DA* 1928 n. pag.).

The complexity of the relations between the primitive and the modern is explored through the figure of Josephine Baker. Paulette Nardal describes her as the erotic and exotic figure par excellence for the modernist artist seeking a neat metaphor to express the affiliations and tensions between the modern and the primitive. Baker represents "le contraste savoureux, pimenté, d'êtres primitifs dans un cadre ultra-moderne de la frénésie africaine de déployant dans le décor cubiste d'une boîte de nuit" (*DA* 1928 n. pag.). It is significant, though, that Nardal, unlike Nancy Cunard in her denunciation of Baker, does not simply condemn the ways in which Baker participated in this commodified exoticisation of herself as a black woman. Rather, she notes that Baker, as an African American, offered the avant-garde "de neuves et truculents images" that, while still crudely primitivist, were less romanticised than those of Morand and Van Vechten:

> Mais Joséphine vint. . . . Voilà que bondit en scène une femme de couleur, aux cheveux laqués, à l'étincelant sourire; elle est bien encore vêtue de plumes ou de feuilles de bananes, mais elle apporte aux Parisiens les derniers produits de Broadway (Charleston, Jazz, etc). La transition entre le passé et le présent, la sourdure entre la forêt vierge et le modernisme, ce sont les noirs américains qui l'accomplissent et la rendent tangible. (*DA* 3 1928 n. pag.)

Here, Nardal recognises that Baker is perceived as the agent of a New World modernity, a presence to be acknowledged and celebrated in cultural history, and further that this agent is a black woman who has traditionally been assigned to the regions of an exotic but silent sexuality. But despite her admiration for Josephine Baker's success in France, Nardal is wary of an uncritical equation of *négrophilie* as an emancipatory political phenomenon. Blacks may be tolerated for the moment, she cautions, but their tenuous position in white society, especially in France and in America, remains one of a subject "destinée à servir à l'amusement" (n. pag.). Thus, despite the potential liberatory effects of *négrophilie,* intellectual and political activity by black diasporic groups in France continues to be strongly marginalised, as this would, Nardal says, "dérange le plan de la nature" (n. pag.). *Négrophilie* restricts black identity to a decorative function, fulfilling "le plaisir esthétique" of the fascinated white gaze. She remarks that despite the abundance of negrophile novels and the enthusiasm for *l'art nègre* and bals *nègres,* there has been less interest in real knowledge of the black subject than in that of a white metropolitan subject who desires to be "assimilé au nègre" in a complicated process of attraction and repulsion (n. pag.). Concluding her discussion of *la vogue nègre* on an optimistic note, she remarks upon the possibilities for future cultural projects that may develop this negrophile interest into a more realistic and less sensational depiction of what it means to be black in the modern world. She calls for white writers to take up this humanist challenge: "Nous attendrons pour cela que quelque Européen attribue au nègre 'littéraire' quelques qualités plus intérieures" (n. pag.). She concludes by calling for a psychological portrait of the black subject ("vu de dedans") who can be allowed to properly enter into human relations (n. pag.).

Responding to the challenge of countering the exoticising excesses of *négrophilie* and constructing new forums for black cultural and intellectual activity, the Nardal sisters were regular contributors to *La Dépêche Africaine,* commenting on a range of cultural issues involving diasporic cultural activities in Paris. For instance, in the August–September 1930 edition, Paulette Nardal reports on the sculpture of the black American artist Augusta Savage, who was all but ignored by the white establishment. In the May 1929 issue of *La Dépêche Africaine,* she writes about a small back-street nightclub in a black working-class area of Paris, La Glacière Boul in Rue Auguste-Blanqui, where people from Martinique, Réunion, and Guadeloupe congregate each weekend to avoid the voyeuristic attention of white negrophiles. The Nardals' remit is to promote the activities of black internationalism, with a particular focus on the ways in which cultural crossovers took place between the colonies and the metropole and on how the idea of racial and cultural *métissage* functioned within this international scene.

In an article entitled "L'internationalisme noir" (*DA* Feb. 1928), Jane Nardal outlines her conception of an inclusive diasporic black identity that deploys a strategic essentialism in order to unite ethnic diversity and mobilise black creativity. This notion of black internationalism would form the basis of much of the work in the later journal *La Revue du Monde Noir.* In this keynote article, Nardal asserts, "Des Noirs de toutes origines, de nationalités, de moeurs, de réligions différentes sentent vaguement qu'ils appartiennent malgré tout à une seule et même race" (n. pag.). A new conceptualisation of ethnicity is clearly emergent here as she works through the ways in which the empirical category of race is no longer an adequate description of the multiple ways in which the modern subject is shaped. Crucially, in this article she also begins to theorise the relationships between metropole and colony, rather than simply between coloniser and colonised. Nardal uses the term *afro-latin* for the first time here, a term that will later catalyse a number of cultural dialogues in *La Revue du Monde Noir* around the complexities of hybridised cultural ethnic identity: "Etre Afro-américain, être Afro-latin, cela veut dire être un encouragement, un réconfort, un exemple pour les Noirs d'Afrique en leur montrant que certains bienfaits de la civilisation blanche ne conduisent pas forcément à renier sa race" (n. pag.). What is posited here is the notion of both racial and cultural *métissage* that stands, at this time, in direct opposition to the empirical positivism of racial science and to the essentialist Africanism of Garveyism.

The Nardals' work attempts to complicate some of the oversimplifications of the negrophile contributors, such as Paul Guillaume and Roger Blin. Guillaume's valorisation of attributes of *l'art nègre* is predicated upon an unreconstructed primitivism that posits the concept of *le nègre* as an a priori negation of Western Enlightenment and Cartesian rationalism (*DA* Feb. 1928: n. pag.). Similarly, in his article "Le scandal du village Canaque," Roger Blin's discovery of the fraud enacted by the organisers of the Exposition Coloniale illustrates the kind of narrow categories of identity permitted to the native subject who, despite the genuine intentions of certain liberal negrophiles like Blin himself, is compelled to demonstrate an authentic racial identity (*DA* Feb. 1928 n. pag.).[10] Jane Nardal's writing on *métissage* in "L'internationalisme noir" argues for a conceptualisation of identity that acknowledges the cultural and political contingencies of individual diasporic identities. Many colonised Francophone subjects straddle two worlds: "L'amour du pays latin, pays d'adoption, et celui de l'Afrique, le pays de leurs ançêtres, ne sont pas incompatibles. L'esprit nègre, si souple, si capable d'assimilation, si subtil, surmontera aisément cette apparente difficulté" (n. pag.). This bifurcated identity formation of *le français du couleur* can function, she argues, as a foundation towards a more collective definition of the term *nègre.* This foreshadows the postcolonial critique of Edouard Glissant's notion of a Caribbean mythopoetics in *Poétique de la Relation* (1990), in which he argues for a less "finished," more fluid Deleuzian definition of identity.

LA REVUE DU MONDE NOIR: "UNE VITRINE DES ARTS NÈGRES"

It has become commonplace to read in anthologies such as Lilyan Kesteloot's *Les Ecrivains noirs de langue française* that *La Dépêche Africaine* paved the way for the later theories of negritude. However, this rush to privilege negritude has tended to occlude the significance of the small publications by diasporic groups in Paris. One of the most influential but short-lived of these journals was *La Revue du Monde Noir,* which went on to develop many of the intellectual concerns begun in *La Dépêche Africaine.* In 1931 Paulette Nardal and Doctor Léo Sajous founded the monthly bilingual journal. Although it would last only six issues, from October 1931 to April 1932, its presence was a significant force in debates taking place amongst black intellectuals and writers in Paris at the beginning of the 1930s. The bilingual format of the journal—all articles and poetry were presented in both French and English—was testament to the cultural internationalism to which the review aspired, specifically to the Franco-American relations that had been established in the previous decade between Harlem and Paris. Philippe Dewitte has suggested that the sisters attempted to import Alain Locke's ideas from the American New Negro movement to a French contest (222). The Nardals' work was central to the expression of this new internationalist racial consciousness that was open to political influences outside the French Empire and to developing cultural dialogues borne out of an already fecund political activism. (Dewitte 263).

It is difficult, however, to define precisely the political alignment of *La Revue du Monde Noir,* unlike that of *Légitime Défense,* which opened by attacking the complacency of "la bourgeoisie de couleur française" in the name of the Communist Third International and revolutionary Marxism (*LD* 34). For the most part, *La Revue du Monde Noir* did not challenge the fundamental legitimacy of colonialism or *assimilation,* continuing the moderate political agendas of *La Dépêche Africaine* and *Les Continents.* The political remit of the review was concerned less with challenging colonial authority than with establishing a position from which the previously silent colonised subject could articulate her own experiences as a racialised subject in the metropole. *Assimilation* would eventually lead to the establishment of a collective notion of black identity, which would in turn result in a degree of cultural autonomy within a liberal and democratic political tradition.[11] The October edition explained the internationalist aims of the review: "To create among the Negroes of the entire world, regardless of nationality, an intellectual and moral tie, which will permit them to better know each other, to love one another, to defend more effectively their collective interests and to glorify their race." The ideals that would secure this were those of "paix, le travail, et la justice," "la liberté, l'égalité et la fraternité" acting in unison to found "une grande démocratie" (1 Oct. 4). However, these laudable aims were struggling in the context of a resurgence of some pernicious ideas about race and biology that were gaining ground amongst more conservative sections of the scientific community in France. *La Revue du Monde Noir* addressed the specific historical contexts of metropolitan France at the beginning of the 1930s, a time when the idea of race was increasingly deployed in the service of a radical conservatism and its attendant xenophobic social policies. This creeping xenophobia spoke to a wider cultural and economic anxiety, what Pierre Laborie has described as the "logique de l'immobilisme, de l'inertie, de la routine, de la défensive" (157).

SCIENCE, RACE, AND RACISM

In "The Equality of Races" (*RMN* 2 Nov. 1931), Jean Louis Finot asserts that France cannot consider itself immune to the economic crisis that had just devastated the United States and Britain.[12] Economic ruin may lead to a more exclusive definition of the French race and nurse a xenophobic cultural nationalism:

> Let us smile at those misinformed individuals who talk of the French "race." France is indeed a superior nation and we are justly very proud of her, but we must admit that she is the product of a peaceful fusion of kindred spirits from different races which not only form the basis of her composition but change her aspect from one day to another. (5)

The glorification of French culture and civilisation is achieved by a narrowly patriotic chauvinism that refuses the idea of cultural diversity for fear of disturbing racial purity and racial degeneration. Significantly, Finot does not name the "misinformed individuals," but the implication is that they are the physical anthropologists and other racial "scientists," such as Dr Papillaut, also mentioned in Georges Gregory's essay "Un Aperçu du Ve Congrès International d'Archéologie préhistorique et d'Anthropologie." Both articles work from the assumption that the nation is on the brink of a crisis that extends beyond that of the purely economic. Although the spectre of degeneration, both racial and moral, has been present in political discourse since the early nineteenth century, the specific socioeconomic conditions of the early 1930s have provided fertile ground for a revival of old debates. The wrangles over national identity have provided a forum for the reemergence of older anthropological traditions "empreinte des tares du gobinisme" and eugenic science (*RMN* 2 Nov. 1931 10–13).[13]

Elsewhere in this issue, Georges Gregory cites the example of a paper given by Dr Papillaut, "Comment une Métropole peut devenir une Colonie de Peuplement," clearly underwritten by debates around racial degeneration and *métissage* (*RMN* 2 Nov. 1931 n. pag.). Papillaut suggests that *métis* are inherently unstable as individuals because they are the products of doubled racial origins. The suggestion is that this is an impurity that may result in insanity or violence, and as such, mixed-race people should not be considered suitable candidates for immigration. The insistence here is on physiological racial differences of skin colour, head shape, posture, and hair texture (32), and they are consonant with the findings of the new racial science, informed by the theories of Georges Montandon writing in the *Revue Anthropologique,* under the directorship of Louis Marin. *La Revue du Monde Noir* gives considerable space to writers challenging the inconsistencies of these theories in order to debunk the very foundations of such a scientifically spurious logic: "[N]o true scientist, without a preconceived opinion respecting scientific laws, could reasonably maintain that it is possible to establish a psychological identity for nearly two hundred million Negroes scattered throughout the world" (34).

Both E. Grégoire-Micheli and Georges Gregory systematically refute the ways in which such spurious theories homogenise all cultural, religious, and ethnic diversities into a single category of racial other. Specifically, Gregory identifies how the category of race has been overstated in support of these arguments: "L'idée des races qui est de nature à fausser touts les recherches, quand on lui donne une place trop importante" (32). Elsewhere, Finot similarly acknowledges the urgency of disproving scientific racism, presciently, warning: "The world is the crucial point concerning the realisation of future pacifism. If a strong desire of alliance is not immediately manifested among its constituents, it will dash headlong into an abyss in which civilisation will be submerged" (7). In his article "La mentalité des noirs est-elle inférieure?" Grégoire-Micheli summarises Gobineau's racial theories (known as Gobinisme) and its spurious racial typologies. He constructs his discussion by outlining the modern history of scientific racism, namely the developments in craniology that sought to explain race by measuring firstly skull sizes and then sizes and weights of the brain (29). In fact, by the time Grégoire-Micheli is writing, the scientific focus has shifted from craniology to serology and the theories of René Martial.[14] The evident shortcomings of empirical measurement as a way of theorising difference are regarded by Grégoire-Micheli as an example of the ideological utilitarianism that such science can be made to serve; in other words, race becomes an ever-expanding signifier that can articulate domestic political crises. Grégoire-Micheli argues that biologist theories of race cannot be taken seriously as they fail to take into account human diversity and "la diversité des psychologies individuales chez les peuples les plus étrangers à nos modes de penser" (33). The powerful or threatened group will invoke these empirical facts at the point of crisis: "Chaque peuple blanc les a accommodées aux besoin de sa politique" (20). This is an obvious point perhaps, but an important reminder of the fact that the notion of racial hierarchy and classification, first developed by George-Louis Leclerc de Buffon in *Histoire naturelle, générale et particulière* (1749), persisted even amongst liberal social scientists like Lévy-Bruhl and Leo Frobenius, who attempted to reinscribe the hierarchies in order to valorise the cultural achievements of African civilisations.[15] The spurious conclusions of craniology, serology, and medical bioethics, the theories of which were extrapolated to entire nations of people, are taken to task by Grégoire-Micheli, who points out their wilful disregard of temporal, geographical, or cultural considerations:

> Pour les peuples noirs, commes pour les peuples blancs, joue la loi de sociologie qui veut que les sentiments et les idées des individus subissent l'influence des conditions sociales dans lesquelles ils vivent. De sorte que ces sentiments et ces idées se modifient, se compliquer, s'étendent ou se restreignent en dedace parfaite avec les variations des conditions sociales qu'ils engendrées. (22)

Concluding his scathing attack on physical anthropology, he describes its ideological utilitarianism: "L'anthropologie, non comme une science vraie, mais comme un moyen de trouver des excuses pour organiser la société, non pas aux mieux intérêts et des besoins de tous les humains, mais uniquement pour le profit des hommes de la race blanche" (21).[16]

POLITICS AND RACE

Philippe de Zara's essay "L'éveil du monde noir" analyses the paradoxical situation in which black writers and intellectuals find themselves after they have made the voyage in to the metropole. Referring to the aftermath of the Exposition Coloniale Internationale, Zara notes that the event created a "très curieuse manifestation intellectuelle" for black intellectuals in Paris (*RMN* 3 Jan. 1932 1). Due to the Exposition's lingering aftereffects, black subjects are once again the focus of white interest, but again circumscribed as fetishised objects of cultural curiosity and prurient fascination rather than as subjects with political and intellectual agency. Echoing the work of Jane and Paulette Nardal, Zara asserts that despite the fact that "la capitale a toujours eu un faible pour les enfants de Cham," there has been a strong tendency to construct "le nègre" in its own image, even in the name of a liberal négrophilie (1). Referring specifically to both the extreme Right in the case of eugenics and cultural conservatism and to the radical Left—primarily the Leninism of the Third International—who viewed the space of a precapitalist continent oppressed by the imperial powers as ripe for revolutionary communism, Zara warns against using the category of the primitive as a politically expedient currency. Either way, for the political Right or Left, he argues, this is not far from the typologies of Gobineau: "Comme si une race aussi variée dans son évolution sociale pouvait être classée tout entière dans un parti électoral

. . . là est le danger: enlever aux hommes de couleur noire leur valeur humaine, authentique et remarquable, pour en faire l'instrument de mesquines politiques" (3).

According to Zara, this instrumental deployment of race and difference into ideological currency has a long tradition in Western political discourses. Recognising this as a variation of Orientalism, he notes that since the discovery of Africa and Asia by Europeans, the continents have been typified in two distinct racialised discourses that have labelled the great unknown geographies of the black and the yellow man (3). Where Asia retains the enigma of "le monde jaune" and "le secret d'un race mature," Africa, he says, has been constructed as an intellectual tabula rasa where the malleable space of sub-Saharan Africa (not the orientalised North) has been constructed to accommodate the ideological aspirations, benevolent or otherwise, of centuries of explorers, anthropologists, colonists, and missionaries who have writ their message large upon the land and the people (2). The danger now, warns Zara, is of a continued political manipulation of the black subject, more nuanced and subtle perhaps in the case of the Exposition but nevertheless dependent on theories of difference that are shaped by domestic ideological requisites (2).

In conclusion, Zara makes a crucial point for the review as a whole. He refutes the efficacy of a large-scale assimilationist policy for France's empire in its entirety when he states that the policy can be reduced to "une thèse ici, se vérifie incomplètement là-bas" (2). Thus, he acknowledges the crucial discrepancies between ideas generated in the metropolitan centre by a centralised colonial administration and the feasibility of those ideas as they are transformed into practical projects in the colonies. Here, then, the stark dissonance between political idealism and administrative pragmatism is unambiguously attacked. Crucially, Zara implies that the recognition of this geopolitical discrepancy is an important consideration for metropolitan anticolonial activities that need to fully comprehend the specific nature of individual colonies and the degrees to which their populations have been assimilated into French culture. In a clear statement of his position, he concludes, "Sans prétendre le moins du monde latiniser le continent noir, pouvons-nous du moins souhaiter d'heureux contacts entre deux vastes fragments d'humanité" (4). These "heureux contacts" produce what the review describes as "l'éveil du monde noir," a political and cultural movement influenced by the renaissance in the black American scene but developed now for the specific contexts of colonial France (4).

L'ÂME NÈGRE

In her article "Éveil de la conscience de la race" (*RMN* 6 Apr. 1932), Paulette Nardal resumes the discussion of diasporic cultures and *métissage* begun in *La Dépêche Africaine*. Race consciousness, she says, is manifested in ways that are not uniformly distributed across the colonies. For instance, the differences in "la conscience de race" between black Americans and Antillians are directly related to the diverse ways in which each group has experienced the dislocations and diasporas of slavery and colonialism (25). Crucially, she also observes that there are great differences in class formations across racial lines between the United States and the Antilles, thus acknowledging the important distinctions between diverse diasporic experiences. These distinctions are expressly refused by the less subtle essentialism of Marcus Garvey's Back to Africa campaign and by some of the writing in the *Negro* anthology that neglects the difficult complexities of internal differences in diasporic cultures and societies.[17] This acknowledgement is significant, as both *La Revue du Monde Noir* and *Légitime Défense* were being produced in Paris by diasporic groups who had left their island communities for the metropole as part of an established trajectory of a highly assimilated élite group, a movement clearly not the equivalent of black American diasporic experiences, which were profoundly marked by both initial dislocation from Africa to the Caribbean and the subsequent horrors of slavery in the diasporic space. Unlike the sustained fury of the contributors in *Légitime Défense,* Nardal's writing does not balk at the diversity of diasporic conditions; rather, she reads the routes of diaspora as part of a reciprocal, if unequal, process of cultural exchange between metropole and colony that produces a gradual metropolinisation of the colonised subject:

> Cependant, la conscience de race s'était éveillée chez certains Antillais, mais il leur avait fallu pour cela, s'éloigner de leur petite patrie. Le déracinement qu'ils ressentirent dans la métropole où le noir n'a pas toujours joui de la considération qu'on semble lui témoigner depuis L'Exposition Coloniale, leur avait fait, en dépit de leur formation, une âme nègre. Pourtant cet état d'âme ne s'éxtériorisait pas. (25)

This statement, which posits the idea of *une âme nègre,* is a crucial one. What actually constitutes this "black soul" will of course become contested ground in later negritudist debates around diaspora, race, and cultural nationalism. Here, Nardal suggests that the immediate social and economic environments, in particular the metropolitan spaces, are crucial determinants of *l'âme nègre,* however fictitious that construct may actually be. What is most striking about this piece is the way in which she distinguishes between white attitudes towards black people in the urban centres of both America and France. In general, the idea that the French attitude towards racial matters is one of tolerant liberalism is reinforced here and contrasted with the American scene, where, as Nardal points out, the extreme polarisation between black and white is born out of the absence of a Republican assimilationist principle that is inevitably bound up with ideas of empire (27). As proof of her thesis, she cites a work by a writer called Sieburg, "Dieu est-il français?" which asserts that racial tolerance in France is entirely based on the principle that anyone can be assimilated into French culture: "l'absence du préjugé du couleur chez les français provoient de leur certitude de faire du Noir, en un temps relativement court, un vrai français" (26). Racial tolerance, or "une amicale bienveillance," is, as Philippe de Zara has pointed out, a "précieux don latin" that, Nardal argues, stands in direct contrast to the bigotry of "White America," which has compelled the black population to forge individual and collective identities in the midst of brutalising hatred and physical segregation (27). As a result, the black American is more race conscious than the average black French subject. Here, she clearly identifies the two oppositional positions in the postslavery United States, that of the moderate liberalism of DuBois versus the essentialism of separatist movements like Garveyism (27). In contrast, the French *sujet de couleur* is not compelled to choose between two extreme responses, as their oppression is tempered by the enlightened principles of *assimilation*.[18] However, it is important to note here that this appraisal of French republicanism is a particularly Antillian point of view, a fact observed by Dewitte: "Il est pourtant frappant de constater à quel point le discours racial domine l'Europe de l'époque a déteint sur les Antillais à Paris" (258).

Jane Nardal's notion of *afro-latinité,* first expounded in *La Dépêche Africaine,* is developed in *La Revue du Monde Noir* into a more complex notion of a *métis* cross-cultural metropolitan subject. Other contributors to the journal, such as Jean Louis Finot, theorise this hybridised creole subject as the ideal combination of the African and the Latin:

> Génie turbulent indépendant et soldatesque d'une part, génie raffiné, amateur des choses de l'esprit, d'autre part, tels sont les traits du caractère créole. Ajouter à cela l'apport de la Race Africaine, tumulteuse elle aussi, et mystique, l'on verra nettement que les deux éléments sociaux qui ont formé la race créole se sont complètes et unifiés puisqu'ils étaient en effet, la française est celle qui a le plus de similitudes, ou d'affinité, avec la génie de la race noire." (2 Nov. 1931 8)

Clearly this view of the construction of the racialised subject shares similarities with the crude essentialism of *négrophilie.* In *négrophilie* the taxonomic binaries of Gobinisme are reinscribed in order to valorise and empower the black subject, a position reinforced by Louis Achille in an article entitled "L'art et les Noirs." Achille proclaims that "le Nègre a L'art dans le sang" and "un instinct artistique, exigeant pour le corps autant que pour l'âme une satisfaction urgente et fréquente" (*RMN* 2 Nov. 1931 1). *La Revue du Monde Noir* gives space to a strategic essentialism that in turn paves the way for the debates around political and cultural agency in the negritude movement in which black subjects become progenitors of their own intellectual and cultural history.

RACE AND GENDER

In much of her work in *La Revue du Monde Noir,* Paulette Nardal traces the literal and symbolic journeys from island colony to metropolitan centre and, along the way, considers the particular circumstances of a gendered and racialised subject. She argues that black women have hitherto been excluded or disregarded in the master narratives of anticolonialism, in which a male heterosexual racialised subject has been assumed to be the normative position of enunciation. Although the attention paid to gender is limited to a single article by Paulette Nardal, this is a crucially important intervention into debates previously dominated by male voices. Nardal's work in the review addresses gender issues through a reading of a short story by Roberto Horth, "Histoire Sans Importance," in which the protagonist of the text is a young mulatto woman who has come to Paris as part of her acculturation into French metropolitan life (*RMN* 2 Dec. 1931). Although she faces the visit with great anticipation and excitement, the reality is that despite encountering little explicit racial discrimination, she gradually becomes aware that her popularity in the salons is that of "une poupée" (49). She remarks that she is exhibited like a charming fetish at fashionable Parisian *soirées* and the reception that she receives renders her as a purely symbolic exotic object, "un fruit étrange que l'on est flatté d'avoir découvert" (50); a position that is little more than decorative and one that systematically excludes her from easy social relations with her white contemporaries.[19] The tone of the story is not confrontational but contemplative and it narrates the slow Fanon-esque dawning of the racialised corporeal schema on the young woman. The sense of her *métis* identity circumscribes all social and sexual relations: "elle ne sera jamais dans ce pays comme toute les autres femmes ayant le droit à un bonheur de femme" (50); thus, her gender identity and sexuality are subsumed by the ways in which external racial signifiers are the overdetermining factors. Nardal later claims that this exoticisation of black women in negrophile Paris also operates to a certain extent amongst mixed-race men who persistently refuse to acknowledge the ways in which gender inflects racial identity and class position among diasporic groups. The writer Jessie Fauset has talked of the implicit restrictions imposed on black women in public space: "[I]n order to offset criticism, the refined colored woman must not laugh too loudly, she must not stare—in general she must stiffen her self-control even though she can no longer humanly contain herself" (*Paris Tribune* 1 Feb. 1923 n. pag.). Nardal concurs with this and cites the "refined colored women's" dilemma in the tight circles of diasporic communities in Paris where male writers and artists inevitably demand and receive more attention than their female counterparts (27).[20]

Nardal narrates the racial awakening of the mulatto woman as a process of at first fierce anger and resentment at her treatment not just by white society but also by her male peers, but this is gradually replaced by a more positive sense of "solidarité raciale" directed towards an emancipatory project of self-discovery (*RMN* 6 Apr. 1932 27). In the final issue of the review, she writes, in "Éveil de la conscience de Race," about the small but growing number of back women in French universities studying writers who address notions of belonging, exclusion, and racial identity. Nardal argues that black women must investigate their own histories in an effort to counter their absurd exoticisation in the metropole, which objectifies them as subjects without agency or voice (27). She cites the example of Grace Walker, the first black woman to give a lecture at Cambridge on African American literature and the works of Countee Cullen, Jean Toomer, Claude McKay, and Langston Hughes in particular (36).[21] Both Nardal sisters acknowledge that the wave of primitivism in interwar Paris has severely circumscribed the available roles for black women to the exotic performative ones of Josephine Baker.[22] However, Nardal argues that black women should not be despondent about this situation as they can find some empowerment in the fact that they occupy the "juste milieu" of contemporary cultural studies on race and gender (30).

The Nardals' work attempted to give a language to the construction of a metropolitan racial identity, both individual and collective, based on the diversity of the diasporic experience and the different oppressions black women encountered both from white negrophiles and from their black male contemporaries. Significantly, however, the Nardals do not prematurely celebrate this kind of hybridity as an optimal space of political agency; rather, they consider it more pragmatically as the inevitable result of *assimilation* and the ongoing process of cross-cultural exchange that operated both positively and negatively for diasporic communities in France.

LÉGITIME DÉFENSE (1932)

In the final issue of *La Revue du Monde Noir,* Paulette Nardal cautiously casts a curious eye on the next generation of Caribbean poets and writers who are no longer satisfied either aesthetically or politically with the polite challenges of their elders:

> Il est à remarquer qu'un certain nombre de nos jeunes amis semble être arrivé spontanément à la dernière phase que nous avons noté dans l'évolution intellectuelle des Noirs américains. S'ils continuent à traiter des sujets occidentaux, c'est aujourd'hui dans une forme extrêmement moderne et ils s'essaient en même temps à mettre en valeur des thèmes raciaux caractéristiques ainsi que nos lecteurs pourront le constater dans une séries de très curieux poèmes que nous allons bientôt publier. (n. pag.)

These "curious poems" will be printed in *Légitime Défense* (1932), a "petite revue incendiaire" that lasted only one issue but that nevertheless made a dramatic impact on the course of black cultural expression in general and on negritude in particular. There has been a great deal written about *Légitime Défense* and its influence on negritude, and in particular about its influence on Léopold Senghor and Aimé Césaire's journal, *L'Étudiant Noir,* which "developed negritude's philosophical foundations of black cultural difference and new cultural orientations towards France" (Lambert 249). The genealogy of influence is undeniable, but we should be wary of assigning *Légitime Défense* an overprivileged place in black intellectual history as the singular catalyst for a new black diasporic consciousness.[23] Rather, *Légitime Défense* is part of a wider trajectory of metropolitan diasporic activities, begun with radical labour journals such as *Le Cri des Nègres* and *La Race Nègre,* cultural reviews like *La Dépêche Africaine* and *La Revue du Monde Noir,* and the works of writers like Marius and Ary Leblond in *Monde Colonial Illustré* (1935). In an internationalist, anticolonial context, the journal reiterates the debates of the Haitian *indigènistes* movement after the American invasion of 1915, as narrated in Jean Price Mars's *Ainsi Parla L'Oncle* (1928) and in the journals *Les Griots* and *La Revue indigène.*[24] Considerable critical space has been devoted to *Légitime Défense* since its publication in 1932, not least because of the reaction of the French authorities to its radical political stance on colonialism, which resulted in the student writers being relieved of their state bursaries to study in Paris. I shall give less consideration to the journal's cultural and political impact on anticolonial movements since this has already been well documented in literary and cultural histories of Francophonie and African independence and nationalism.[25] Here, I consider only a selection of pieces from the journal that elaborate upon issues that both *La Revue du Monde Noir* and *La Dépêche Africaine* began to mobilise earlier; in particular a critique of *assimilation,* both as a colonial policy and as a disabling form of cultural hegemony in the Antilles.

Légitime Défense is well known for its rejection of cultural assimilation through a radical political agenda espousing the Marxism of the Communist Third International, Surrealism, and Freudian psychoanalysis, taking in the Marquis de Sade, Hegel, Rimbaud, and Mallarmé en route, in its attack on the "bourgeoisie de couleur franchises" in the Antilles (2). The journal addresses similar issues to those of its predecessors but does so in a unified polemic made explicit in the opening "Avertissement." The privileged position of *Légitime Défense* in black cultural history is due, in part, to its affiliations with the particular aesthetics of the avant-garde or, more precisely, with the aestheticised politics of the moment. However, the wholesale espousal of Communist politics and the coruscating attacks on the black bourgeoisie glosses the enormous tensions and difficulties that existed at this time between Surrealism and communism; to read

Légitime Défense uncritically would be to accept that the relations between revolutionary communism and Surrealism were harmonious, productive, and entirely coincident with the larger struggle of an oppressed colonised proletariat. This, however, is far from the true realpolitik and the remonstrations of the journal do not fully acknowledge the complexities of the contemporary historical moment or the messy political struggles that led up to the formation of this political and aesthetic alliance. The fact that the young writers chose Surrealism as an aesthetic vehicle for its anticolonial polemics lent the work a contemporary metropolitan resonance, linking it with the emergent negritudism of *L'Etudiant Noir*. What remains striking about *Légitime Défense* are the ways in which the writers unify complex issues of culture, *métissage*, and metropolitan diasporic identities into a singular unifying polemic. In the opening "Avertissement," readers are warned of this polemic and the editors even go so far as to apologise for the negativity of the journal's tone (2). However, the writers are willing to accept this negativity as they regard the Third International as the only political organisation that explicitly denounces colonial abuses (1).

In the opening piece the political agenda is made explicit. According to the collective of *Légitime Défense*, Third International communism and its programmatic dialectical materialism offer the possibility of dismantling bourgeois conventions and the privileged unit of the nuclear family. As noted above, the writers preface the entire text with an apology for the negative tone of the text, but they argue that it is entirely necessary in order to present a legitimate case against imperial capitalism. Accordingly, an inventory of oppressive capitalist structures and institutions is systematically demolished, culminating in an impassioned and scathing denunciation of the black bourgeoisie who travel to Paris as part of the inevitable assimilationist trajectory from colony to centre: "[N]ous addressons à ceux qui ne sont pas encore tués placés foutus universitaires réussis décorés pourris purvus décoratifs pudibonds opportunistes marqués . . . " (2). The sense of frustrated contradiction around the colonial policy of *assimilation* is palpable in these opening pages, in which the writers acknowledge their own emancipated position of metropolitan locution, one that is inevitably bound up with a particular class formation in the Antilles. Simultaneously, they attack the structures that put those class and race divisions into the colonies in the first place, an argument that points up the inherently paradoxical nature of the processes of *assimilation* and reveals the intrinsic double bind of colonial ideology.[26]

With the exception of Etienne and Thélus Léro, the contributors to *Légitime Défense*, René Ménil, Jules-Marcel Monnerot, Michel Pilotin, Maurice-Sabas Quitman, Auguste Thésée, and Pierre Yoyotte, have originated from the *mulâtre* bourgeoisie in the Antilles and have all come to Paris to pursue courses of higher education in prestigious French academic institutions. The writers attempt to address their own privileged position of enunciation from within an elite mixed-race class, refusing to shy away from the fact that they themselves are implicated in "ce monde capitaliste, chrétien, bourgeois," but nevertheless urging their readers to imagine the possibility of a class based revolution. However, the possibility of a black proletarian audience for the journal's revolutionary message is immediately discounted as they have been denied the means of comprehension of this kind of revolution by the capitalist system that oppresses them and refuses them viable political alternatives. In fact, the imagined audience for *Légitime Défense* is a highly specific one; the writers address their plea for enlightenment against "l'hypocrysie humanitaire" that has produced massive inequalities in European civilisation to the children of "la bourgeoisie noire" (2).

In contrast to *La Revue du Monde Noir* and *La Dépêche Africaine*, the notion of cultural assimilation is unequivocally rejected in *Légitime Défense*. The journal's attack on the policy of *assimilation* uses Martinique as the exemplary metonymic space representative of wider colonial practices where the discrepancies between the theories and practice of *assimilation* are played out. The island's unique historical position within the French Empire has produced a clearly defined middle class and mixed-race élite. In an ironically entitled article, "Paradis Sur Terre," a scathing reference to ways in which the island has been (and continues to be) represented as a tropical playground for European tourists, Maurice Sabas-Quitman dissects the French *mission civilisatrice* in Martinique by contrasting the situations of the impoverished majority of exploited workers, "la masse est vite prise dans les longs et pénibles travaux de rhum nécessaire à l'Europe," with the elite position of the *assimilés* (9). The majority of the island's population are, he argues, functionally illiterate and, as they begin work at the age of six or eight years old, have no opportunity of equality with the small group of islanders, mostly Creole, who benefit from "la culture intellectuelle" of France's highly selective civilising mission. Quitman identifies the limitations of cultural assimilation as a metropolitan rhetorical device that demands "qu'elle ne civilise trop"; for instance, schools are built by the French authorities, but the mass of the labouring population cannot afford to send their children to these schools because their wages are desperately needed for their families (6). In contrast, the elite *assimilés* from Martinique are sent to France to learn the lessons of French culture but remain as racial outsiders in the metropole, where the final goal is to maintain an invisibility: "ne pas se faire remarquer" (4), a situation depicted in Jules Monnerot's article "Note Touchant la bourgeoisis de couleur française." To blend into the mass of the population as undifferentiated subjects, to become a "maigre imitation" of the coloniser, and at all costs to avoid the charges of "faire comme un nègre" (10)—this invisible mimicry is the final goal of the properly assimilated racial subject, a subject that the writers in *Légitime Défense* take to task through their critique of cultural production in Martiniquean poetry.[27]

POETRY AND MIMICRY

In "Misère d'une Poésie," Etienne Léro argues that the production of culture in the Antilles reverberates with the unequal power relations of colonialism, a situation most evident in the uneasy mimicry of its most celebrated poets in which "Le charactère exceptionnel de médiocrité de la poésie antillaise est donc nettement lié à l'ordre sociale existant" (10). In his scathing indictment of Antillian poets, particularly Gilbert Gratiant and Henri Flavia-Léopold, Léro explicates the relationships between cultural production and consumption and social and economic relations in a society profoundly divided by both race and class. The imagined geopolitical spaces of *la vieille France* are repeatedly invoked in the work of both Flavia-Léopold and Gratiant, as each poet refuses to confront the material realities of labour and language in the Antilles through a construction of the 1789 Republican spirit and classical literary humanism (11). Specifically, Léro takes one of Gratiant's poems, "Poèmes en vers faux," as emblematic of the historically myopic voices of the assimilationist poets whose sycophantic celebration of metropolitan French-ness is blind to its own conditions of production in a colonised society. In contrast to the fawning panegyrics of Gratiant and Flavia-Léopold, Léro warns of the imminent literary sea-change from the more engaged poets of the Harlem Renaissance who eschew the ideals of assimilation in favour of more politically engaged texts: "Le vent qui monte de l'Amerique noire aura vit fait, espérons-le, de nettoyer nos Antilles des fruits avortés d'une culture caduque" (12). Black Americans such as Claude McKay and Langston Hughes are held up as examples of writers who refuse the cultural mimicry of their predecessors in favour of a new aesthetic that is negotiable across cultures without becoming consumed by the colonising culture itself, and which is capable of maintaining a political stance in the aesthetic. Elsewhere, René Menil bluntly identifies this relationship between culture and colonisation: "Il est certain que les livres dont les Antillais sont nourris ont été écrits dans d'autre pays et pour d'autres lecteurs" (7). Thus, according to Ménil, the detrimental acculturating processes of colonialism in the Antilles are played out most prominently in their national literature, where poets such as José Maria de Héredia, Théodore Faullain de Banville, Albert Victor Samain, and Henri François Régnier have influenced Antillean poets who immerse themselves in a "bric à brac gréco-latin" in order to create a "maigre imitation de la littérature française" (8). These writers, who assume the voice of their colonising masters, write themselves out of their indigenous world in an attempt to perform an idealised version of French identity that is a miasma, a nostalgic fantasy. Ménil goes on to claim that the simulacrum of metropolitan French-ness set up in this poetry of mimicry constructs the Antillian subject as ridiculous in the eyes of the "français moyen" as "celui-ci rencontre en celui-là son image déformée et foncée" (7). Furthermore, he says that the writer who writes himself into the master's text lives in "une domaine irréel déterminé par les idées abstraites d'une autre peuple" (7). The writers in *Légitime Défense* reject this textual and political idealism and conceive of literary mimicry as symptomatic of a colonial history that has relegated the native voice to an archive of nostalgic repetition from where it can never obtain the real subject of its own narrative.

In "Misère d'une Poésie," Etienne Léro likewise uses the example of Flavia-Léopold in a poem called "Le Vagabond" as a poet so far removed from his subject that his central poetic metaphor is "un bifteck bien grillée" (12). Just as daffodils became emblematic of a bucolic England in the exported literary curriculum of the British Empire in India, so here the typical bourgeois foodstuff stands synecdochically for the tastes and mores of a complete nation in Léopold's poem (12). The way out of this cultural impasse is, according to Ménil, in "Généralities sur l'écrivain de couleur antillais," a decisive sweeping aside of the old régime and a movement towards literary realism through the reappropriation of indigenous narratives (12). Ménil identifies what has been erased from Antillian poetry:

> Sentiment du coupeur de cannes devant l'usine implacable, sentiment de solitude du noir à travers le monde, révolte contre les injustices dont il souffre souvent dans son pays surtout, l'amour de l'amour, l'amour des rêves, l'amour des rêves d'alcool, l'amour des danses inspirées. l'amour de la vie et de la joie, le refus de puissance et l'acceptation de la vie etc. etc. . . . voilà de quoi de nos distingués écrivains ne parlent jamais et qui toucherait noirs, jaunes, et blancs comme les poèmes des nègres d'Amérique touchent le monde entier. (8)

Writers, declares Ménil, must express the material of their own lives and histories in their own voices and refuse the tyranny of the refining voice of the assimilated centre, thereby breaking the cycle of class privilege in order to emancipate poetry and literature from the exclusive domains of the bourgeoisie (10). Concurring with this, Etienne Léro remarks that the kind of poetry that Gilbert Gratiant has produced in the 150 verses of "Poémes en vers faux" is typical of the cultural conservatism of the Antilles. He cites others, such as Salvina, Daniel Thaly, and Duquesnay in Martinique; Vieux and Moravia in Haiti and Lara in Guadaloupe are also typical of a bourgeois mediocrity in Antillian literature because they refuse to acknowledge that the majority of the population in the Antilles speak Creole and do not read or write or even speak French (11). The tiny handful of people who can write French reproduce their assimilationist ideologies for a successive minority of élite *évolués*.

The metropolitan space of Paris in the interwar era cannot be read simply as a utopian cosmopolitan geography of political and cultural exchange between diasporic groups and others, a position that James Clifford has tended towards in his work on *négrophilie*. Rather, the journals discussed above demonstrate a collection of voices that emerged from the fundamentally antagonistic cultural spaces of imperial France in order to point up the inequities of power relations between colonised and coloniser; these relations, although weighted firmly against the colonised subject, did not preclude the possibilities of resistance to the project of empire by testing the boundaries of *assimilation* to the full. Homi Bhabha's idea of minority discourse is useful here, as he characterises it as an "act of emergence in the antagonistic in-between of image and sign" where accumulative voices produce an "alternative subaltern signification that attempts to wrest some agency from colonial authority" ("DissemiNation" 307). This is not to suggest, however, that diasporic communities at this time can be reduced to a univocal, homogeneous set of responses to this authority—for example, the ideological stances of *La Dépêche Africaine* and *Légitime Défense* are clearly quite distinct from one another—nor that diasporic cultural and intellectual activities were crudely systematised forerunners of the negritude movement that has largely overshadowed this earlier work. The diversity of the black diaspora in France at this time cannot, then, be seen as an embryonic version of negritude and its Surrealistic aesthetic but as a variegated expression of what Paul Gilroy calls the "discontinuous histories of diaspora" itself (91).

In different ways, *La Revue du Monde Noir, La Dépêche Africaine,* and *Légitime Défense* all attempted to instil a multidimensionality to the term *nègre* that had been taken up by white negrophiles as a metaphor to articulate the condition of a postwar nation exhausted by its own modernity. Whatever discrepancies and tensions existed between the various groups and factions of political and cultural diasporic activism in interwar France, they shared a broad thematic communality around the rehabilitation of the term *nègre*—a term that had hitherto been manipulated as a malleable sign of alterity, evacuated of all but the most perfunctory sense of history. *Négrophilie* continued this fascinated manipulation of cultural alterity in ways that ostensibly reinvested the term *nègre* with a significance and value of its own but that perpetuated the dehistoricisation of cultural difference through racial essentialism. Such essentialism, although largely benign in intention, negated any real agency of colonised populations and paid scant attention to the material conditions of colonial rule. This reclamation of diasporic history and agency did not then begin with the strategic orthodoxies of negritude that celebrated a common inherited culture but with these earlier, often more radical, groups, whose writing insisted on the political contexts of race and colonialism. *La Voix des nègres*, founded by Lamine Senghor in 1927, began to reclaim (*ramasser*) the term *nègre* for political purposes, to imbue it with a set of meanings now familiar to histories of Francophone literature:[28]

> Nos terres, nos droits et notre liberté ne nous appartenant plus, nous nous cramponnons sur ce qui, avec l'éclat de la couleur de notre épiderme sont les seuls biens qui nous restent de l'héritage de nos aieux. Ce nom est à nous; nous sommes à lui! . . . Oui, messieurs vous avez voulu vous servir de ce nom comme mot d'ordre scissioniste. Nous, nous en servons comme mot d'ordre de ralliement: un flambeau. Nous nous faisons honneur et gloire de nous appeler Nègres avec un N majuscule en tête. C'est notre race nègre que nous voulons guider sur la voie de sa libération totale du joug esclavagiste qu'elle subit. (1 Jan. 1927: n. pag.)

From the liberal humanism of René Maran in *La Dépêche Africaine* to the radical leftism of *Légitime Défense,* each journal broke the ground for the later, more-celebrated negritude movement, but perhaps more importantly each contributed to the emergent anticolonial politics that was beginning to challenge the fundamental legitimacy of European colonial rule.

NOTES

1. See Dewitte; Fabre; Stovall; and Jules-Rosette and Sharpley-Whiting on women writers such as the Nardal sisters and Suzanne Lacascade.

2. See C. Miller, *Nationalists* 9–55.

3. The abbreviations *RMN, DA,* and *LD* will be used for each reference to individual journal articles.

4. Student groups from Indo-China were also politically active in Paris during the interwar years. In particular, Nguyen Van Tao and other radical Vietnamese students were arrested for their part in anti-Exposition demonstrations in 1931. See Lebovics 108–10; Ageron 571–73; and Norindr 61–62.

5. Maran's searing indictment of French colonialism in the preface to *Batouala* claims that France constructed its empire from the sweated labour of Africa: "Tu bâtis ton royaume sur des cadavres, Quoi que tu veuilles, quoi que tu fasse, tu te meus dans le mensonge. . . . Tu n'est pas un flambeau mais un incendie. Tout ce à quoi tu touches tu le consumes" (n. pag.). This indictment of French colonialism caused Maran's immediate decommission from his post as colonial administrator in Oubangui-Chari (Chad) and the novel was summarily banned in all French colonies.

6. In September 1924 *Les Continents* published an article by Alain Locke, entitled "New African-American Poetry," that examined the works of Langston Hughes, Jean Toomer, and Claude McKay. In December 1925 Maran wrote a piece, "Mouvement negro-littéraire aux États-Unis," that considered the work of Jessie Fauset and Walter White's *Fire in The Flint* (1924). For detailed studies of the relationships between black American and French writers, see Stovall and Fabre.

7. For certain issues of journals, there are no page numbers on the archival material in the Bibliothèque Nationale. This is denoted by the abbreviation n. pag.

8. Blaise Diagne, deputy of Sénégal at this time, objected to Maran's comments

about the circumstances surrounding his appointment and took *Les Continents* to court in 1924. The trial united disparate leftist groups and assimilationists against the *parti colonial* and was a crucial moment in the history of black solidarity in France. Maran lost the trial and was ordered to pay almost 3,000 francs. See C. Miller, *Nationalists* 24.

9. The leaders of the CDRN were Maurice Satineau and Georges Forgues.

10. Blin narrates the deception that the organisers of the Exposition Coloniale perpetrated on its unsuspecting visitors. The natives of Nouvelle Calédonie were exhibited in villages in which they performed war dances, pretended to be cannibals, and enacted various savage rituals. However, Blin discovered that most of the "savages" spoke fluent French, and some of them had even attended military school and had fought for France in the First World War. Most had been educated under a French system and were either practising Catholics or Protestants in their own country. More troubling was the fact that the impresarios who had recruited these so-called natives failed to pay them and many went hungry during their time in France.

11. In theory, *association* replaced *assimilation* in 1900 as an official colonial policy. However, there was no discernible difference between the two policies. The following description of the goals of *association* points up the almost identical nature of the programme: "To elevate, civilize the native, to associate him with our program of colonization. To make him a beneficiary of his own land, there is our program" (qtd. in Betts 49).

12. Although the economic crisis took longer to have an effect in France, its impact was as devastating as it had been in the United States and in Britain. On June 24, 1928, and again on October 2, 1936, the franc was devalued in order to reduce the national debt.

13. See Lebovics 40.

14. On craniology see Gould 8–100 and 73–112. On French physical anthropology see Poliakov 264–67 and Barzun 116–32. For an overview of racial and social sciences in this period in France, see Schneider *Quality*.

15. In fact, Leo Frobenius contributed an article to the journal, "Le spiritisme à l'intérieur de l'Afrique" (3 Jan. 1931).

16. Micheli does point out that there were social scientists such as Maurice Delafosse who were not convinced by the biologism of these approaches.

17. The most obvious example of internal distinctions such as these is W. E. B. DuBois's notion of the "talented tenth" in America.

18. There is a great deal of attention given to Garveyism and the creation of Liberia in the second edition of the review. Léo Sarjous has written a piece, called "Les noirs américains au Libéria," that roundly condemns the "splendid isolement" of Garveyism, the Universal Negro Improvement Association (UNIA), and the African Communities League. Sarjous concludes by saying, "Ce n'est pas en semant la discorde autour de lui que le Libéria peut espérer entrer dans la voie du progrès" (*RMN* 2 Dec. 1931: 14).

19. This has strong parallels with Nella Larsen's novel *Quicksand* (1928).

20. Indeed, it is only relatively recently that serious scholarship has been done to recover the lives and works of black women in Paris at this time, including those of Augusta Savage, Jessie Fauset, Gwendolyn Bennett, Margaret Rose Martin, Clara Shepherd, and even the Nardal sisters themselves. See Fabre 114–29 and

more recently Sharpley-Whiting on black women writers in Paris and their contributions to negritude.

21. Paulette Nardal completed an MA dissertation on Harriet Beecher Stowe at the Sorbonne.

22. The lesser-known Nardal sister, Andrée, contributed one piece to *La Revue du Monde Noir,* "Étude sur la Biguine Créole," in which she examines the upsurge in the popularity of this exotic dance after the Exposition and Josephine Baker's performances. However, she concludes that the version of the dance offered to Montparnasse patrons has "un aspect obscène" with its endless frisson of erotic taboo (*RMN* 2 Dec. 1931: 51).

23. Hereafter referred in references as *LD.*

24. See Dewitte 261–62 and Kestleloot 40–43. Christopher Miller sees Kesteloot's decision to begin her study of Francophone literary history in 1932 with the publication of *Légitime Défense* as erroneous because he says that "the idea of the 1930s as the exclusive decade of origin is faulty" (*Nationalists* 12).

25. See Kesteloot; Langley; and Dewitte.

26. This, of course, foreshadows Césaire's later work in which he uses Hegel, Marx, and Freud to incriminate Western civilisation.

27. See Thomas on Bhabha's ideas of ambivalence, desire, and disavowal between coloniser and colonised (39–49).

28. See C. Miller, *Nationalists* 35–37.

Bibliography

Abatino, Pepito. *Joséphine Baker vue par la presse française.* Paris: Pirandello, 1931.

Abatino, Pepito, and Félix de la Camra. *Mon Sang dans tes veines, roman d'après une idée de Joséphine Baker.* Paris: Isis, 1931.

Achebe, Chinua. "Out of Africa." *The Guardian.* 22 Feb. 2003. http://books.guardian.co.uk/review/story

Adorno, Theodor W. *Minima Moralia: Reflections from Damaged Life.* Trans. E. F. N. Jephcott. Stanford, CA: Stanford UP, 1974.

Adorno, Theodor, and Max Horkheimer. *Dialectic of Enlightenment.* London: Verso, 1979.

Ageron, Charles-Robert. *Les Lieux de mémoire.* Vol. 1 de *La République.* Ed. Pierre Nova. Paris: Gallimard, 1984.

Alexandre, Maxime. *Mémoires d'un surréaliste.* Paris: Jeune parque, 1968.

Alloula, Malek. *The Colonial Harem.* Trans. Myra and Wlad Godzich. Minneapolis: U of Minnesota P, 1980.

Anderson, Benedict. *Imagined Communities.* London: Verso, 1991.

Anderson, Perry. "Modernity and Revolution." *New Left Review* 144 (1984): 96–113.

Andrew, Christopher M., and A. S. Kanya-Forster. *France Overseas: The Great War and the Climax of French Imperial Expansion.* London: Thames, 1981.

Antoine, Régis. *Les écrivains français et les Antilles: Des premiers pères blancs aux surréalistes noirs.* Paris: Maisonneuve, 1978.

Apter, Emily, and William Pietz, eds. *Fetishism As Cultural Discourse.* Ithaca, NY: Cornell UP, 1993.

Arac, Jonathan, ed. *Macropolitics of Nineteenth Century Literature.* Philadelphia: U of Pennsylvania P, 1991.

Archard, Paul. "Tout en Noir ou La Revue Nègre." *Paris-Midi,* 27 Sep. 1925.

Archer Shaw, Petrine. *Negrophilia: Avant Garde Paris and Black Culture in the 1920s.* London: Thames, 2000.

Arendt, Hannah. *Imperialism*. Pt. 2 of *The Origins of Totalitarianism*. San Diego: Harcourt, 1968.

Arnold, James. *Modernism and Negritude*. Cambridge, MA: Harvard UP, 1981.

Arp, Hans. *On My Way: Poetry and Essays 1912–1967*. New York: New Directions, 1971.

Asad, Talal, ed. *Anthropology and the Colonial Encounter*. London: Ithaca, 1973.

August, T. G. *The Selling of the Empire—British and French Imperialist Propaganda 1890–1940*. Westport, CT: Greenwood, 1985.

Balibar, Etienne, and Immanuel Wallerstein. *Race, Nation and Class: Ambiguous Identities*. London: Verso, 1991.

Ball, Hugo. "Dada Fragments 1916–1917." *The Dada Painters and Poets: An Anthology*. Ed. Robert Motherwell. Cambridge, MA: Harvard UP, 1989. 49–54.

Bancel, Nicholas, and Pascal Blanchard. "De l'indigène à l'immigré: Images, Messages et réalités. *Homme et Migration*. 1207 (mai–juin 1997): 133–56.

Barkan, Elazar. *The Retreat from Scientific Racism: Changing Concepts of Race in Britain and the United States between the World Wars*. Cambridge: Cambridge UP, 1992.

Barkhan, Elazar, and Ronald Bush. *Prehistories of the Future: The Primitivist Project and the Culture of Modernism*. Stanford, CA: Stanford UP, 1995.

Barzun, Jacques. *Race: A Study in Superstition*. New York: Harper, 1965.

Baudelaire, Charles-Pierre. *Les fleurs du mal*. Trans. Richard Howard. Boston: David R. Godine, 1982.

Baudrillard, Jean. "The Beaubourg Effect." Trans. Rosalind Krauss and Annette Michelson. *October* 20 (Spring 1982): 3–13.

Bauer, Gérard. *Annales*. September 1930.

Bauman, Zigmunt. *Modernity and Ambivalence*. Cambridge: Polity, 1991.

Baumgart, William. *Imperialism: The Idea and Reality of British and French Colonial Expansion*. Oxford: Oxford UP, 1982.

Benjamin, Walter. *Illuminations*. London: Fontana, 1973.

———. *One Way Street and Other Writings*. Trans. Edmund Jephcott and Kingsley Shorter. London and New York: Verso, 1977.

———. "Surrealism: The Last Snapshot of the European Intelligentsia." *Reflections*. New York: Harcourt, 1978. 177–92.

Berliner, Brett. *Ambivalent Desire: The Exotic Black Other in Jazz-Age Paris*. Amherst: U of Massachusetts P, 2002.

Berman, Marshall. *All That Is Solid Melts into Air: The Experience of Modernity*. London: Verso, 1995.

Bernstein, Serge. *La France des années trente*. Paris: Colin, 1988.

Berry, Faith. *Langston Hughes: Before and Beyond Harlem*. Westport, CT: Hill, 1983.

Betts, Raymond. *Tricouleur: The French Overseas Empire*. New York: Gordon, 1978.

Bhabha, Homi K. "DissemiNation: Time, Narrative, and the Margins of the Modern Nation." *Nation and Narration*. London: Routledge, 1990. 291–323.

———. "Of Mimicry and Men: The Ambivalence of Colonial Discourse." *The Location of Culture*. London: Routledge, 1994. 85–92.

———. "The Other Question." *Screen* 24.6 (1983): 18–36.

———. "The Other Question: Difference, Discrimination and the Discourse of Colonialism." *Literature, Politics, and Theory: Papers from the Essex Conference, 1976–84*. Eds. Francis Barker et al. London: Methuen, 1986. 148–72.

———. "The Postcolonial Critic." *Arena* 96 (1991): 47–63.

Blachère, Jean Claude. *Le modèle nègre: Aspects littéraires du mythe primitiviste au vingtième siècle chez Apollinaire, Cendrars, Tzara.* Dakar: Nouvelles Editions Africaines, 1981.

Blake, Jody. *Le Tumulte Noir: Modernist Art and Popular Entertainment in Jazz-Age Paris 1900–1930.* University Park: Pennsylvania State UP, 1999.

Blanchard, Pascal, et al. *L'Autre et Nous: "Scènes et Types."* Paris: Syros/ACHAC 1995.

Bloch, Ernst, et al. *Aesthetics and Politics.* London: NLB, 1977.

Boas, Franz. *Kwakiute Tales: A Handbook of American Indian Language.* New York: Bureau of American Ethnography, 1911.

Bogle, Donald. *Brown Sugar: Eighty Years of America's Black Female Superstars.* New York: Harmony, 1980.

———. *Toms, Coons, Mulattoes, Mammies, and Bucks: An Interpretative History of Blacks In Films.* New York: Continuum, 1989.

Bone, Robert A. "The Background of the Negro Renaissance." *Black History* 12 (1979): 408–21.

Bongie, Chris. *Exotic Memories: Literature, Colonialism, and the Fin de Siècle.* Stanford, CA: Stanford UP, 1991.

Bonnet, Jean-Charles. *Les pouvoirs publics français et l'immigration dans l'entre-deux-guerres.* Lyon, France: Université Lyon II, Centre d'histoire économique et sociale de la région lyonnaise, 1976.

Brach, Paul. *Comoedia.* Nov. 1925: 15.

Bradbury, Malcolm, and James McFarlane, eds. *Modernism 1890–1930.* Harmondsworth: Penguin, 1976.

Brassai, Georges. *The Secret Paris of the 30's.* Paris: Gallimard, 1976.

Breton, André. "La force d'attendre." *Clarté* 79 Dec. 1925: 10–15.

———. *Manifestoes of Surrealism.* Trans. Richard Seaver and Helen R. Lane. Ann Arbor: U of Michigan P, 1972.

———. "Ne visitez pas l'Exposition Coloniale." *Tractes Surréalistes et déclarations collectives.* Ed. J. Pierre. Paris: Terrain Vague, 1931.

———. *Qu'est ce que le surréalisme?* Brussels: Henriquez, 1934.

———. *What Is Surrealism?* London: Pluto, 1978.

Brewer, Anthony. *Marxist Theories of Imperialism: A Critical Survey.* London: Routledge, 1980.

Brown, William Wells. *The Black Man, His Antecedents, His Genius.* New York: Hamilton, 1863.

Brunschwig, Henri. *Mythes et réalités de l'impérialisme coloniale français 1871–1914.* Paris: Colin, 1960.

Bürger, Peter. *Theory of the Avant Garde.* Trans. Michael Shaw. Manchester: Manchester UP, 1984.

Butler, Judith. *Bodies That Matter: On the Discursive Limits of Sex.* New York: Routledge, 1993.

———. *Gender Trouble: Feminism and the Subversion of Identity.* New York: Routledge, 1990.

Carr, Helen. "Imagism and Empire." *Modernism and Empire.* Ed. Howard J. Booth and Nigel Rigby. Manchester: Manchester UP, 2000. 64–92.

Carter, Paul. *The Road to Botany Bay: An Essay in Spatial History.* London: Faber, 1987.
Célestin, Roger. *From Cannibals to Radicals.* Minneapolis: U of Minnesota Press, 1996.
Cendrars, Blaise. *Comment les Blancs sont les anciens Noirs.* Argenteuil: Coulouma, 1930.
———. *Magie Noire.* Paris: Grasset, 1928.
———. *Petits Contes Nègres Pour les Enfants des Blancs.* Paris: Vigneau, 1946.
Certeau, Michel de. *The Practice of Everyday Life.* Berkeley: U of California P, 1984.
———. *The Writing of History.* New York: Columbia UP, 1988.
Césaire, Aimé. *Notebook of a Return to My Native Land [Cahier d'un retour au pays natal].* Trans. Mireille Rosello and Annie Pritchard. Newcastle: Bloodaxe Books, 1995.
Champly, Henry. *White Women. Coloured Men.* London: Lang, 1936.
Chisholm, Anne. *Nancy Cunard.* London: Sidgwick, 1979.
Clifford, James T. "Negrophilia." *A New History of French Literature.* Ed. Denis Hollier. Cambridge, MA: Harvard UP, 1989. 901–08.
———. *The Predicament of Culture.* Cambridge, MA: Harvard UP, 1988.
Cobban, Alfred. *France of the Republics 1871–1962.* London: Cape, 1965. Vol. 3 of *A History of Modern France 1871–1962.* 3 vols.
Cohen, W.B. "Nature Exotic and the Science of French Colonialism." *Journal of Interdisciplinary History* 26.4 (1996): 701–08.
Collins, Patricia Hill. *Black Feminist Thought.* Boston: Unwin Hyman, 1990.
Condé, Maryse, and Madeleine Cottenet-Hage. *Penser la créolité.* Paris: Karthala, 1995.
Conklin, Alice J. *Mission to Civilize: The Republican Ideal of Empire in France and West Africa, 1895–1930.* Stanford, CA: Stanford UP, 1997.
Cooke, James J. *France 1789–1962.* Hamden, CT: Archon, 1975.
———. *New French Imperialism 1880–1910: The Third Republic and Colonial Expansion.* Hamden, CT: Archon, 1973.
Coombes, Annie. *Reinventing Africa: Museums, Material Culture and Popular Imagination in Late Victorian and Edwardian England.* New Haven: Yale UP, 1994.
Coty, François. *Contre le Communisme: Sauvons nos colonies, Le péril rouge en pays noir.* Paris: Grasset, 1931.
Crespelle, Jean Paul. *La Grande Époque 1905–1930.* Paris: Hachette, 1976.
Crowder, Henry. *As Wonderful As All That?* Navarro, CA: Wild Trees, 1987.
Crowder, Michael. *Senegal: A Study in French Assimilation Policy.* London: Methuen, 1967.
Cunard, Nancy. *Black Man, White Ladyship: An Anniversary.* London: Utopia, 1931.
———. *Grand Man: Memories of Norman Douglas.* London: Secker, 1954.
———. *Negro: An Anthology.* New York: Negro Universities P, 1934.
Curtin, Philip D. *The Image of Africa.* Madison: U of Wisconsin P, 1964.
———. *Imperalism.* New York: Walker, 1971.
Damase, Jean. *Sidi de Banlieue.* Paris: Fasquelle, 1937.
De Buffon, Comte George Louis le Clerc. *A Natural History, General and Particular.* Trans. William Smellie. London: Kelly, 1866.
De Flers, Robert. *La Semaine Dramatique.* 16 Nov. 1925.
Delafosse, Maurice. *L'Âme Nègre.* Paris: Payot, 1922.

Delteil, Joseph. *La Deltheillerie.* Paris: Grasset, 1968.
Demaison, André. "Addresse au visiteur." *Guide Officiel de l'Exposition Coloniale Internationale.* Paris: Albin Michel, 1931.
Dewitte, Phillipe. *Les mouvements nègres en France 1919–1939.* Paris: Harmattan, 1985.
Doane, Mary Anne. *Femmes Fatales: Feminism, Film Theory and Psychoanalysis.* New York: Routledge, 1991.
Dunbar, Ernest. *The Black Expatriates.* New York: Dutton, 1968.
Eagleton, Terry. *The Ideology of the Aesthetic.* Oxford: Blackwell, 1990.
Eagleton, Terry, Fredric Jameson, and Edward Said. *Nationalism, Colonialism and Literature.* Minneapolis: U of Minnesota P, 1990.
Einstein, Carl. *Negerplastik: La Sculpture Africaine.* Paris: Crès, 1922.
Eisenman, Stephen F. *Gauguin's Skirt.* London: Thames, 1997.
Ewen, Frederic. *Bertolt Brecht: His Life, His Art, His Times.* London: Citadel, 1967.
Ezra, Elizabeth. *The Colonial Unconscious: Race and Culture in Interwar France.* Ithaca, NY: Cornell UP, 2000.
Fabian, Johannes. *Time and the Other: How Anthropology Makes Its Objects.* New York: Columbia UP, 1983.
Fabre, Michel. *From Harlem to Paris.* Chicago: U of Chicago P, 1991.
Fanon, Frantz. *Black Skin, White Masks.* London: Pluto, 1986.
———. *Peau noire; masques blancs.* Paris: Seuil, 1952.
Fanoudh-Siefer, L. *Le mythe du nègre et de l'Afrique noire dans la littérature française de 1800 à la deuxième guerre mondiale.* Paris: Klincksieck, 1968.
Fauset, Jessie. *Paris Tribune.* 1 Feb. 1923.
Ferguson, Blanche E. *Countee Cullen and the Negro Renaissance.* New York: Dodd, 1966.
Fielding, Daphne. *Emerald and Nancy.* London: Eyre, 1968.
Flanner, Janet. *An American in Paris.* New York: Simon, 1940.
———. *Paris Was Yesterday.* New York: Viking, 1972.
Ford, Hugh, ed. *Negro: An Anthology Collected and Edited by Nancy Cunard.* New York: Ungar, 1970.
Foster, Hal. "The 'Primitive' Unconscious of Modern Art." *October* 34 (1985): 181–233.
Frascina, Francis, and Jonathan Harris. *Art In Modern Culture.* London: Phaidon, 1992
Frobenius, Leo. *Das Sterbende Afrika.* München [Munich]: Recht, 1923.
Fry, Edward. *Cubism.* London: Thames, 1966.
Fuss, Diana. *Essentially Speaking: Feminism, Nature and Difference.* New York: Routledge, 1989.
Gates, Henry Louis, Jr., and Karen C. C. Dalton. "Josephine Baker and Paul Colin: African American Dance Seen through Parisian Eyes." *Critical Inquiry* 24.4 (1998): 903–34.
Gauguin, Paul. "Un lettre inedité de Gauguin." *Les Marges* 14 (May 1918).
Gide, André. *Voyage au Congo: Carnets de route.* Paris: Gallimard, 1927.
Gikandi, Simon. "Race and the Modernist Aesthetic." *Writing and Race.* Ed. Tim Youngs. London: Longman, 1997. 159.
Gilman, Sander. "Black Bodies, White Bodies." *"Race," Writing and Difference.* Ed. Henry Louis Gates, Jr. Chicago: Chicago UP, 1986. 223–61.

———. *Difference and Pathology: Stereotypes of Sexuality, Race and Madness*. Ithaca, NY: Cornell UP, 1985.

Gilot Françoise, and Carlton Lake. *Life with Picasso*. New York: McGraw, 1964

Gilroy, Paul. *The Black Atlantic: Modernity and Double Consciousness*. London: Verso, 1993.

Girardet, Raoul. *L'idée coloniale en France de 1871 à 1962*. Paris: Table Ronde, 1972.

Gobineau, Joseph Arthur Comte de. *Essai sur l'inégalité des races humaines*. Paris: Michel, 1853.

Goldberg, David Theo, ed. *Anatomy of Racism*. Minneapolis: U of Minnesota P, 1990.

———. *Racist Culture*. Oxford: Blackwell, 1993.

Goldwater, Robert. *Primitivism in Modern Art*. Cambridge, MA: Harvard UP, 1986.

Gould, Stephen Jay. *The Mismeasure of Man*. New York: Norton, 1981.

Grant, Madison. *The Passing of the Great Race or the Racial Bias of European History*. New York: Scribners, 1918.

Greenhalgh, Paul. *Ephemeral Vistas: The Expositions Universelles, Great Exhibitions and Worlds Fairs 1851–1939*. Manchester: Manchester UP, 1988.

Guillaume, Paul. "African Art at the Barnes Foundation." *Opportunity* 2.17 (May 1924): 140–41.

———. "Opinions sur l'art nègre." *Action* 3 (avril 1920): 23–26.

———. "A propos de l'art des noirs." *Première exposition d'art nègre et d'art océanien, organisée par M. Paul Guillaume du 10 mai au 31 mai 1919*. Paris: Galerie Devambez, 1919.

Guillaumin, Colette. *L'Idéologie raciste: genèse et langage actuel*. Paris: Mouton, 1972.

———. "Race and Nature: The System of Marks. The Idea of a Natural Group and Social Relationships," *Feminist Issues*, 8:2 (1988): 25–43.

———. *Racism, Sexism, Power and Ideology*. London: Routledge, 1995.

Habermas, Jürgen. "Modernity—An Incomplete Project." *The Anti-Aesthetic: Essays on Postmodern Culture*. Ed. Hal Foster. Seattle: Bay, 1983. 3–15.

Hall, Catherine. "Histories, Empires and the Post-Colonial Moment." *Common Skies, Divided Horizons*. Eds. Iain Chambers and Lidia Curti. London: Routledge, 1996. 65–78.

Hall, Stuart. *The Hard Road to Renewal*. London: Verso, 1988.

———. "New Ethnicities." *Black Film: British Cinema*. Ed. Kobena Mercer. ICA Document 7. London: British Film Institute, 1988. 27–31.

———. "Pluralism, Race and Class in Caribbean Society." *Race and Class in Post-Colonial Society*. New York: UNESCO, 1977.

———. *Representation: Cultural Representations and Signifying Practices*. London: Sage/O.U.P., 1997.

———. "What Is This 'Black' in Black Popular Culture?" *Black Popular Culture: A Project*. Ed. Michele Wallace. Seattle: Bay, 1992. 21–36.

———. "The Whites of Their Eyes: Racist Ideologies and the Media." *Silver Linings: Some Strategies for the Eighties*. Eds. George Bridges and Rosalind Brunt. London: Lawrence, 1981. 28–52.

Hammond, Brian, and Patrick O'Connor. *Josephine Baker*. London: Cape, 1988.

Hampton, Anne-Marie. "Gide, Maran, Céline et l'Afrique: Exotisme, Colonialisme et Humanisme." Diss. U of California, Los Angeles, 1995.

Haney, Lynn. *Naked at the Feast: A Biography of Josephine Baker.* New York: Dodd, 1981.
Hanotaux, Gabriel. *Histoires des Colonies françaises et de l'expansion de la France dans le monde.* Paris: Plon, 1929.
Hargreaves, Alec G. *The Colonial Experience in French Fiction.* London: Macmillan, 1981.
Harmond, Jules. *Domination et Colonisation.* Paris: Flammarion, 1910.
Harris, Marvin. *The Rise of Anthropological Theory: A History of the Theories of Culture.* London: Routledge, 1968.
Harvey, David. *The Condition of Postmodernity.* Oxford: Blackwell, 1989.
Heath, Stephen, and Teresa de Lauretis, eds. *The Cinematic Apparatus.* New York: St. Martin's, 1985.
Hebdige, D. "Postmodernism and the 'the Other Side'." Eds. David Morley and Kuan-Hsing Chen. *Stuart Hall: Critical Dialogues in Cultural Studies.* London: Routledge, 1996.
Hemery, Daniel. "Du patriotisme au marxisme: L'immigration vietnamienne en France." *Le Mouvement social* 90 (janv.–mars 1975): 3–54.
Hobsbawm, Eric. *The Age of Empire 1875–1914.* London: Weidenfeld, 1987.
Hobson, J. A. *Imperialism: A Study.* Ann Arbor: U of Michigan P, 1972.
Hodeir, Catherine, and Michel Pierre. *L'Exposition Coloniale.* Bruxelles: Complexe, 1991.
Hoffmann, Léon-François. *Le Nègre Romantique: Personnage Littéraire et Obsession Collective.* Paris: Payot, 1973.
Hollier, Denis. *Le Collège de Sociologie.* Paris: Gallimard, 1979.
———. *A New History of French Literature.* Cambridge, MA: Harvard UP, 1989.
hooks, bell. *Black Looks: Race and Representation.* London: Turnaround, 1992.
———. *Yearning: Race, Gender and Cultural Politics.* London: Turnaround, 1991.
Huelsenbeck, Richard. "Dada Lives." *Transition* 23 (Fall 1936): 77–80.
———. *Memoirs of a Dada Drummer.* Ed. H. J. Kleinschmidt. New York: Viking, 1974.
Hue-tam, Ho Tai. *Radicalism and the Origins of Vietnamese Revolution.* Cambridge, MA: Harvard UP, 1992.
Huggins, Nathan. *Harlem Renaissance.* New York: Oxford UP, 1971.
Hughes, Langston. *The Big Sea.* London: Pluto, 1986.
———. *Fine Clothes to the Jew.* New York: Knopf, 1927.
Hulme, Peter. *Colonial Encounters: Europe and the Native Caribbean 1492–1797.* London: Routledge, 1986.
Huyssen, Andreas. *After the Great Divide: Modernity, Mass Culture and Postmodernity.* Bloomington: Indiana UP, 1986.
Jack, Belinda. *Francophone Literatures: An Introductory Survey.* Oxford: Oxford UP, 1997.
Jackson, Julian. *The Popular Front in France: Defining Democracy.* Cambridge: Cambridge UP, 1988.
Jahn, Janheinz. *A History of Neo-African Literature.* London: Faber, 1966.
Jameson, Fredric. *Modernism and Imperialism: The Field Day Pamphlets.* Derry: Field Day, 1988.
———. *The Political Unconscious: Narrative As a Socially Symbolic Act.* London: Methuen, 1981.

———. "Third World Literature in the Era of Multinational Capitalism." *Social Text* 15 (Fall 1986): 65–88.

Jamin, Jean. "De L'humaine conditione de Minotaure," *Regards sur Minotaure*. Ed. Charles Georg. Geneva: Musée d'art et d'histoire, 1987. 78–87.

———. "Un sacré collège ou les apprentis sorciers de la sociologie." *Cahiers Internationaux de sociologie* 66. (1980): 5–30.

Jencks, Charles. *Le Corbusier and the Tragic View of Architecture*. London: Penguin, 1973.

Johnson, Lemuel A. *The Devil, the Gargoyle and the Buffoon*. New York: National University Publications, 1971.

Johnson, James Weldon. *Black Manhattan*. Knopf: New York, 1930.

Jules-Rosette, Benetta. *Black Paris: The African Writers' Landscape*. Chicago: U of Chicago P, 1998.

Kahnweiler, Daniel Henry. "L'Art Nègre et le cubisme." *Présence Africaine* 3 (mars–avril 1948): 367–77.

———. *Confessions Esthétiques*. Paris: Gallimard, 1963.

Kanneh, Kadiatu. *African Identities*. London and New York: Routledge, 1998.

Kellner, Bruce, ed. *The Harlem Renaissance*. New York: Methuen, 1984.

Kessler, Harry. *The Diaries of a Cosmopolitan: Count Harry Kessler, 1913–1937*. Trans. and ed. Charles Kessler. London: Wiedenfeld, 1971.

Kesteloot, Lilyan. *Black Writers in French: A Literary History of Negritude*. Philadelphia: Temple UP, 1974.

———. *Les Ecrivains Noirs de langue française: Naissance d'une littérature*. Bruxelles: Editions de l'Institit de Sociologie de l'Université de Bruxelles, 1961.

Kiernan, Victor G. *The Lords of Humankind: European Attitudes to the World in the Imperial Age*. London: Weidenfeld, 1969.

Kiernan, V. J. *Imperialism and Its Contradictions*. London: Routledge, 1995.

Kimoni, Iyay. *Destin de la littéarature négro-africaine ou problematique d'une culture*. Zaire: Presses Universitaires, 1975.

Koebner, R., and H.D. Schmidt. *Imperialism: The Story and Significance of a Political Word*. Cambridge: Cambridge UP, 1964.

Kolocotroni, Vassiliki, Jane Goldman, and Olga Taxidou. *Modernism: An Anthology of Sources and Documents*, Edinburgh: Edinburgh University Press, 1998.

Krauss, Rosalind. *The Originality of the Avant-Garde and Other Modernist Myths*. Cambridge, MA: MIT P, 1985.

———. "Giacometti." *Primitivism in Twentieth Century Art: Affinity of the Tribal and the Modern*. Ed. William Rubin. New York: MOMA, 1984. 503–635.

Kuhn, Annette. *The Power of the Image: Essays on Representation and Sexuality*. New York: Routledge, 1985.

Kuper, Adam. *The Invention of Primitive Society: Transformations of an Illusion*. London: Routledge, 1988.

Laborie, Pierre. *L'Opinion française sous Vichy*. Paris: Seuil, 1990.

La Capra, Dominic. *The Bounds of Race*. Ithaca, NY: Cornell UP, 1991.

Lambert, F. *Léopold Sedar Senghor: un poéte, itineraires et contacts de cultures*. Paris: L'Harmattan, 1988.

Langley, John Ayele. *Pan-Africanism and Nationalism in West Africa 1900–1945: A Study in Ideology and Social Class*. Oxford: Clarendon, 1973.

———. "Pan-Africanism in Paris 1924–36." *Journal of Modern African Studies* 17.1 (1969): 69–94.

Laude, Jean. *La peinture française 1905–1914 et 'l'art nègre.'* Paris: Klincksieck, 1968.

Lazereff, Pierre. *Paris-Midi.* 20 Apr. 1925: n. pag.

Lebel, Roland. *Histoire de la Littérature coloniale en France.* Paris: Kra, 1931.

Leblond, Marius Ary. "La race inférieure." *Revue de Paris* 4 (1 July 1906): 104–30.

Lebovics, Herman. *True France: The Wars over Cultural Identity 1900–1945.* Ithaca, NY: Cornell UP, 1992.

Leiris, Michel. *Brisées.* Paris: Mercure de France, 1966.

———. *Brisées: Broken Branches.* Trans. Lydia Davis. San Francisco: North Point, 1989.

———. *L'Afrique fantôme.* Paris: Gallimard, 1934.

Lenin, Vladimir. *Imperialism: The Highest Stage of Capitalism: A Popular Outline.* New York: International Publishers, 1939.

LeTourneau, Charles, *La Psychologie Ethnique.* Paris: Schleicher Frères, 1901.

Lévi-Strauss, Claude. *Tristes Tropiques.* New York: Atheneum, 1975.

Lewis, David Levering, ed. *The Portable Harlem Renaissance Reader.* Penguin: New York, 1994.

Lewis, David Levering. *When Harlem Was in Vogue.* Knopf: New York, 1981.

Lewis, Helena. *Dada Turns Red: The Politics of Surrealism.* Edinburgh: Edinburgh UP, 1990.

Lewis, Martin Deming. "100 Million Frenchmen." *Comparative Studies in Society and History* 4.2 (January 1962): 129–43.

Liauzu, Claude. *Race et Civilisation: L'autre dans la culture occidentale. Anthologie critique.* Paris: Syros, 1992.

Lionnet, Françoise. *Autobiographical Voices: Race, Gender, Self-Portraiture.* Ithaca, NY: Cornell UP.

Locke, Alain, ed. *The New Negro.* New York: Boni, 1925.

Londres, Albert. *Terre d'ébene: La traite des noirs.* Paris: Albin Michel, 1929.

Loti, Pierre. *Roman d'un spahi.* Paris: Calmana Levy, 1925.

Loutfi, Martine Astier. *Littérature et colonialisme: L'expansion coloniale vue dans la littérature romanesque française.* Paris: Mouton, 1971.

Manganaro, Marc, ed. *Modernist Anthropology: From Fieldwork to Text.* Princeton, NJ: Princeton UP, 1990.

Mantagnon, Pierre. *La France Coloniale.* Paris: Pygmalion, 1988.

Maran, René. *Batouala, véritable roman nègre.* Paris: Albin Michel, 1921.

Marcus, Jane. Paper given to Modernism Research Seminar. University of London, 23 Mar. 1994.

Marriot, David. "Bordering On: The Black Penis." *Textual Practice* 10.1 (1996): 9–28.

Marseille, Jacques. *Empire colonial et capitalisme français, histoire d'un divorce.* Paris: Albin Michel, 1984.

Martin, Wendy. *Idealism and Objectivity: Understanding Fichte's Jena Project.* Stanford, CA: Stanford UP, 1997.

Martinkus-Zemp, Ada. "Européocentrisme et exotisme: l'homme blanc and la femme noire dans la littérature de l'entre-deux-guerres." *Cahiers d'Etudes Africaines* 49 (1973): 40–81.

Mauco, Georges. *Les Etrangers en France.* Paris: Colin, 1932.

Mauss, Marcel. *The Gift.* London: Routledge, 1990.

McKoy, Shelby T. *The Negro in France.* Lexington: U of Kentucky P, 1961.

Memmi, Albert. *The Colonizer and the Colonized.* Boston: Beacon, 1967.

Mercer, Kobena. *Welcome to the Jungle.* London: Routledge, 1994.

Michel, Andreas. "Europe and the Problem of the Other." Diss., U. of California, 1992.

Millbury-Stein, Sarah L. *European and African Stereotypes in Twentieth Century Fiction.* London: Macmillan, 1980.

Miller, Christopher L. *Blank Darkness: Africanist Discourse in French.* Chicago: U of Chicago P, 1985.

———. *Nationalists and Nomads: Essays on Francophone Literature and Culture.* Chicago: U of Chicago P, 1998.

Miller, Tyrus. *Late Modernism: Politics, Fiction, and the Arts between the World Wars.* Berkeley: U of California P, 1999.

Mirzoeff, Nicholas. *Bodyscape: Art, Modernity, and the Ideal Figure.* London: Routledge, 1995.

Montaigne, Michel de. "Des Cannibales." *Essais.* Eds. J. C. Chapman and Frederic Mouret. New York: Atlene, 1979.

Montefiore, Janet. *Men and Women Writers of the 1930's: The Dangerous Flood of History.* London: Routledge, 1996.

Monti, Nicholas, ed. *Africa Then: Photographs 1840–1918.* New York: Knopf, 1987.

Morand, Paul. *Black Magic.* London: Heinemann, 1929.

Morrison, Toni. *Playing in the Dark: Whiteness and the Literary Imag*ination. Cambridge, MA: Harvard UP, 1992.

Motherwell, Robert, ed. *The Dada Painters and Poets: An Anthology.* 2nd ed. Cambridge, MA: Harvard UP, 1989.

Moynagh, Maureen. "Cunard's Political Lines: Political Tourism and Its Texts." *New Formations* 34 (Summer 1998): 70–91

Mudimbe, V. Y. *The Surreptitous Speech: Présence Africaine and the Politics of Otherness 1947–1989.* Chicago: Chicago UP, 1992.

Mulvey, Laura. "Visual Pleasure in Narrative Cinema." *Screen* 10.3 (Autumn 1975): 6–18.

———. *Visual and Other Pleasures.* Bloomington: Indiana UP, 1989.

Nadeau, Maurice. *Histoire du Surréalisme.* Paris: Seuil, 1964.

Nicholls, Peter. *Modernisms: A Literary Guide.* London: Macmillan, 1995.

——— "Anti-Oedipus? Dada and Surrealist Theatre 1916–35." *New Theatre Quarterly* VII.28 (Nov. 1991): 331–47.

Norindr, Panivong. *Phantasmic Indochina: French Colonial Ideology in Architecture, Film, and Literature.* Durham, NC: Duke University, 1996.

North, Michael. *The Dialect of Modernism: Race, Language, and Twentieth Century Literature.* New York: Oxford UP, 1994.

Nye, Robert. *Crime, Madness and Politics in Modern France.* Princeton, NJ: Princeton UP, 1984.

———. "Savage Crowds, Modernism and Modern Politics." *Prehistories of the Future.* Eds. Elazar Barkan and Ronald Bush. Stanford, CA: Stanford UP, 1995.

O'Connor, Patrick, and Bryan Hammond, eds. *Josephine Baker.* London: Bullfinch, 1988.

Ory, Pascal, and Jean François Sirinelli. *Les Intellectuels en France, de l'affaire Dreyfus à nos jours.* Paris: Colin, 1986.

Ory, Pascal, and Olivier Barnot. *Entre-deux guerres: La création française 1919–1939.* Paris: François-Bourrin, 1990.

Osborne, Peter. *The Politics of Time: Modernity and Avant-Garde.* London: Verso, 1995.

O'Shaughnessy, Martin. "*Pépé Le Moko* or the Impossibility of Being French in the 1930s." *French Cultural Studies* vii (1996): 247–58.

Panassié, Hugues. *Hot Jazz: The Guide to Swing Music.* New York: Whitmark, 1934.

Papich, Stephen. *Remembering Josephine.* New York: Bobbs, 1976.

Parker, Andrew. *European Imperialism 1860–1914.* London: Macmillan, 1994.

Parry, Benita. "Narrating Imperialism: Nostromo's Dystopia." *Cultural Readings of Imperialism: Edward Said and the Gravity of History.* Eds. Keith Ansell Pearson, et al. London: Lawrence, 1997. 227–67.

———. "Problems in Current Theories of Colonial Discourse." *Oxford Literary Review* 9 (1987): 27–58.

Pala, Sylvie. *Documents sur L'Exposition Coloniale de Paris 1931.* Paris: Bibliothèque de la Ville de Paris, 1981.

Paulhan, Jean. *Le Nègre.* Paris: Cercle du Livre Précieux, 1966.

Paz, Octavio. *Alternating Current.* New York: Viking, 1973.

Persell, Stuart M. *The French Colonial Lobby.* Stanford, CA: Hoover Institute, 1983.

Pick, Daniel. *Faces of Degeneration: A European Disorder c.1848–c.1918.* Cambridge: Cambridge UP, 1989.

Pieterse, Jan Nederveen. *White on Black.* London: Yale UP, 1992.

Poliakov, Léon. *Le mythe aryen. Essai sur les sources du racisme et des nationalismes.* Paris: Complexe, 1987.

Powell, Richard J. *Black Art and Culture in the Twentieth Century.* London: Thames, 1997.

Pratt, Mary Louise. *Imperial Eyes: Travel Writing and Transculturation.* London: Routledge, 1992.

Price, Richard and Sally. *Primitive Art in Civilized Places.* 2nd ed. Chicago: U of ChicagoP, 2001.

Proctor, Henry Hugh. *Between Black and White.* Boston: Pilgrim, 1925.

Psichari, Ernest. *Oeuvres complètes de Ernest Psichari: Vol 1 Carnets de routes.* Paris: Conard, 1948.

Rabinow, Paul. "Beyond Ethnography: Anthropology As Nominalism." *Cultural Anthropology* 3 (1988): 350–64.

Rader, Dotson. Interview with Josephine Baker. "Down but Not Out at the Palace." *Esquire* June 1974: 80.

Reclus, Maurice. *Grandeur de la troisième: de Gambetta à Poincaré.* Paris: Hachette, 1948.

Régnier, Pierre de. "La Revue Nègre." *Candide* 12 Nov. 1925: n. pag.

Rennert, Jacques. *100 Posters of Paul Colin.* New York: Images Graphiques, 1977.

Ridley, Hugh. *Images of Imperial Rule.* London: St. Martin's Press, 1983.

Rivollet, André. "Conférence sur le phonographe." *Université Annales* 3 avril 1930.

Rose, Phyllis. *Jazz Cleopatra: Josephine Baker in Her Time.* London: Chatto, 1990.

Rosello, Mireille. *Littérature et identité créole aux Antilles.* Paris: Karthala, 1992.

Rosenblum, Mort. *Mission to Civilize: The French Way.* New York: Harcourt, 1986.

Rouverge, André. *Mercure de France.* 1 Sep. 1926: n. pag.
Rubin, William, ed. *"Primitivism" in Twentieth Century Art: Affinity of the Tribal and the Modern.* 2 vols. New York: MOMA, 1984.
Rudbeck, I. de. "Une demi-heure intime avec Joséphine Baker et sa panthère 'Chichita'." *Marseille Matin* 20 Sep. 1933: n. pag.
Said, Edward W. *Culture and Imperialism.* London: Vintage, 1993.
———. *Orientalism.* New York: Vintage, 1979.
Sampson, Harry T. *Blacks in Blackface: A Source Book on Early Black Musical Shows.* London: Scarecrow, 1980.
Sangari, Kumkum "The Politics of the Possible." *Cultural Critique* 7 (Fall 1987): 157–86.
Saurel, Hélène. "La petite 'idole noire' nous raconte quelques pages de sa vie artiste." *Marseille Matin* 21 Nov. 1931: n. pag.
Saurraut, Albert. *Grandeur et servitude coloniales.* Paris: Sagittaire, 1931.
———. *Mise en valeur des colonies françaises.* Paris: Michel, 1923.
Sauvage, Marcel. *Les mémoires de Joséphine Baker, recueillis et adaptés par Marcel Sauvage.* Paris: Kra, 1927.
Schneider, William H. *An Empire for the Masses: The French Popular Image of Africa, 1870–1900.* London: Greenwood, 1982.
———. *Quality and Quantity: The Quest for Biological Regeneration in Twentieth Century France.* Cambridge: Cambridge UP, 1990.
Schor, Ralph. *L'Antisemitisme en France pendant les années trente.* Paris: Complexe, 1992.
Schwartz, Bill. "Black Metropolis, White England." *Modern Times: Reflections on a Century of English Modernity.* Eds. Mica Nava and Alan O'Shea. London: Routledge, 1996. 176–207.
Scott, Bonnie Kime. *The Gender of Modernism.* Bloomington: Indiana UP, 1990.
Semidei, Manuela. "De L'Empire à la decolonisation à travers les manuels scolaires." *Revue française de science politique* 1.1 (Feb. 1961).
Sharpley-Whiting, Tracey Denean. *Negritude Women.* Minneapolis: U of Minnesota P, 2002.
Silverman, Max, ed. *Deconstructing the Nation: Immigration, Racism and Citizenship in Modern France.* London: Routledge, 1992.
———. *Race, Discourse and Power in France.* Aldershot, United Kingdom: Gower, 1991.
Smith, Bernard. *European Vision and the South Pacific, 1768–1850.* Oxford: Clarendon, Oxford, 1960.
Smith, Neil. *Uneven Development: Nature, Capital, and the Production of Space.* Oxford: Blackwell, 1984.
Sontag, Susan. *Against Interpretation and Other Essays.* New York: Farrar, 1966.
Soupault, Phillipe. *Le Nègre.* Paris: Kra, 1920.
Spector, Jack J. *Surrealist Art and Writing 1919–1937: The Gold of Time.* Cambridge: Cambridge UP, 1997.
Spengler, Oswald. *The Decline of the West.* New York: Knopf, 1926.
Spivak, Gayatri. *The Post-colonial Critic: Interviews, Strategies, Dialogues.* New York: Routledge, 1990.
Spurr, David. *The Rhetoric of Empire: Colonial Discourse in Journalism, Travel Writing, and Imperial Administ*ration. Durham, NC: Duke UP, 1993.

Steins, Martin. "Entre l'exotisme et la négritude: La littérature coloniale." *L'Afrique littéraire* 58 (1981): 71–82.
Stepan, Nancy. *The Idea of Race in Science.* London: Macmillan, 1982.
Stocking, George W. *Victorian Anthropology.* New York: Free Press, 1987.
Stovall, Tyler. *Paris Noir: African-Americans in the City of Light.* New York: Houghton, 1996.
Stuart, Jeffrey, ed. *The Critical Temper of Alain Locke.* New York: Garland, 1983.
Suleri, Sara. *The Rhetoric of English India.* Chicago: U of Chicago P, 1992.
Suret-Canale, Jean. *Afrique noire: L'ère coloniale, 1900–1945.* Paris: Editions Sociales, 1964.
Sweeney, James Johnson, ed. *African Negro Art: Catalogue of an Exhibition.* New York: Arno, 1973.
Taguieff, Pierre-André. *Discours sur le bioéthique.* Paris: Découverte, 1995.
———. "Le debat sur l'immigration dans l'entre-deux-guerres." *Vingtième Siècle* 47 (July–Sep. 1995): 103–32.
Taussig, Michael. *Mimesis and Alterity.* London: Routledge, 1993.
———. *Shamanism, Colonialism, and the Wild Man: A Study in Terror and Healing.* Chicago: U of Chicago P, 1987.
Thirion, André. *Revolutionaries without Revolution.* Trans. Joachim Neugroshel. New York: Macmillan, 1975.
Thomas, Nicholas. *Colonialism's Culture: Anthropology, Travel and Government.* Cambridge: Polity, 1994.
Todorov, Tzvetan. *Nous et les autres: La réflexion sur la diversité humaine.* Paris: Seuil, 1989.
Torgovnick, Marianna. *Gone Primitive: Savage Intellects, Modern Lives.* Chicago: U of Chicago P, 1990.
Tzara, Tristan. "Note 6 sur l'art Nègre." *Sic* 21–22 Sep.–Oct. 1917: 279–84.
Ungar, Steven, and Tom Conley, eds. *Identity Papers: Contested Nationhood in Twentieth Century France.* Minneapolis. U of Minnesota P, 1996.
Vaillant, Janet G. *Black, French, and African: A Life of Léopold Sédar Senghor.* Cambridge, MA: Harvard UP, 1990.
Van Vechten, Carl. *Nigger Heaven.* New York: Knopf, 1926.
Vergès, Françoise. *Monsters and Revolutionaries: Colonial Family Romance and Métissage.* Durham, NC: Duke UP, 1999.
Vergo, Peter, ed. *The New Museology.* London: Redaktion, 1989.
Viollis, André. *Gringoire.* 3 Oct. 1930.
Wallace, Michele. *Invisibility Blues: From Pop to Theory.* London: Verso, 1990.
Warwick, Paul. *The French Popular Front: A Legislative Analysis.* Chicago: U of Chicago P, 1977.
Williams, Raymond. *Culture and Society 1780–1950.* London: Chatto, 1958.
———. *The Politics of Modernism.* London: Verso, 1996.
Withol de Wenden, Catherine. *Les immigrés et la politique: Cent cinquante ans d'évolution.* Paris: Fondation Nationale des Sciences Politiques, 1988.
Young, Lola. *Fear of the Dark: 'Race', Gender and Sexuality in the Cinema.* London: Routledge, 1996.
Young, Robert. *Colonial Desire: Hybridity in Theory, Culture and Race.* London: Routledge, 1995.
Zavala, Iris. *Colonialism and Culture.* Bloomington: Indiana UP, 1993.
Zeldin, Theodore. *France 1848–1945.* 2 vols. New York: Oxford UP, 1977.

Archival Collections, Bibliothèque Nationale, Paris

L'Action Coloniale.
La Dépêche Africaine, 1928–1932.
La Race Nègre.
La Revue du Monde Noir [Paris]. 1931–1932.
Légitime Défense [Paris]. 1932.
Le Libéré.
Le Paria.
Les Continents.

Index

About the Author

CAROLE SWEENEY is a Lecturer in French and Transnational Studies at the University of Southampton. She has written on race, colonialism, and interwar European modernism. She is currently working on a comparative literary project looking at the Francophone Americas and international avant-gardism.